THE PRINCIPLES OF INTERNATIONAL TAX PLANNING

by

INTERNATIONAL FISCAL SERVICES

Published in 2005 by
Corpus Publishing Limited
PO Box 8, Lydney, Gloucestershire, GL15 6YD
Tel: 01594 560600 Fax: 01594 560550
Email: corpus@firststonepub.co.uk

DISCLAIMER

While every care was taken to ensure the accuracy of the contents of this book, no responsibility for any loss occasioned to any person acting or refraining from action as a result of any statement or material in it can be accepted by the authors or publishers.

All names of individuals, companies or other entities used in the examples contained in the book are fictitious and are not intended as references to any actual individuals, companies or entities. Any resemblance to the names of actual individuals, companies or entities is purely coincidental.

British Library Cataloguing in Publication Data
A CIP record for this book is available from the British Library

ISBN 1 903333 22 9

THE PRINCIPLES OF INTERNATIONAL TAX PLANNING

by

INTERNATIONAL FISCAL SERVICES

ROY SAUNDERS

MILES DEAN

RICHARD WILLIAMS

DIANA VAN DER MERWE

CORPUS PUBLISHING

Acknowledgements

We wish to thank the following companies for their financial contribution towards publishing this book:

- Andreas Neocleous & Co., Limassol, Cyprus.
- Jersey Trust Company Ltd, St Helier, Jersey.
- Marrache & Co., Gibraltar.
- Praxis Fiduciaries Ltd, St Peter Port, Guernsey.

We wish to thank the following people in particular for their direct input into the writing of this book:

- All the contributors of *International Tax Systems and Planning Techniques.*
- Mike Aitken, Minter Ellison, Sydney, Australia.
- David Bevir, Andreas Neocleous & Co., Limassol, Cyprus.
- Olivier Couraud, Morgan Lewis & Bockius, Paris, France.
- Nancy Cruickshanks, AGN Shipleys Chartered Accountants, London, UK.
- Lucky De Silva, Regent University, Virginia Beach, Virginia, USA.
- Michael Fromstein, SF Partnership, Toronto, Canada.
- Derek Gilman, Day Berry & Howard, Stamford, Connecticut, USA.
- Alon Kaplan, Alon Kaplan Law Firm, Tel Aviv, Israel.
- Marios Kyprianou, Kyprianou & Co., Limassol, Cyprus.
- Mike Luckett, AGN Shipleys Chartered Accountants, London.
- Philippe Malherbe, Liedekerke Wolters Waelbroeck & Kirkpatrick, Brussels, Belgium.
- Maurizio Marullo, Cristofori & Partners, Milan, Italy.
- Andreas Neocleous, Andreas Neocleous & Co., Limassol, Cyprus.
- Elias Neocleous, Andreas Neocleous & Co., Limassol, Cyprus.
- Adam Perry, Halliwells LLP, London, UK.
- Matteo Rapinesi, Cristofori & Partners, Milan, Italy.
- Jørn Qviste, Rønne & Lundgren Law Firm, Copenhagen, Denmark.
- Robert Schneider, Schneider's Rechtsanwalts-KEG, Vienna, Austria.
- Karl-Ruediger Steeb, Stehle Hollaender & Partner, Stuttgart, Germany.
- Christian Strik, Strik & Dunnewijk, Amsterdam, the Netherlands.
- Herman Troskie, Maitland & Co., Luxembourg, Luxembourg.
- Lex van der Zande, Strik & Dunnewijk, Amsterdam, the Netherlands.

Contents

Table of Cases

United States

Table of Statutes and EU Legislation

Table of Statutory Instruments

Table of International Instruments

Double Tax Treaties

Treaties

Abbreviations

AStG	Aussensteueurgesetz
BTW	Omzetbelasting (VAT, Netherlands)
BV	besloten vennootschap met beperkte aansprakelijkheid
BVI	British Virgin Islands
CDT	Consolidated Tax Decree (Italy)
CFC	controlled foreign company
CFO	chief financial officer
CGI	Code Générale des Impôts (France)
CIR	Code des Impôts sur les Revenus (Belgium)
CP	cost plus
CRA	Canada Revenue Agency
CUP	comparable uncontrolled price
EBT	employee benefit trust
ECJ	European Court of Justice
FAPI	foreign accrual property income
FATF	Financial Action Task Force
FAPT	foreign asset protection trust
FIE	foreign income exemption
FOB	free on board
FURBS	funded unapproved retirement benefit scheme
GAAP	generally accepted accounting principles
GAAR	general anti-avoidance rules
GIE	groupement d'intérêt economique
GST	Goods and Services Tax (Australia, Canada)
HMRC	Her Majesty's Revenue and Customs
ICTA	Income and Corporation Taxes Act 1988 (UK)
IFS	International Fiscal Services
IR	Inland Revenue
IRC	Internal Revenue Code
IRS	Internal Revenue Service (US)
ISP	internet service provider
ITEPA	Income Tax (Earnings and Pensions) Act 2003 (UK)
ITTA	Income Tax Assessment Act 1936 (Australia)
ITTOIA	Income Tax (Trading and Other Income) Act 2005 (UK)
KStR	Körperschaftsteuer-Richtlinien
LLC	limited liability company
LLP	limited liability partnership
LOB	limitation on benefits
LP	limited partnership
MARD	Mutual Assistance Recovery Directive (Council Directive 76/308/EEC)
MEC	modified endowment contract
MLR	Money Laundering Regulations 2003 (UK)
MLRO	money laundering reporting officer
NAFTA	North American Free Trade Association
NCIS	National Criminal Intelligence Service
NIC	national insurance contribution
NV	naamloze vennootschap
OECD	Organisation for Economic Co-operation and Development
OEIC	open-ended investment company
PAYE	Pay As You Earn
PCC	protected cell company
PE	permanent establishment
POCA	Proceeds of Crime Act 2002 (UK)
PPB	personal portfolio bond
PS	profit split
RP	resale price
RST	retail sales tax
SA	société anonyme; South Africa
SAR	suspicious activity report
SCI	société civile immobilière
SDLT	stamp duty land tax
SIPP	self-invested pension scheme
SpA	Società per azioni
SPV	special-purpose vehicle
STAR	Special Trusts (Alternative) Regime (Law of 1997)
TCGA	Taxation of Chargeable Gains Act 1992 (UK)
TNM	transactional net margin
TVA	taxe sur la valeur ajoutée
UNI	undistributed net income
VAT	value added tax
VISTA	Virgin Islands Special Trusts Act (Law of 2003)

Foreword

I first met Maurice Brightman (whom readers will encounter as the principal character in this work, when they read beyond this Foreword) some 16 or 17 years ago. I'd just started in practice at the Tax Bar, and was interested in international taxation, and was advised to attend a conference at which he was speaking. I recall being incredibly impressed by Maurice's presentation. It wasn't just the energetic style of the presentation, or the incredible amount of material relating to a large number of countries that he deployed. It was his youth that impressed me more than anything else. How had someone so young learnt so much about so many different jurisdictions?

In subsequent years, I have got to know Maurice rather well. He has appeared in other works – *Structuring International Real Estate Transactions* by Roy Saunders for example. We have served on committees together, spoken together at conferences and advised clients together. I have never ceased to be impressed by the range of knowledge that he has at his disposal. But – and in many respects this is more surprising – I don't think he has aged in those 16 or 17 years that I have known him. I am convinced that, somewhere in the attic of the Brightman household in Belsize Park or wherever, there is a painting showing a portrait of a wizened, elderly gentleman, which ages day by day, while Maurice Brightman, international tax adviser extraordinaire, maintains his youthful looks. (In fact, there are probably two portraits, one of Maurice and one of Mrs Brightman, who equally maintains her youthful looks.)

Readers of this work will be introduced to some of the breadth and depth of Maurice Brightman's international tax knowledge. The book introduces the reader to a number of factors which are crucial in delivering effective and practical international tax planning advice. To even contemplate a book which covers so many areas is an ambitious task, and I congratulate the authors on undertaking it. A beginner to the subject of international tax planning will learn a great deal of value from this book: even an old practitioner (like me) would have to admit that he has learnt much from reading the pages.

I wish Maurice and his colleagues the very best with this publication. I look forward to encountering him in his different guises on future occasions, though I shall continue to be astonished and in awe of his undiminishing youthfulness.

Philip Baker QC
Gray's Inn
June 2005

Preface

The purpose of this book is to give you, the reader, and no doubt avid follower of international tax planning, an excellent read. Most tax books are notoriously dry, dull, unimaginative and, above all, boring. We hope this book is the exception to the rule. We also hope that it proves what we already know: that international taxation *is* a fascinating subject and practice area; it's just that most books and journals – especially textbooks, which are often the starting point on our journey in taxation – tend to focus on specific legislation and case law. While it is vital that any international tax practitioner (and those involved in professions where international taxation is just one of many disciplines, e.g. private banking and trust administration) knows about and understands sections and cases, it is equally important to look at the commercial practicalities of each client case we encounter. We often tell clients that it is they who hold the key to the solution they are seeking. We merely assist in the 'unlocking' of the problem, but to do so we need to understand not only the tax issues, but also the commercial or family issues and circumstances that are relevant to them. It is not enough simply to be able to repeat *verbatim* sections of the various tax codes; it is much more relevant to be able to relate to clients' circumstances and to give advice which meets all of their objectives, not simply tax.

It is with this in mind that we have written, or rather updated, this book. In 1977, our founder and Chairman, Roy Saunders, wrote a little black book called the *Principles of Tax Planning*. While the book did not reach the heady heights of our flagship title, *International Tax Systems and Planning Techniques*, published by Sweet & Maxwell, it succinctly identified and explained the basic principles of international tax planning.

When I first joined Roy at IFS in 1997 as an obedient and somewhat awestruck 20-something, this little black book was thrust upon me. It soon became clear that Roy had new and greater plans for his virgin work, and it is solely down to me that you have been deprived for so long. The opportunity for updating the little black book arose when Roy was asked by a not-so-small Swiss private bank to write, produce and deliver a course on the principles of international taxation for 60 in-house lawyers and financial planners. The basis of the course was, you guessed it, the little black book. When we dusted off the last office copy, it was evident that while the laws in most countries had changed since 1977, the principles had more often than not remained the same.

This book is therefore an updated version of our first book, but with a twist. We wanted to write a book that not only explained the principles of international tax planning, but also brought the subject to life. We have done this by basing the book around a fictional family: not the Simpsons, not the Addams, but the Filipes, an Italian family whose affairs (quite literally!) and business interests encompass many of the tax issues we tax advisers encounter. Their history, on which this book is based, is set out in the Case Study. This is not, however, a tax novel *per se*; rather, it is a textbook which has been split into ten chapters, with each chapter being split into two parts: the first part is the tax principle in theory, the second part, the principle in practice, and this is done by way of reference to the Filipes.

We want this book to inspire you to take this subject to heart. We hope that the Filipes bring the subject to life, and that through them you gain an understanding of this most fascinating, demanding and stimulating subject.

Miles Dean
Managing Director of International Fiscal Services Ltd
www.interfis.com
info@interfis.com

Case Study
The Filipe Family

Papa Filipe, aged 85, is the grandfather of the Italian Filipe family. He has been resident in Lucca his entire life. He is now a widower and has just one son, Giuliano.

Giuliano is now 57 and divorced his wife five years ago, at which stage he left Lucca and went to live in London where he took responsibility for running the UK operation of the family firm that he created many years ago, Lucca Software. However, Giuliano also has a flat in Paris where he spends much of his time looking after the French operation of Lucca Software.

Giuliano and his ex-wife have two children, a son and a daughter. Their son, Paolo Filipe, is 23 and has reached stardom in international football through his recent signing by Belsize Wanderers FC. Their daughter, Renata Filipe, is 21 and renowned already as a top model. She currently spends much of her time in the US, although her base is at her mother's house in Lucca.

One of Papa Filipe's long-term friends and confidants is Maurice Brightman, an extremely knowledgeable and reputable international tax adviser based in London. The other Filipes have all had the pleasure of making Maurice Brightman's acquaintance during their various visits to the city. On occasion, the Filipes consult Maurice Brightman on matters related to their international tax planning, but a distinct problem is this: for the sake of providing a diversion from their day-to-day activities, the Filipes are all very fond of trying their hands at a bit of international tax planning themselves. Not wishing to seem over-anxious to increase the professional consulting fees he earns from his Italian friends (Maurice Brightman is, in addition to his other outstanding characteristics, also a modest man), he cautions the Filipes on occasion that international tax is best left to the experts. After all, it is a complicated and ever-changing field, and amateur international tax planning will more likely than not lead to trouble. However, the Filipes, whose determination has no doubt resulted in some excellent things, not least their professional and financial success, all seem quite set on continuing their hobby of international tax planning. This is causing Maurice headaches on a fairly regular basis. As a tax adviser subject to the laws of the United Kingdom, Maurice often finds himself in the unenviable position where he has to decide whether the Filipes' most recent tax planning antics create a requirement to report the relevant family member to the authorities...

Diagram 1

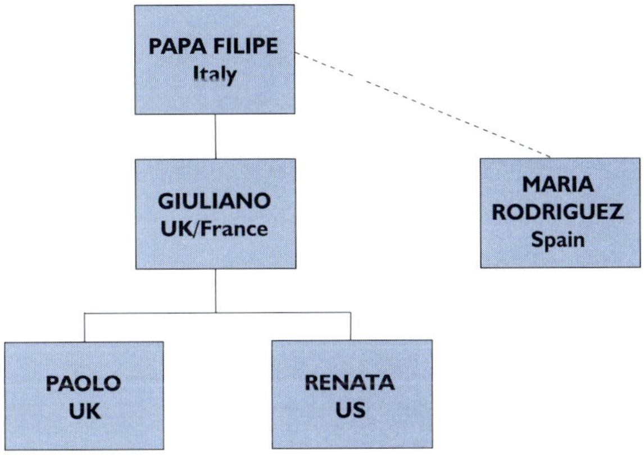

THE FILIPE FOUNDATION

Papa Filipe created a small fortune when he sold his soft furnishing business in Lucca, with much of the sale proceeds being directed to the Filipe Foundation, established in Liechtenstein in 1980 at the time of the sale. Since then, the Filipe Foundation has created a substantial investment portfolio expertly looked after by Banco Fortuno in Zurich.

The company secretary of Lucca Soft Furnishings SpA was Maria Rodriguez, a beautiful Spanish lady in her forties with whom Papa Filipe had been having an affair for over ten years. On selling the soft furnishing business, Papa Filipe lived up to his promise and bought her a dream villa in her home town of Mijas on the Costa del Sol. The villa was acquired through a Gibraltar company, which was created as a wholly owned subsidiary of the Filipe Foundation. Maria has the right to occupy the villa until her death, and this she does, enjoying the year-round sun with her children. Sadly, Papa Filipe's regular visits to the Costa del Sol became less regular in the 1990s, and have virtually ceased as his health further deteriorates.

Diagram 2

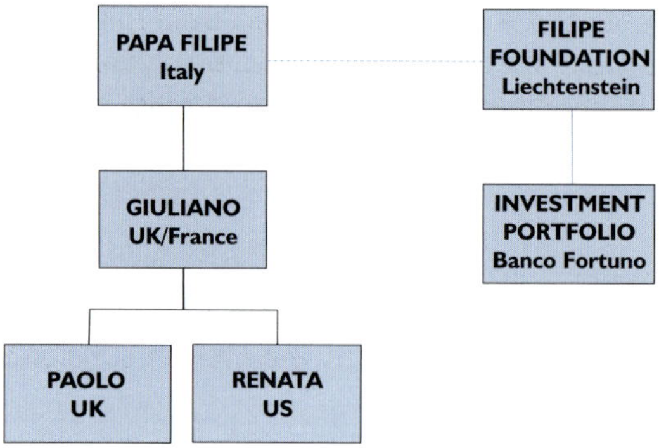

Diagram 3

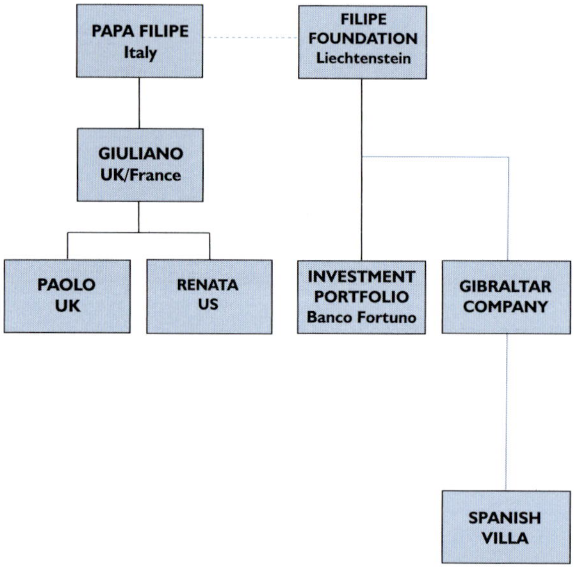

THE GIULIANO TRUST

Giuliano decided many years ago that he did not wish to follow his father's footsteps into the soft furnishing business, and had no interest whatsoever in the company when it was sold in 1980. Instead, a few years earlier, he created his own company to develop software for business systems, for Italian banks in particular. In the belief that this was likely to develop into an international business operation requiring subsidiaries in several countries, Giuliano sought advice as to the creation of a holding structure. He was advised to create the Giuliano Trust as a Jersey trust, which would own Lucca NV, a Netherlands Antilles company, which in turn would own Lucca BV, a Dutch holding company. The Dutch company would be the central holding company for future growth and expansion, but initially it would restrict its investment to one subsidiary, namely Lucca Software SpA in Italy. The initial capital requirement was not too significant, and this was advanced by Papa Filipe from personal funds to the Giuliano Trust, with the trustees then using the funds to incorporate the relevant entities. Subsequently, as the group developed and required more capital, further funds were advanced to the Giuliano Trust by the then created Filipe Foundation.

In the late 1980s, Giuliano expanded into the UK with the creation of Lucca Software Ltd as a direct subsidiary of the Dutch holding company, and in the mid-1990s created Lucca Software SA as the French subsidiary of the Dutch holding company.

Diagram 4

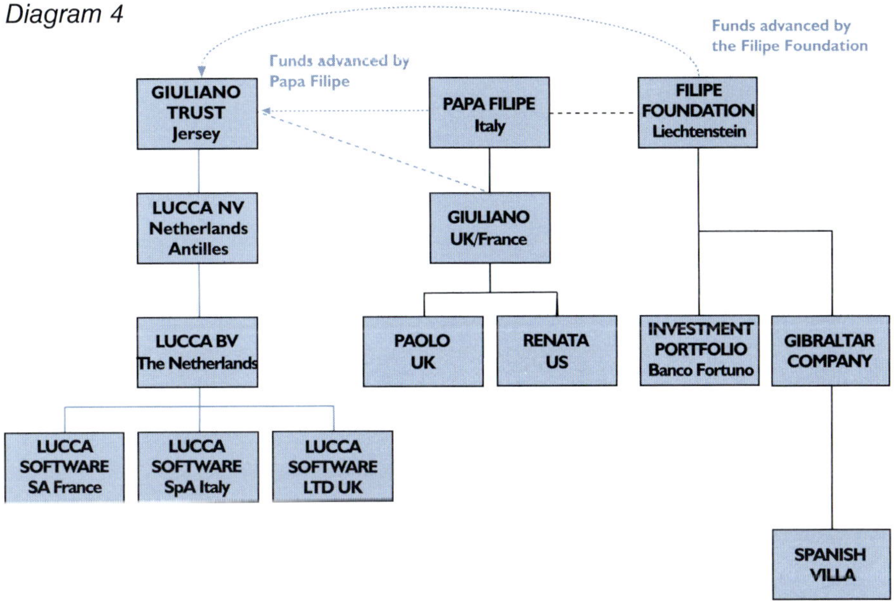

Following the distribution of dividends from the Italian subsidiary through the Dutch and Antilles companies to the Giuliano Trust, the trustees acquired a house near London through a British Virgin Islands (BVI) company in anticipation of Giuliano needing to move to London to pursue the development of Lucca Software in the UK. When Giuliano left Lucca after his divorce, he used the BVI company to charge his salary to the Italian company which had previously employed him personally, and now uses the BVI company to charge the Italian, the UK and the French companies with the relevant proportions of his total salary.

The Italian company became very profitable during the early 1990s, and Giuliano started to use the BVI company more extensively, employing third-party consultants who were working on the software development for the Lucca Group and charging for their services at a significant premium to the Italian company, thus reducing taxable profits in Italy. However, rather than using another direct invoicing arrangement from the BVI company to the Italian company, the BVI company used a third-party UK nominee company to render the invoices to the Italian company on its behalf.

Finally, after the French subsidiary of Lucca Group was created, Giuliano temporarily moved to Paris where he rented a flat for a three-year rolling period, but maintained his UK property in order to ensure (hopefully) that he remained a tax resident of the UK rather than France.

Diagram 5

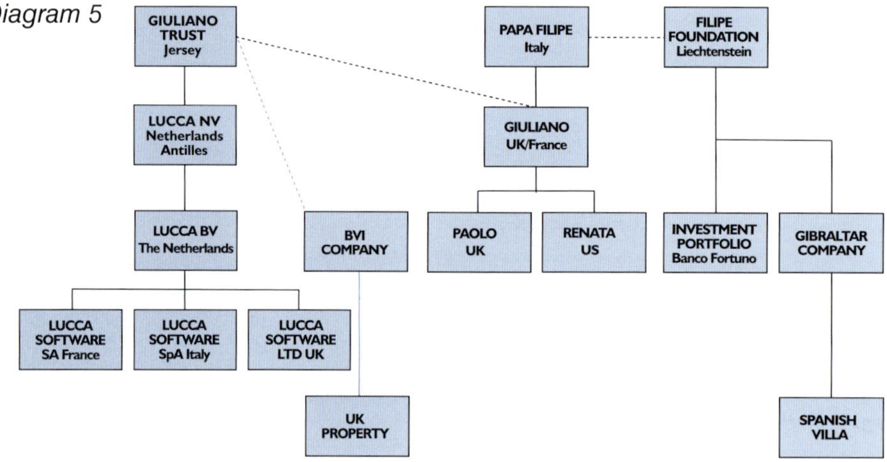

Diagram 6

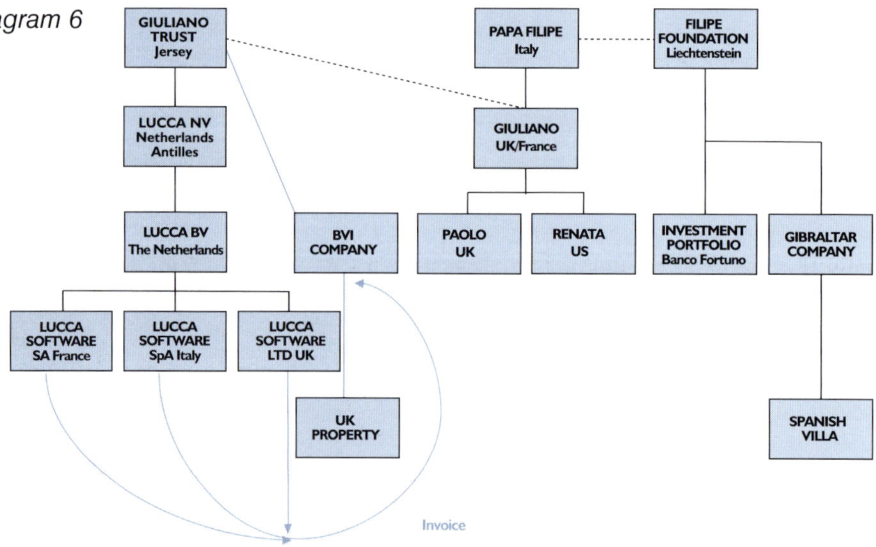

Diagram 7

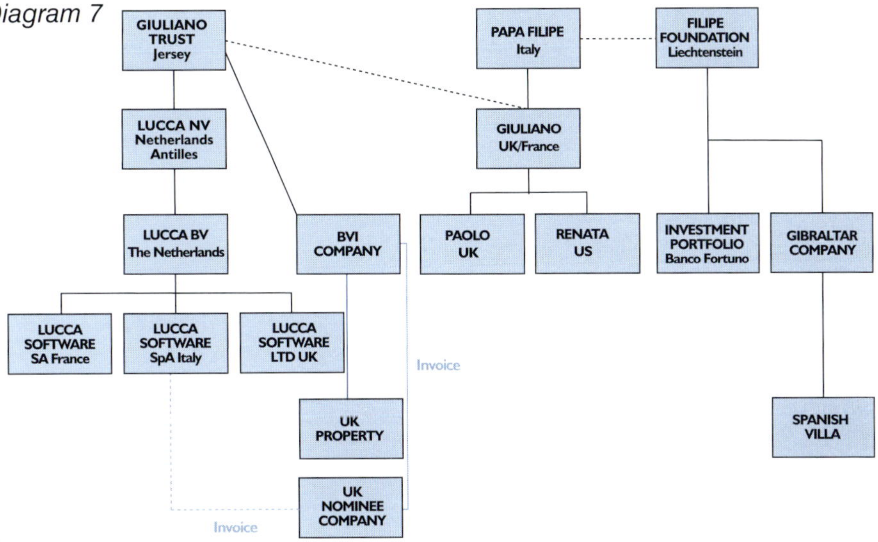

PAOLO'S FOOTBALL CONTRACT

Paolo recently moved from Athletico Roamer to Belsize Wanderers FC for a record fee, propelling him into international stardom. His face became one of the most widely recognised faces in the footballing world, and the No. 11 shirt became one of the hottest merchandising assets for the club. Belsize Wanderers were therefore prepared to enter into two separate contracts when they signed Paolo, the first being for Paolo's footballing performances for Belsize Wanderers, and the second being with a third-party Swiss company, Opus AG, for his image and merchandising rights.

RENATA'S MODELLING CAREER

Another well-known face is Renata Filipe, known worldwide simply as 'Renata', who has a freelance arrangement with a famous model agency, and is required to model clothes (and sometimes not many clothes) all over the world. She spends about three months of the year in the US, two months in the UK, one month in France, one month in Germany, approximately two months in the Far East and the rest of her time in Italy at her mother's home. Her catwalk fees are paid to her subject to local withholding taxes, and she expects to derive considerable income from commercial endorsements and merchandising rights.

Renata has taken out a life insurance policy in Italy, the proceeds of which will provide for her mother in the event of Renata's untimely death.

Diagram 8

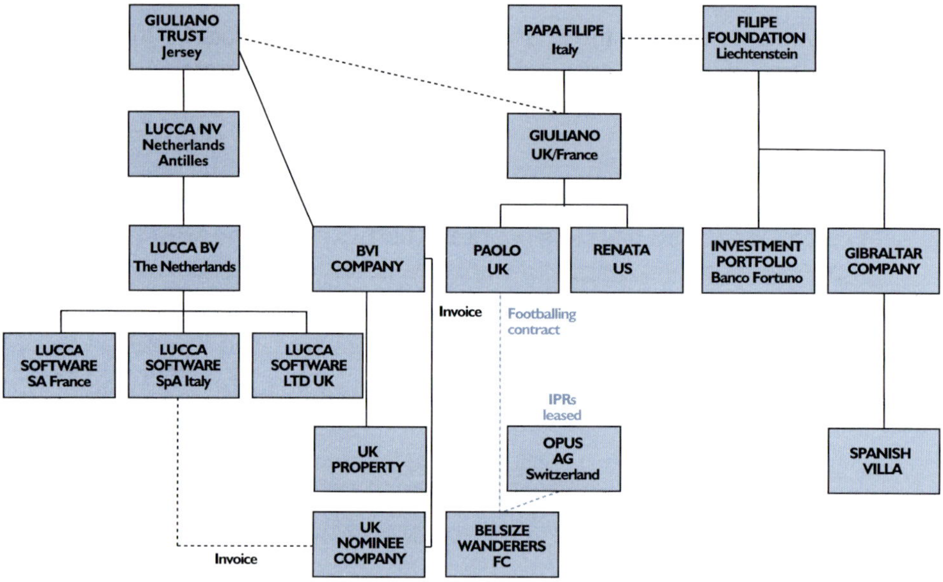

Diagram 9

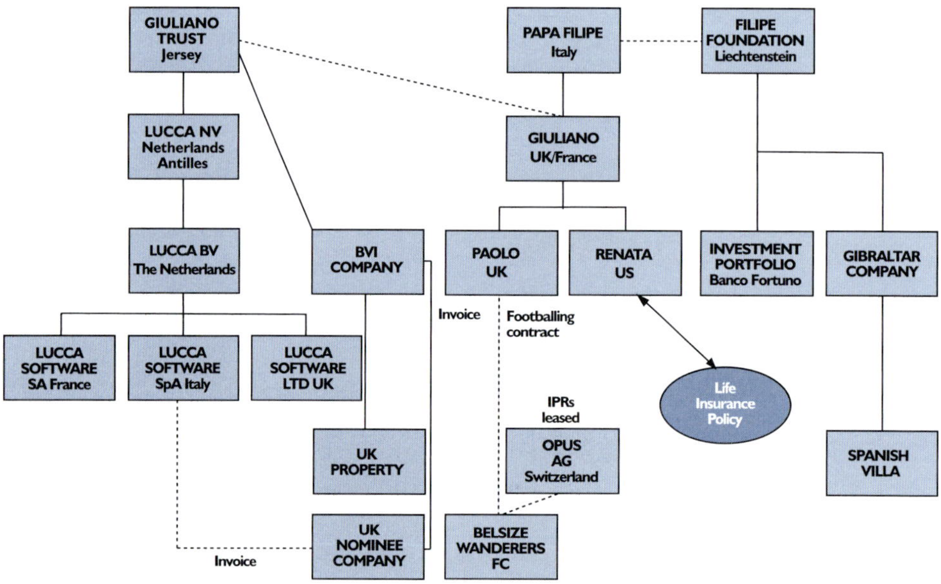

OVERSEAS REPRESENTATIVE OFFICE OF LUCCA SOFTWARE SpA

Giuliano wants to expand the scope of his distribution outlets for the software for business systems, and has decided to concentrate the group's development into the Far East because of the huge potential, initially in Australia and New Zealand. Lucca Software SpA opens a representative office in Sydney:

(a) to provide a fixed base to store documentation, promotional material, etc. and to display them on computers, demonstrating the range of the software to potential clients;

(b) to circulate literature relating to the software to interested potential customers in China and Japan as well as Australia and New Zealand; and

(c) to pass on any enquiries or other information which may affect potential sales of the software programme to Giuliano and his staff in Italy, UK and France.

As a result of being inundated with enquiries, additional staff have to be employed locally. They are principally technicians able to demonstrate the software programmes. The promotion of Lucca Software is so successful in Australia that Lucca Software SpA now appoints independent agents throughout Australia and the Far East to sell the software systems to customers who became aware of the systems through the representative office.

Diagram 10

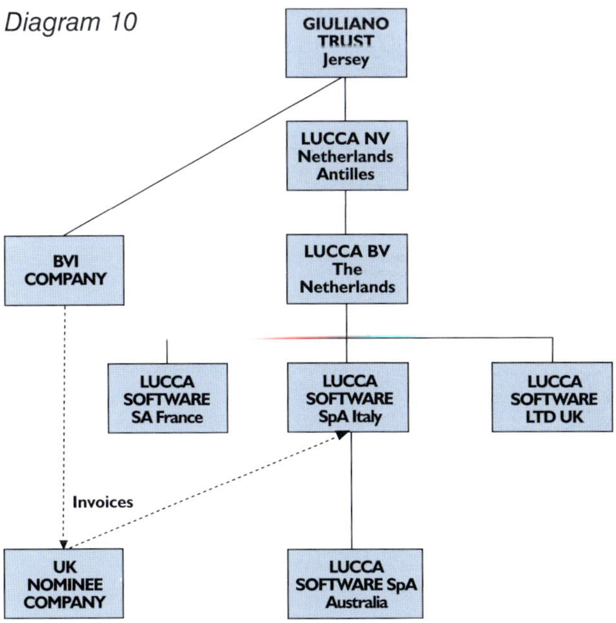

Diagram 11

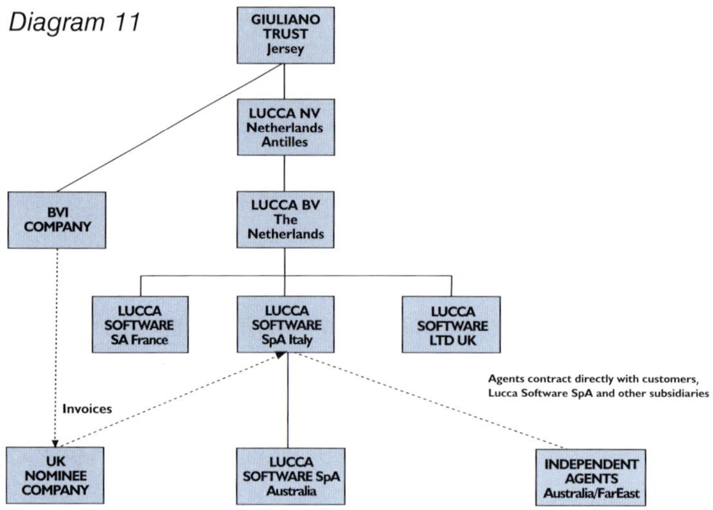

CREATING A RESEARCH AND DEVELOPMENT UNIT IN INDIA

Now that the group is expanding into various different territories, a decision has been taken to commit a significant amount of research and development funds into how businesses in different countries can adapt to the basic Lucca software system. As a result, Lucca Software creates a research and development centre in Mumbai, India, and employs 20 personnel there whose job it is to develop both different language and different accounting system adaptations of the Lucca business system. A local company is formed with the name of Lucca Developments which charges Lucca NV, the Netherlands Antilles parent company, on a cost-plus basis, i.e. costs of premises, all equipment, staff salaries and other overheads, plus a 10% mark-up for such activities, the mark-up being subject to Indian tax.

Diagram 12

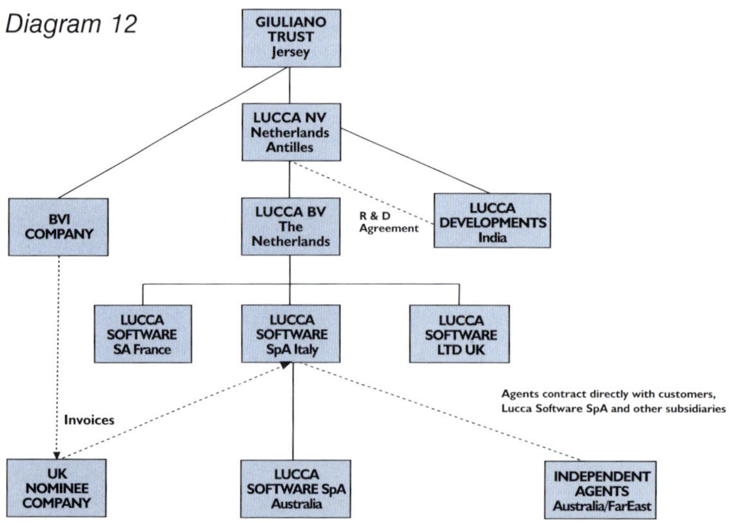

FINANCING THE DEVELOPMENT OF LUCCA SOFTWARE GROUP

Until now, the Filipe Foundation has advanced funds to the Giuliano Trust for the initial development of the Lucca Software Business, but Papa Filipe has now decided to fund the businesses direct rather than through the trust. This is to enable interest income to be owned by the Filipe Foundation for the benefit of other beneficiaries of the foundation than Papa Filipe's direct lineage, such as the second family he has created with Maria Rodriguez. Giuliano is happy with this development since he is sure that he and his children will also benefit from tax-free interest derived from financing the Lucca business, but is concerned about thin capitalisation issues. Giuliano is also concerned that the tax exposure for the Lucca Group in respect of inter-company sales and purchases may become considerable if adjustments are made under transfer pricing arrangements. In order to structure loans to the various subsidiaries of Lucca BV, the Filipe Foundation forms Filipe Finance BV as a Dutch finance company.

CREATING A LICENSING STRUCTURE

With Lucca Developments India having contracted directly with Lucca NV for research and development expenditure, Lucca NV is the owner of all rights relating to the development of the software business for Japan, China and the rest of the Far East. By creating Lucca License BV, Lucca NV hopes to maximise royalty returns from a subsequent relicence of the rights to Lucca Software Pty Ltd in Australia, a company that was formed to expand on the functions initially performed by the Australian representative office of Lucca Software SpA. However, Giuliano realises that there may be a dispute as to what rights are owned by Lucca NV (or the sub-licensee Lucca License BV) and what rights are the initial rights already owned by Lucca Software SpA.

Diagram 13

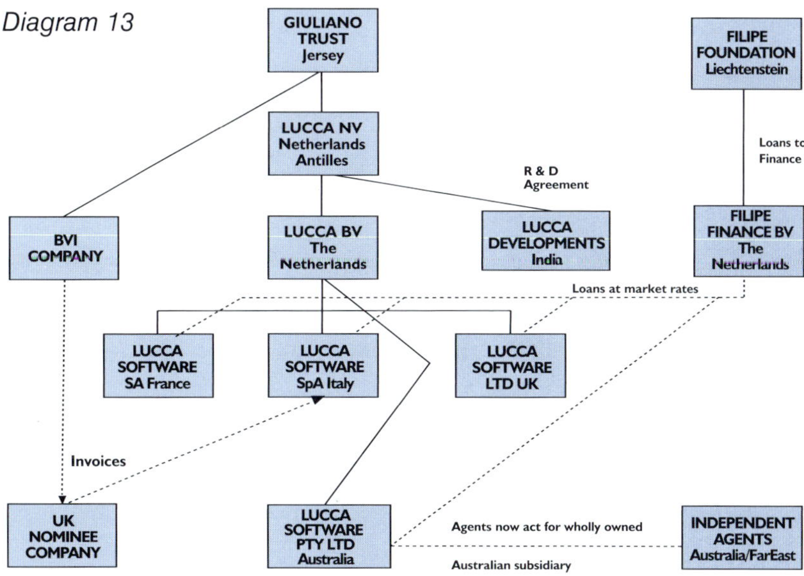

Diagram 14

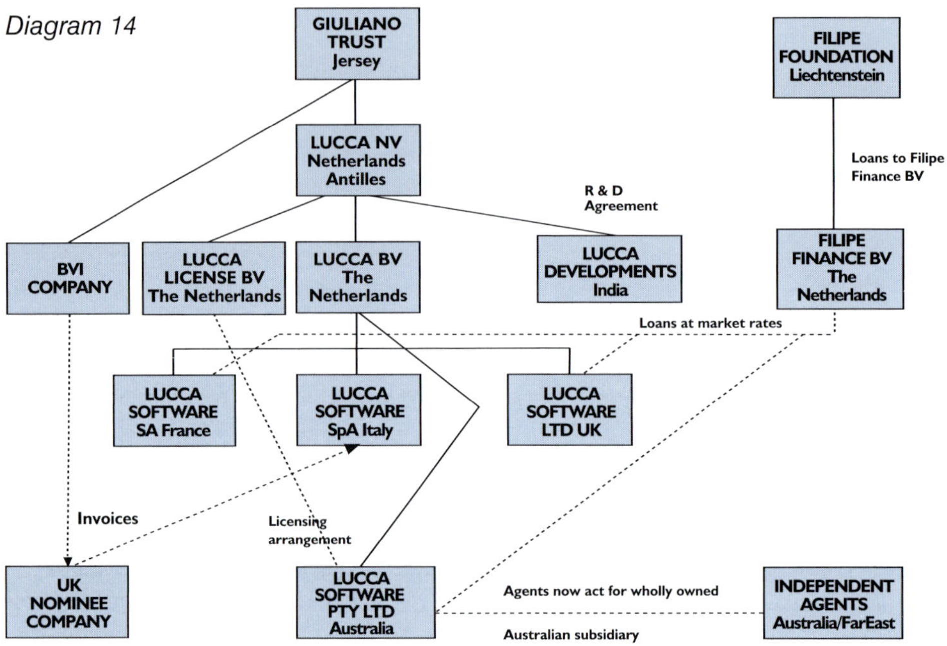
GIULIANO TRUST Jersey
FILIPE FOUNDATION Liechtenstein
LUCCA NV Netherlands Antilles
Loans to Filipe Finance BV
R & D Agreement
BVI COMPANY
LUCCA LICENSE BV The Netherlands
LUCCA BV The Netherlands
LUCCA DEVELOPMENTS India
FILIPE FINANCE BV The Netherlands
Loans at market rates
LUCCA SOFTWARE SA France
LUCCA SOFTWARE SpA Italy
LUCCA SOFTWARE LTD UK
Invoices
Licensing arrangement
UK NOMINEE COMPANY
LUCCA SOFTWARE PTY LTD Australia
Agents now act for wholly owned
Australian subsidiary
INDEPENDENT AGENTS Australia/FarEast

Chapter 1
Is the Advice Lawful?

The first chapter of this book concentrates on probably the most fundamental question of all, and one which all tax advisers must consider before giving advice to their clients. As will be discussed later in the book, and in particular with reference to the Filipe family, the distinction between legal tax avoidance and illegal tax evasion is sometimes blurred.

1.1 TAX AVOIDANCE V. TAX EVASION

It is easy to see why taxpayers (and often their advisers, too) are not certain about what may and may not be done in their efforts to reduce their contributions to the *fiscus*:

Tax avoidance was to be distinguished from tax mitigation. The hallmark of tax avoidance is that the taxpayer reduces his liability to tax without incurring the economic consequences that Parliament intended to be suffered by any taxpayer qualifying for such reduction in his tax liability. The hallmark of tax mitigation, on the other hand, is that the taxpayer takes advantage of a fiscally attractive option afforded to him by the tax legislation, and genuinely suffers the economic consequences that Parliament intended to be suffered by those taking advantage of the option.[1]

From the above it is clear that the concepts surrounding tax minimisation are clouded by jargon. We shall attempt to bring some clarity to the relevant concepts and to their importance in the process of tax planning. Simplistically put, tax avoidance is the attempt to minimise tax within the confines of the law and may often involve a transaction entered into in order to obtain a certain tax benefit. This includes tax planning, tax mitigation, and both acceptable and unacceptable forms of tax avoidance. Conversely, evasion relates to illegal attempts to minimise tax.

1. Lord Nolan in *IRC v. Willoughby* [1997] STC 995 (HL), [1995] STC 143 (CA).

1.1.1 Avoidance

Tax avoidance generally includes situations where a person's liability to pay tax is avoided, reduced or deferred. However, unlike mitigation, tax savings results are achieved in a way that government did not intend.

Tax mitigation

Anyone may arrange his affairs so that his taxes shall be as low as possible; he is not bound to choose that pattern which best pays the Treasury. There is not even a patriotic duty to increase one's taxes. Over and over again the Courts have said that there is nothing sinister in so arranging affairs as to keep taxes as low as possible. Everyone does it, rich and poor alike and all do right, for nobody owes any public duty to pay more than the law demands.

Thus proclaimed US Court of Appeals Judge Learned Hand in *Helvering v. Gregory.*[2]

It is widely accepted[3] that taxpayers who mitigate their tax liability are not likely to be subject to anti-avoidance legislation. Mitigation amounts to a reduction of a taxpayer's tax liability not by entering into an 'arrangement', but by a reduction of income or by an increase in expenses. Tax mitigation often is the result of forward tax planning.

Acceptable tax avoidance

In some cases government promulgates laws that are aimed at a reduction, often permanent, of tax liability for taxpayers. Where taxpayers avail themselves of such opportunities by directing their affairs in such a way as to reduce taxes, the tax avoidance is acceptable. Tax incentives and tax holidays are examples of such measures introduced by government.[4]

Unacceptable tax avoidance

Some tax avoidance is within the confines of the law, but was not intended by government. Such kind of tax avoidance often results from loopholes or defects in the law, and is contrary to what government intended. A common example is treaty shopping, which will be discussed in more detail in §4.4.

Tax mitigation and avoidance relate to the question of whether a tax liability has arisen, but with tax evasion a tax liability has always arisen but has been hidden from the tax authorities, with or without intent. Innocent tax evasion exists where the intent to defraud the tax authorities does not exist (e.g. where reportable income remains forgotten in a *bona fide* manner), and may lead to a reassessment.

2. 69F.2d 809.
3. See also Judge Templeman in *CIR v. Challenge Corporate Ltd* (1986) 8 NZTC 5,219.
4. Another example is that a married couple can reduce their exposure to inheritance tax by ensuring their wills are drafted in such a way that on the death of the first spouse all assets vest in the surviving spouse, on whose death inheritance tax will be due. Alternatively, it may be possible for a married couple resident in a civil law jurisdiction to separate their assets.

Fraudulent evasion exists where the taxpayer formed the intent to defraud the tax authorities, and may lead to a criminal prosecution together with a reassessment.

1.1.2 Constituent elements of avoidance and evasion

In determining whether a tax avoidance scheme exists, tax authorities look for certain elements when analysing the facts. Some of these elements are discussed below:

- Tax minimisation or elimination: the onus is on the tax authorities to prove that the tax paid was less than would otherwise have been the case.

- Lawfulness or legality of the transaction: tax planning, tax mitigation and tax avoidance are carried on within the confines of the law; however tax evasion, for example the non-declaration of profits, is illegal. The difference between tax avoidance and tax evasion is often a very thin line.

- Relevance of the purpose or motive of the taxpayer: generally, tax arrangements of which the primary motive and/or purpose is tax minimisation can be rebutted by the tax authorities.[5]

- Artificiality: where steps that have no other purpose than the avoidance of tax are inserted into a transaction, artificiality exists, but on its own is usually not enough to justify sanction by the tax authorities. In this respect, common law developed the 'business purpose' rule and the 'substance over form' rule. Under the former, a transaction must have a main purpose other than tax avoidance to be acceptable to the tax authorities. Under the latter doctrine, the facts must be assessed according to *bona fide* economic and commercial substance and not the formal content. Comparable concepts under civil law are the *abus de droits* and *fraus legis* concepts.[6]

- Exploitation of loopholes: this involves the exploitation of defects in the law, and in itself is usually not enough to justify sanction by the tax authorities.

- Economic reality of transactions: generally, taxpayers are not entitled to tax advantages resulting from legal means that are different from the economic reality.

- Legislative intent or purpose: it is generally held[7] that a tax avoidance scheme is an attempt to reduce the tax liability to a level below which the legislature

5. It should be noted, however, that where a taxpayer's primary motive and/or purpose is to avail himself of certain incentives provided by government, the authorities would not rebut a transaction. This element thus involves a subjective test, which should be determined on the basis of the merits of each individual case.
6. These concepts are discussed in further detail in Chapter 6.
7. For example, by the OECD Committee on Fiscal Affairs.

intended and legislative intent is generally decisive of the question of legitimacy of the result.

1.1.3 The tax adviser's role

In order to assess whether tax advice is lawful, the tax adviser must have a client who is willing to divulge all the relevant facts. It is an impossible task to give meaningful tax advice if what is being disclosed is only half the story. This, however, creates difficulties in itself, because if the tax adviser is aware of circumstances that constitute, for example, 'money laundering' (this wide topic is discussed in §1.3), he is duty bound to make an official report[8] to the relevant authorities.[9] Not only that, but 'tipping off' the client that a report is being made is also an offence. The tax adviser's role and responsibilities have come a long way since September 2001, when the tax advisers' profession, along with many others, changed overnight. Money laundering legislation introduced subsequent to that date has imposed upon each tax adviser an overriding obligation to ensure that all aspects of the advice given are legal. The consequences are very penal[10] and, as such, 'know your client' policies and internal take-on and review procedures are vitally important to ensure and maintain the integrity of the office.

Now that the concepts of 'avoidance' and 'evasion' have been clarified, we turn the discussion to measures promulgated by government to counter avoidance techniques. Much of the anti-avoidance legislation referred to throughout this book is rooted in the 'transfer of assets'. In addition to anti-avoidance legislation, exchange control provisions (discussed in §1.6 of this chapter) are still a method of preventing assets, in particular cash, from being dissipated overseas.

1.2 ANTI-AVOIDANCE LEGISLATION

The topic of anti-avoidance legislation is key to this (and for that matter any international taxation) book. It is not possible to tax-plan without reference to anti-avoidance legislation. Understanding what the client can and cannot do within the bounds of the law, and indeed what constitutes 'acceptable tax avoidance' is of fundamental importance.

---

8. Known as a Suspicious Activity Report (SAR). A copy of an SAR form can be found at http://www.ncis.co.uk/disclosure.asp.
9. In the UK, the Economic Crime Branch of the National Criminal Intelligence Service (NCIS) will analyse the SARs it receives.
10. In the UK, for instance, under the Money Laundering Regulations (MLR) 2003 that came into effect on 1 March 2004, thereby implementing the requirements of the Second EC Money Laundering Directive in national law, the penalty for non-compliance could mean a maximum of two years in prison and/or a maximum fine of £5,000 (MLR 3 and 20). See §1.3 below for a further discussion in this respect, including potential penalties introduced by the Proceeds of Crime Act 2002.

Ever-increasing globalisation has greatly increased the international flow of cash and assets. Most developed countries, particularly those with worldwide systems of taxation, have anti-avoidance legislation to counter:

(a) the transfer of assets outside their borders;

(b) the non-declaration of income and capital arising outside their borders; and

(c) the non-declaration of rights in respect of overseas assets.[11]

The UK and the US have led the way in countering tax avoidance by the use of anti-avoidance legislation, and this has been the basis on which other developed countries have based similar legislation. This is an important point to note: while the international tax adviser cannot hope, or indeed profess, to know the tax laws in all the countries he encounters, he will know that there is a degree of similarity between the anti-avoidance provisions of, say, the US and France. In other words, while he may not know the detailed provisions of Article 209B,[12] he should know that similar laws exist in the US[13] to prevent domestic companies creating low or no-taxed subsidiaries and allowing these to shelter income from taxation. This is a fairly simple example, but it does make the point that the developed and developing tax systems around the world often follow the same format, and it is likely that if Country A has Controlled Foreign Company (CFC) legislation, then Country B will also have provisions, if not the same, then very similar.

The rules concerning the attribution of income and gains to individuals in the UK are discussed in Chapter 5. However, they are briefly reviewed here as examples of typical anti-avoidance measures.

1.2.1 United Kingdom[14]

Income and profits arising outside the UK as a result of a transfer of cash or other assets abroad by an individual subject to UK tax are nevertheless taxable under Sections 739 and 740 of the Income and Corporation Taxes Act (ICTA) 1988 and various sections of the Taxation of Chargeable Gains Act (TCGA) 1992.[15] It should also be noted that for these purposes *any* transfer of

11. For example, as a beneficiary of an offshore trust, usufruct rights, foreign partnership income and income from a foreign fiduciary arrangement.
12. French CFC legislation – for more on this topic see §5.3.2.
13. Section 951 of the Internal Revenue Code (IRC), and in particular subpart F income provisions.
14. The reader will notice that throughout this book reference is made to aspects of the law in selected countries. The jurisdictions were specifically chosen on the basis of such factors as particular relevance, illustrative value, interest, distinct characteristics and also the frequency with which issues in respect of these jurisdictions end up on the desks of international tax advisers.
15. Sections 13, 86, etc. These anti-avoidance provisions are discussed in greater detail in §5.4.

intellectual property rights outside the UK will be subject to the above provisions, or any services provided by an individual resident in the UK where the income flows to an offshore company that he owns (or when income can be applied for his benefit).

Also, the Chancellor of the Exchequer announced on 17 March 2004 new disclosure rules to require promoters and users of certain tax schemes and arrangements to disclose details relating to those arrangements to the Inland Revenue under part 7 of the Finance Act 2004. The Tax Avoidance Schemes Regulations took effect on 1 August 2004. The required report should include a summary of the proposal and the name by which it is known, as well as information on each element of the proposed arrangement from which the tax advantage is expected to be obtained. The Regulations outline certain transactions that have to be reported accordingly. These include arrangements under which tax advantages are obtained, based on the employment relationship (by using securities or associated rights, payments to trustees, or loans), or based on arrangements in relation to financial products where the tax advantage follows from using loans, derivatives, stock lending arrangements, etc.[16]

Additionally, it should be noted in this respect that it is illegal for a UK company to cause or permit a non-resident company over which it has control to create or issue any shares or debentures without Treasury consent, unless the transaction is covered by one of the General Consents. Similarly, if the company transfers such shares or debentures, other than to a non-related third party for full consideration, without Treasury consent, it will again commit a criminal offence.[17] The penalty for this is £10,000 or two years' imprisonment, imposed on both the directors and those advisers involved in recommending the arrangements. These restrictions do not apply to movements of capital between residents of member states of the EU.

1.2.2 United States

The Internal Revenue Service (IRS) and the US Treasury have been highly active in the passing of new legislation, together with the use of Treasury Notes, in an attempt to redress the balance of tax mitigation and planning in the favour of the US authorities. Anyone with US clients should ensure that they are up to date with the latest publication by the above agencies in order to comply with an environment increasingly hostile to tax planning. The US has also been highly active in attacking the promoters of tax 'shelter' schemes, often naming and shaming individuals whom it has yet to prove guilty of any wrongdoing. Examples of such transactions are those described by the US Treasury, generally effective from 28 February 2003:

16. More information on this in §6.2 under United Kingdom.
17. See ICTA 1988, Section 765.

(a) listed transactions (those involving tax shelters);

(b) those transactions 'offered under terms of confidentiality';

(c) those transactions which benefit from contractual protection;

(d) those transactions which create a loss ('loss transactions') that exceeds prescribed levels;

(e) those transactions which create a large 'book-tax difference';

(f) those transactions for which the asset has only been held for 45 days or less.

In addition to these, the US has also acted to close down specific schemes, such as those focused on creating paper losses,[18] and deferring tax through using stock options.

The IRS also continues to publish its annual list of 'dirty dozen' tax scams, which highlights tax schemes that do not work. For 2004, such schemes include the 'misuse of trusts' (the transfer of assets to trusts in order to achieve tax breaks such as reductions in income tax, gift or estate tax), 'offshore transactions' such as trusts and offshore employee leasing, as well as 'employment tax evasion' and identity theft.

One of the areas in which legislation is most likely to be reviewed is that concerning the relocation of company headquarters to tax havens. The debate reached its climax following the relocation of the headquarters of a number of companies, including Stanley Works, a US company, to Bermuda, thereby reducing tax due in the US. The ability of non-US companies to obtain taxation advantages over their US counterparts was viewed as a barrier to competitiveness for US companies.

Such inversions prompted the US Treasury to release a report entitled *Corporate Inversion Transactions: Tax Policy Implications*, which aims to curb some of the tax advantages mentioned above. The report concluded that a 'comprehensive review of the US tax system, particularly the international tax rules, is both appropriate and timely', with a mission statement of maintaining 'the position of the US as the most desirable in the world for incorporation, location of headquarters, and transaction of business'. The report itself looks at the nature of 'corporate inversions' and the tax consequences, as well as looking to end the tax advantages benefiting non-US companies operating in the US, including earnings stripping, income shifting and cross-border reorganisations. Finally, the report considers ways of ending the tax disadvantages felt by US-based multinationals.

18. This scheme was closed down under Notice 2002-65.

1.3 ANTI-MONEY LAUNDERING LEGISLATION

1.3.1 What is money laundering?

Money laundering can best be defined as the conversion of money derived from criminal activities into legitimate funds, or more simply the 'washing' of dirty money. The methods used for laundering dirty money can be extremely complex, and often involve trusts, companies (both offshore and onshore) and even the use of complex bank instruments.

In cases where employees of a financial institution suspect that they are being asked to deal with monies that have originated from illegal sources, they are obliged to inform the authorities. If they turn a blind eye, or 'wilfully neglect' to report a suspicious transaction, it is possible a criminal prosecution could ensue. There have been a number of high-profile cases in the US involving large investment houses that were in breach of US money laundering reporting requirements,[19] and the infamous BCCI was fined a total of $15 million for its involvement in money laundering. However, in today's climate, the fight against money laundering has reached new heights.

As the EU and other developed countries become more and more aggressive in their stand against money laundering, the criminal will target softer options. It is a fact that banks and financial institutions in the developing world are now being targeted as places to launder money. The answer to this problem is hard to find. Each country must be diligent in its policing of financial transactions and to this end the Financial Action Task Force (FATF), set up by the OECD, is regarded as the leading international anti-money laundering authority. The battle against money laundering is ongoing, and the regulations differ from country to country. Furthermore, the continuing evolution of the problem means that the rules themselves are constantly being rewritten and updated.

19. Contained in the Money Laundering Control Act 1986; the reader should note that the US has introduced substantial new anti-money laundering provisions under the guise of the USA PATRIOT Act 2001. This Act provides wide powers to federal officials to track and intercept communications, and vests the Secretary of the Treasury with regulatory powers to combat corruption of US financial institutions for foreign money laundering purposes. Under the Act, the Secretary is empowered to promulgate regulations under which securities dealers and persons in similar professions are to file Suspicious Activity Reports (SARs), require businesses to file SARs as well, establish minimum new customer identification standards, require financial institutions to maintain money laundering programmes and encourage financial institutions to share information concerning suspected money laundering activities. Sanctions under the Act include prohibiting laundering in the US of the proceeds of foreign crimes, increasing penalties for counterfeiting and providing authority to prosecute overseas fraud involving American credit cards.

1.3.2 Money laundering in the 21st century

The term money laundering conjures up the image of a sophisticated criminal who has the resources to go to great lengths to cover his tracks (after all, those who employ the services of a professional money launderer will generally not tolerate failure!). Historically, this would be correct, and the laundering of money would be the final step in the criminal chain, that is the conversion of the proceeds of crime and reintroduction thereof into the economy.

A. European Union

First Money Laundering Directive[20]

The EU introduced its Money Laundering Directive in 1993. The effect of this was that new rules concerning 'know your client' were introduced, together with record-keeping and the introduction of systems within firms for reporting suspicious transactions or knowledge of money laundering activities to a specially appointed and trained Money Laundering Reporting Officer (MLRO). However, these were mainly confined in their effect to so-called regulated sectors, namely those dealing primarily with investment activities.

Second Money Laundering Directive[21]

The EU required member states to put its Second Money Laundering Directive into effect by 15 June 2003. The importance of the Second Directive to most accountants and tax advisers is that it specifically includes those individuals in the previously regulated sector.

Money laundering, according to the new provisions, means:

> *... the following conduct when committed intentionally:*
>
> *(a) the conversion or transfer of property, knowing that such property is derived from criminal activity or from an act of participation in such activity, for the purpose of concealing or disguising the illicit origin of the property or of assisting any person who is involved in the commission of such activity to evade the legal consequences of his action;*
>
> *(b) the concealment or disguise of the true nature, source, location, disposition, movement, rights with respect to, or ownership of property, knowing that such property is derived from criminal activity or from an act of participation in such activity;*

20. 91/308/EEC.
21. 2001/97/EC.

(c) the acquisition, possession or use of property, knowing, at the time of receipt, that such property was derived from criminal activity or from an act of participation in such activity;

(d) participation in, association to commit, attempts to commit and aiding, abetting, facilitating and counselling the commission of any of the actions mentioned in the foregoing incidents.

The Directive uses an objective test, stating that 'knowledge, intent or purpose' can be inferred from the factual circumstances.

Article 3 of the Directive states:

1. *Member States shall ensure that the institutions and persons subject to this Directive require identification of their customers by means of supporting evidence when entering into business relations, particularly, in the case of the institutions, when opening an account or savings accounts, or when offering safe custody facilities.*

2. *The identification requirement shall also apply for any transaction with customers other than those referred to in paragraph 1, involving a sum amounting to €15,000 or more, whether the transaction is carried out in a single operation or in several operations which seem to be linked. Where the sum is not known at the time when the transaction is undertaken, the institution or person concerned shall proceed with identification as soon as it or he is apprised of the sum and establishes that the threshold has been reached.*

Article 6 states:

Member States shall ensure that the institutions and persons subject to this Directive and their directors and employees co-operate fully with the authorities responsible for combating money laundering:

(a) by informing those authorities, on their own initiative, of any fact which might be an indication of money laundering;

(b) by furnishing those authorities, at their request, with all necessary information, in accordance with the procedures established by the applicable legislation.

These increased requirements, already established in the regulated sector, include ensuring:

(a) that staff are properly trained to prevent money laundering;

(b) that systems are in place to counter money laundering;

(c) that all 'know your client' due diligence information has been gathered before a new client is taken on, and this must be maintained; and

(d) that internal reporting procedures are set up and maintained.

Many firms previously outside the regulated sector will already have such procedures in one form or another; however, if such procedures are not in place by the time that the regulations fully come into effect, the employer faces the prospect of a fine and even imprisonment.

B. OECD

As mentioned before, the OECD set up the FATF to co-ordinate its fight against money laundering. Through this body the OECD has forced compliance on many of the world's tax havens using its blacklist and the threat of sanctions for those who fail to comply with information exchange and the like. The OECD's purge of tax havens which it deems to contribute to harmful tax practices appears to have been highly successful, with just Andorra, Liberia, Liechtenstein, the Marshall Islands and Monaco failing to make the required commitment. There have of course been doubts raised, quite properly, by such jurisdictions over the level of safeguards in place in the developed countries that constitute the OECD.

C. United Kingdom

The UK Criminal Justice Act 1988 changed the face of UK anti-money laundering legislation. This Act and its successors[22] brought with them swingeing powers against money laundering. It is, however, misleading to assume that the relevant provisions apply only to money laundering; this is not true and in fact the extent of the provisions goes much further than any previous laws have done by creating offences with respect to the proceeds of criminal conduct, namely:

- assisting others in the retention of proceeds of criminal conduct;
- acquiring, possessing or using the proceeds of criminal conduct; and
- concealing or transferring the proceeds of criminal conduct.

The key phrase in this context is 'criminal conduct'. 'Criminal conduct' not only includes drug trafficking and terrorism (which one usually associates with money laundering), but indictable offences in general, which of course includes tax offences in most countries. Relevant provisions of the Proceeds of Crime Bill stirred a degree of panic among professionals in the UK, not least because of the 14-year maximum sentence[23] that could apply if found guilty. Debate raged as to whether

22. Most notably the Proceeds of Crime Act 2002, which came into force on 24 February 2003. The new Money Laundering Regulations offences have been created under part 7 of POCA 2002.
23. Now POCA 2002, Section 334.

tax offences were indeed covered, but the prudent adviser had to assume they were. This all became academic when the Proceeds of Crime Bill received Royal Assent on 24 July 2002, which brought with it a definition of money laundering so wide that tax evasion is undoubtedly caught. Not only that, but each firm must:

(a) appoint a suitably qualified Money Laundering Reporting Officer (MLRO);

(b) train staff in respect of their obligations under the new law;

(c) introduce or revise money laundering checks and 'know your client' policies;

(d) ensure that 'know your client' and due diligence information is maintained in respect of each client.

The international tax adviser might be under a further obligation, in that it does not matter where his client is based in the world; if he knows or suspects that tax has not been paid when it should have, he is duty-bound to make a report to the relevant authorities.[24] With the proliferation of mutual assistance treaties and bilateral and multilateral agreements, it is common for such information to be passed from one administration to another. The age in which we live is driven by transparency, and it is technology that permits this transparency to exist.

1.4 INFORMATION EXCHANGE

The exchange of information is of itself a fascinating subject, although it is something that the majority of tax advisers will not experience first hand. Not only that, but most clients will be unaware of the ability of one country to exchange detailed information with another, let alone appreciate that they may be willing to help one another with the collection and enforcement of tax debts.

1.4.1 EU Directive and EC/OECD Convention on Mutual Assistance

The Mutual Assistance Directive in the Field of Direct Taxation has been extended to value-added tax and excise duties.[25] Where exchange of information can be provided under a treaty or under the Directive, revenue authorities are likely to use whichever route for the exchange of information is most likely to give them the required result.

The Mutual Assistance Directive provides specifically for an exchange *on request* of a competent authority of a member state, or the *automatic* exchange of information and the *spontaneous* exchange of information where there is

24. Some are of the opinion, however, that based on the decision in *Government of India v. Taylor* [1955] AC 491 no report is required in respect of evasion of foreign taxes.

25. 77/799/EEC, as amended by Council Directives 79/1070/EEC and 92/12/EEC.

reason to believe there may be a loss of tax to the other member state.

Information exchange is arranged where there has been a reduction of or exemption from tax in one state which gives rise to an increase or liability in the other, or where transactions take place through another country to produce a tax saving in another member state. In particular, where there have been artificial transfers of profits within groups of enterprises, or where information has been obtained which could be relevant in assessing liability to tax in the other member state, the competent authorities exchange information. In this context, the OECD/Council of Europe Convention on Mutual Administrative Assistance in Tax Matters[26] provides for the collaboration of officials from both countries, consultation and the pooling of experience by revenue authorities. Information has to be kept secret in the same manner as information obtained by the local fiscal authorities.

Exchanges of information very often take the form of an exchange of computer data and this is a process that is likely to increase substantially. Fiscal authorities have co-operated in other ways, for example through the simultaneous examination of a company's branches or subsidiaries in two or more states, with each revenue authority making enquiries under its local provisions, but with a view to exchanging the results of their enquiries as may be relevant to the other jurisdiction.

In addition to the exchange of information, the Mutual Assistance Convention covers tax examinations abroad. This last provision is unusual, and it is provided that the decision as to whether the foreign representative may be allowed to be present lies exclusively within the hands of the competent authority of the state where the examination is to take place.

1.4.2 Information-gathering powers

In order to exchange information, the fiscal authority in any country has first to obtain it, but that information might be statute-barred, depending on the terms of the local legislation. The UK HMRC, for example, has power to obtain information from agents, and about employees' emoluments, fees and commissions paid, payments to agency workers, interest paid by banks, interest paid without deduction of tax, and in connection with rents. They can also obtain particulars of lodgers and licensees. The main powers given to the Inland Revenue to obtain information allow documents to be obtained from taxpayers and other parties. Particulars of Stock Exchange transactions carried on by a market maker may also be obtained.

26. European Treaty Series number 127; opened for signature by the EU member states and the member countries of the OECD at Strasbourg on 25 January 1988 and entered into force on 1 April 1995. Note that this convention has, at the time of writing, been signed by only around ten countries.

Under self-assessment, the Revenue's powers of enquiry and audit are extended still further. The disclosure of information may also be necessary to enable a credit to be obtained for UK tax in a foreign jurisdiction.

1.4.3 Other multilateral treaties

The most likely exchange, in practice, is under the appropriate bilateral double taxation treaties, or the Mutual Assistance Convention mentioned above. However, within Europe, there are other options that the authorities can pursue. For instance there is a Convention between Denmark, Finland, Iceland, Norway and Sweden on Administrative Assistance in Tax Matters, which is based on the Mutual Assistance Convention.

The calls for greater information exchange have been growing steadily stronger for some time now, with bodies such as the OECD increasingly supported by their members, usually developed western economic powers, seeking to prevent the loss of income and capital from their respective tax nets through non-declaration. With the ever-increasing threat of terrorism, fresh impetus has been added to the drive by the tax authorities and the criminal investigation units of most developed countries. This has been borne out by the following:

(a) an increasing number of newly negotiated information exchange treaties, particularly by the US and notably with jurisdictions such as the Isle of Man, Jersey and a number of other 'tax havens' in the Caribbean, including the BVI, Antigua and Barbuda, the Bahamas and the Cayman Islands;

(b) the continued attempts of the OECD to enforce its will on tax havens using its black list. In this regard the OECD published its report on harmful tax practices relating to financial activities on 9 April 1998, updated in 2004;

(c) the powers of the domestic authorities such as the IRS to attack tax schemes and their 'promoters' to break down the barrier of professional privilege between advisers and clients, and to obtain offshore credit card information on its citizens;

(d) the EU's much publicised Savings Tax Directive.[27]

The result of these measures is that 'tax planning' (and this term is used very loosely) based on non-disclosure (which is tantamount to tax fraud or evasion) is no longer an option in the vast majority of jurisdictions. As a side effect of the above, individuals with tax neutral issues, for example, confidentiality, will have witnessed a substantial erosion of their rights. This has relevance in particular to the EU Savings Tax Directive, over which there has been much debate during the

27. 2003/48/EC of 3 June 2003 on taxation of savings income in the form of interest payments. See also §3.2 for a more detailed discussion.

first years of the new millennium. However, not only is there an erosion of the rights of the taxpayer, but the quest for federalism within the EU has led to a number of jurisdictions agreeing to impose a withholding tax rather than hand over information to the EU. As discussed in Chapter 3, this follows the agreement struck with Switzerland and subsequently three EU member states.[28]

1.4.4 Double tax treaties

Perhaps of as much relevance and importance to the international tax practitioner as anti-avoidance legislation, double tax treaties play a vital role in our work. They allow the tax adviser and client to plan with a degree of certainty, they provide a framework within which to work and they permit the flow of international trade. These aspects of double tax treaties are discussed in greater detail in Chapter 4; this section is devoted to Article 26 of the OECD Model Treaty,[29] which allows for mutual exchange of information between those states party to a particular treaty.

The OECD's Model Treaty provides for wide powers in respect of exchange of information. Administrative assistance is dealt with in the Mutual Assistance Directive mentioned above. Under the Commentary to Article 26 of the OECD Model Treaty, the main rule is that the competent authorities of the applicable Contracting State will exchange information necessary to ensure the correct application of the provisions of the Model Treaty or of the domestic laws of the Contracting States concerning taxes covered by the Model Treaty.

1.5 MUTUAL COLLECTION OF TAXES[30]

1.5.1 European Union

The general rule that the courts of one state will not enforce tax debts owed by residents of that state to the revenue authorities of another state[31] is countered by both an EU Directive and the OECD Model Treaty.

Council Directive 76/308/EEC, otherwise known as the Mutual Assistance Recovery Directive (MARD), allows the taxation authority of one EU member state to recover tax owed to it by a person resident in another member state by direct action.

---

28. Austria, Belgium and Luxembourg.
29. The OECD Model Convention with respect to Taxes on Income and on Capital, of which there have been various versions and updates, the latest being 2005, which are vital reading to any international tax adviser.
30. Also note the comments in respect of the Mutual Assistance Convention discussed under §1.4.1, which provides for the recovery of taxes due in other treaty countries.
31. For example, this principle was confirmed by the English courts in the case of *Re Delhi Electric Supply and Traction Co. Ltd, Government of India, Ministry of Finance (Revenue Division) v. Taylor* [1955] AC 491.

MARD was originally restricted in its application to only a small number of taxes; however, its effect was broadened by Council Directive 2001/44/EC, following which it covers a number of taxes including VAT, income tax, corporation tax and capital gains tax.

The Directive provides the authorities of each member state with the authority to recover tax due to another state and apply interest and penalties in the same way as they would do so if the tax were owed to the member state. Article 6 of the original Directive states:

> *At the request of the applicant authority, the requested authority shall, in accordance with the laws, regulations or administrative provisions applying to the recovery of similar claims arising in the Member State in which the requested authority is situated, recover claims, which are the subject of an instrument permitting their enforcement.*

The application for recovery 'must be accompanied by an official or certified copy of the instrument permitting its enforcement, issued in the Member State in which the applicant authority is situated and, if appropriate, by the original or a certified copy of other documents necessary for recovery.'

The taxation authority of a member state cannot instigate recovery proceedings against a person in circumstances where the person can prove that proceedings concerning the outstanding tax claimed are ongoing, or will shortly commence in the appropriate member state. However, in circumstances where such proceedings are not followed through in a timely manner, it will then be possible for the member state in question to commence proceedings.

The request for recovery must indicate:

(a) the name, address and any other relevant information relating to the identification of the person concerned and/or to the third party holding his or her assets;

(b) the name, address and any other relevant information relating to the identification of the applicant authority;

(c) a reference to the instrument permitting its enforcement issued in the member state in which the applicant authority is situated;

(d) the nature and the amount of the claim, including the principal, the interest, and any other penalties, fines and costs due indicated in the currencies of the member states in which both authorities are situated;

(e) the date of notification of the instrument to the addressee by the applicant authority and/or by the requested authority;

(f) the date from which and the period during which enforcement is possible under the laws in force in the member state in which the applicant authority is situated;

(g) any other relevant information.

In circumstances where the claimant state has failed to apply appropriate recovery procedures, it may not be possible to request the application of MARD.

1.5.2 Non-European Union assistance in the collection of taxes

Agreements providing for the recovery of taxes are not restricted to the EU and the OECD Model Treaty also includes provisions similar to those contained within MARD. Article 27 of the OECD Model Treaty (condensed version) 2003 requires contracting states to assist each other in the collection of revenue claims. Furthermore, it is interesting to note that like Article 26 (Exchange of Information), the article is not restricted by Articles 1 (Persons Covered) and 2 (Taxes Covered). Paragraph 2 of Article 27 explains that the provisions encompass amounts owed in respect of taxes of any description as well as interest, administrative penalties and costs of collection or conservancy related to such amount. Paragraph 3 of Article 27 provides that the outstanding amount will be collected by one state on request of the other state in accordance with the provisions of the first-mentioned state's laws applicable to the enforcement and collection of its own taxes as if the revenue claim were a revenue claim of that state.

1.6 EXCHANGE CONTROL

The restrictions placed on the transfer of cash abroad used to be centred on exchange control. Exchange control was a common feature in the post-Second World War era, but is declining in its use as anti-avoidance legislation becomes more sophisticated and as the impediments to global trade and therefore economic prosperity becomes realised. However, it is important to remember that certain jurisdictions continue to impose exchange control restrictions. Although in practice the vast majority of tax advisers will seldom come into contact with exchange control, it is important that they are taken into account and not simply overlooked.

1.6.1 South Africa

There are a number of countries throughout the world that still impose exchange control, for example South Africa,[32] Russia and Zimbabwe. As an illustration as to how the exchange control mechanisms work, the main features of the applicable laws[33] in South Africa are briefly reviewed.

32. Administered by the Exchange Control Department of the South African Reserve Bank on behalf of the Minister of Finance.
33. In particular, the Exchange Control Regulations 1961 and the Exchange Control Rulings.

A. Residence

Exchange control has effectively been abolished over a period of time in relation to non-residents, and the government has expressed the intention of a gradual relaxation of the remaining exchange controls applicable to residents.[34] Where a non-resident transacts with a resident, it is the resident who is constrained under the exchange control legislation, as opposed to the non-resident. All South African residents are subject to the exchange control measures, and a conviction under the exchange control rules can amount up to R250,000 and/or five years in prison.[35]

Transactions between a subsidiary in South Africa and its holding company outside South Africa are regarded as being between a resident and non-resident, and are subject to the approval of the exchange control authorities.

In terms of the South African exchange control regulations, it is possible for a local entity to invoice in a foreign currency. However, payment made in the foreign currency must be converted to South African rand by an authorised bank upon receipt.

B. Fundamental exchange control restrictions

Authorised dealers

Regulation 2 extends authority to deal in foreign currency only to persons approved by the Reserve Bank as authorised dealers. No transaction or agreement to import and exchange foreign currency into rand, nor any transaction for the purchase of foreign currency with rand, nor agreements to exchange different denominations of foreign currency may therefore be concluded without an authorised currency dealer as an intermediary.

Export prohibition and 'financial assistance'

Regulation 3 prohibits the export of any currency from the Republic, whether in a direct or indirect manner, or any transaction which may have that effect (subject to exceptions in 'Approved remittances from the Republic' below). This regulation also prohibits residents from gaining financial assistance from non-residents. 'Financial assistance' is very widely defined in this context and includes the lending of currency, the granting of credit (except where the credit is granted for the purchase of goods or services), the taking up of securities, the conclusion of a hire purchase or a lease, the financing of sales or stocks, discounting, factoring, the guaranteeing of acceptance of credits, the guaranteeing or acceptance of any

34. As, for example, signified by the amnesty announced in early 2003 for South African residents who have contravened the Exchange Control Regulations on or before 28 February 2002.
35. Regulation 22.

obligation, a suretyship, a buy-back and a leaseback.

C. Local borrowing restrictions[36]

Although exchange control measures typically only constrain transactions between residents and non-residents, the ability of a resident South African company to borrow locally may be restricted in certain circumstances. Where 75% or more of the voting stock, capital or earnings of a local company is held or controlled directly or indirectly by a non-resident, the local company's ability to obtain financial assistance in the domestic market is subject to certain restrictions. The local company becomes an 'affected company' for exchange control purposes. 'Financial assistance' is widely defined, as referred to above. The primary purpose of these restrictions is to ensure the adequate capitalisation of foreign investments and to prevent excessive gearing.

An affected company's ability to borrow money from a South African lender is determined by the application of a prescribed formula that depends on both the composition of the company and the extent of the shareholder funds. The exchange control authorities at present permit an entirely foreign-owned company to borrow locally up to 300% of the shareholder investment in the affected company, i.e. the paid-up equity capital, preference shares, undistributed earned profits, shareholders' loans from abroad and, in certain instances, the shareholders' trade credit.

D. Approved remittances from the Republic

The following payments from the Republic are generally allowed under the circumstances specified for each, as exceptions to the restrictions imposed on the export of currency under Regulation 3.

Remittance of management fees

The remittance of management fees to a non-resident only requires exchange control approval if charged as a percentage of turnover or profit. Consequently, where management fees are charged on a basis similar to the methods applied by consultants (e.g. at a fixed hourly tariff), no exchange control approval is required. Instead, payments may be approved directly by any authorised dealer (i.e. a bank).

Remittance of dividends

South African exchange control regulations permit the remittance of dividends to non-resident shareholders. Dividends may be transferred to non-resident

36. Regulation 3.

shareholders without prior Reserve Bank approval. The payment of the dividend should, however, not cause the entity to exceed the allowable debt to equity ratio of 3:1. This situation may occur where dividends are declared out of retained income or other distributable reserves.

Remittance of interest

The rate and terms at which interest may be remitted to a non-resident must be approved by Exchange Control at the time of introduction of the loan. If the loan is denominated in rand, the rate must usually approximate the South African prime lending rate, currently around 12.5% per annum. This is in addition to the transfer pricing guidelines on interest for related parties, in terms of which the interest rate cannot exceed the relevant interbank rate plus 4% (for non-rand denominated loans) or prime plus 2% (for rand loans). Approval for the terms of repayment of the capital portion of the loan are also required.

[I.] CASE STUDY I

In this section of each chapter, some of the laws and rules explained in the preceding pages are applied to the tax plans made and advice received by the Filipes.

Chapter 1 deals with the first fundamental principle of international tax planning: *is the advice lawful?* This question has relevance to three issues in particular in the case study:

(a) the creation of the Filipe Foundation on the sale of Lucca Furnishings (Diagram 2);
(b) the creation of the Giuliano Trust to own the Lucca Software empire-to-be (Diagram 4);
(c) the use of a UK nominee company for invoicing operations (Diagram 7).

Diagram 2

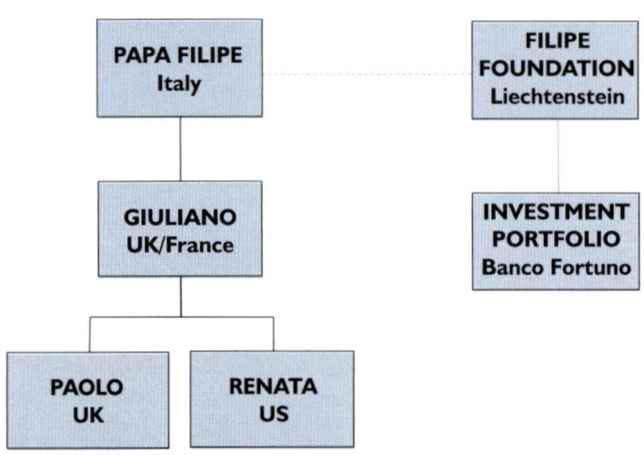

Diagram 4

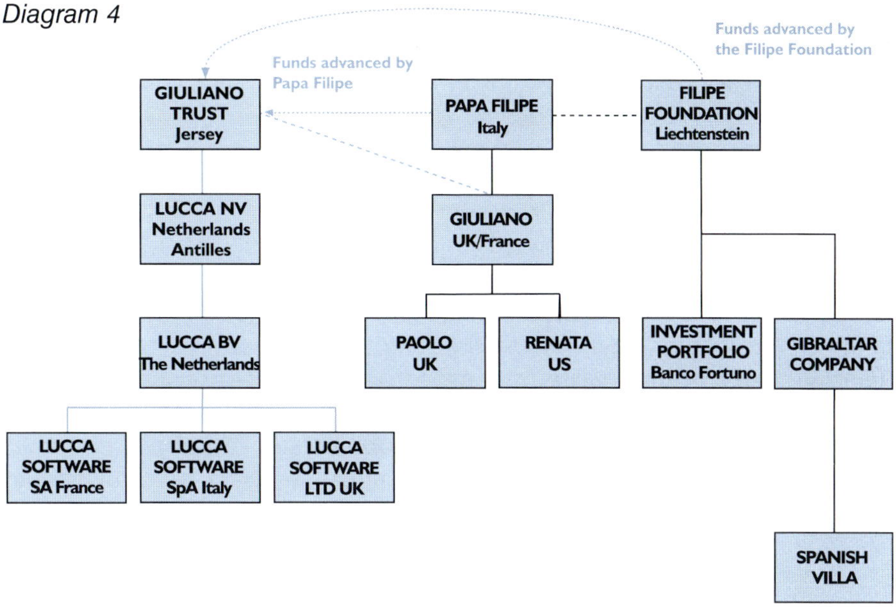

Diagram 7

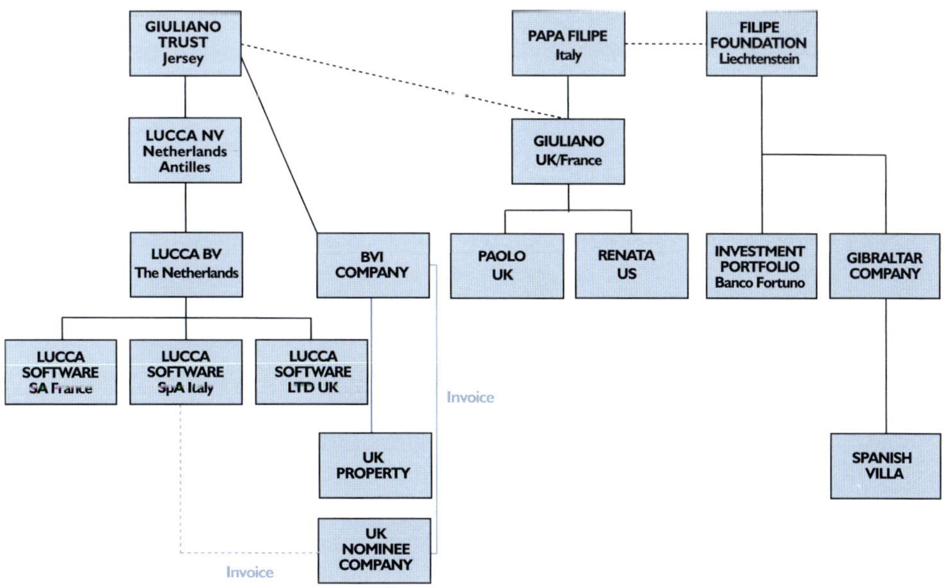

How does what was learnt in the first chapter apply to the actions that the Filipes and, where applicable, Maurice Brightman took to reduce their tax burden?

[I.a] Exchange control

You will recall that Papa Filipe, resident in Italy at the time, created the Filipe Foundation in Liechtenstein in 1980 during the sale of Lucca Furnishings. The Filipe Foundation creation was followed by the transfer of a small fortune of cash from Italy to the foundation.

Recently, Papa Filipe, who has never left the northern hemisphere, experienced a yearning to explore both new horizons and new business opportunities. He thought of creating a subsidiary in South Africa, 100% owned by the foundation. He would then use the subsidiary to borrow money from South African banks to fund his intended business of *biltong* manufacturing.

Papa Filipe ran this idea past Maurice Brightman. The tax adviser, always keen to ensure that his friends' and clients' tax plans are lawful, had to point out that South Africa still has strict exchange control measures in place. These need to be considered at all times, but in particular in the following instances:

(a) in transactions between the South African subsidiary and the Liechtenstein Foundation; and

(b) when the South African subsidiary is planning to borrow money from South African banks.

[i.] Transactions between the SA subsidiary and the foundation

Maurice explained that for tax purposes, the South African subsidiary would be a resident of South Africa, whereas the foundation would be resident in Liechtenstein. The South African exchange control measures are aimed at controlling outward investment, which means that they are focused on the exchange control transactions of South African residents, in our case the SA subsidiary. In practical terms, this means that Papa Filipe would need approval by the South African Reserve Bank under Regulation 3 to advance any of the locally borrowed money to the foundation, or conversely, before any money can be lent to the SA subsidiary by the foundation. However, once the *biltong* business starts being profitable, the SA subsidiary can remit dividends to the non-resident Liechtenstein Foundation without approval by the Reserve Bank. Papa Filipe was very happy to learn this news, since, born with a bit of a head for business, he expects the *biltong* business to become profitable in no time at all.

[ii.] SA subsidiary borrowing money from SA banks

Maurice had to remind Papa Filipe that the old businessman's plan of borrowing large amounts of rand to leverage the SA subsidiary may not be as simple as initially intended. He had to inform Papa Filipe that the local borrowing restrictions mean that the SA subsidiary, which is more than 75% held by a non-resident, will be an 'affected company'. This means that the SA subsidiary will only be able to borrow an amount equal to 100% of the investment that the foundation had made in the SA subsidiary.

The old Filipe, greatly discouraged at the prospects of such complications on far-away shores and too busy missing Maria Rodriguez to think of plans to circumvent South African exchange control laws, decided to spend his time investigating local business opportunities in *panettone* manufacturing instead.

[I.b] Anti-avoidance legislation

When Papa created the foundation back in 1980, Maurice was away on an extensive backpacking trip to the Far East, and could not be contacted for his expert international tax advice. However, Papa learnt from an Italian business contact that a large amount of lire (at the time) could be saved by transferring the money from Italy to Liechtenstein, provided that the Italian tax authorities did not find out about this. Papa proceeded with the Filipe Foundation creation. Had Maurice, on his return, heard of Papa's latest international tax planning spree, he would have had to rely heavily on the Buddhist relaxation techniques he acquired during his recent holiday abroad. What Papa had done amounted to tax evasion and was, moreover, fraudulent.

If Maurice had known, he would have had to advise Papa that all future income resulting from the Filipe Foundation and the expertly-looked-after Swiss investment portfolio should be declared in his annual Italian income tax return. If not, he would certainly have to deal with Italian anti-avoidance legislation, which could mean that Papa would no doubt need to pay the tax due on the income from Liechtenstein and Switzerland, and, more likely than not, some hefty interest and penalty charges. Maurice would have had to advise Papa that he was not keen on bailing clients out of jail, and that he would prefer Papa to stay within the bounds laid down by current Italian tax law – in keeping with many other developed countries' policy of increased attention to tax avoidance, Italian tax law, too, contains specific provisions aimed at counteracting specific tax-motivated transactions.

[I.c] Money laundering legislation

It was seen above that the Filipe Foundation was established under dubious circumstances. Had Maurice suspected that the money made from the sale of the soft furnishings business in Lucca had slipped through the fingers of the

Italian tax authorities untaxed, he would probably have been aware that non-payment of tax due in Italy at the time was a criminal offence. If only Papa had availed himself of the Italian tax amnesty![37] Maurice knew that under the *current* law in the UK he would have had a duty to report the non-payment of Italian tax to the National Criminal Intelligence Service, but he hoped that the *Government of India* decision relieved him of this duty since the applicable tax was foreign.

Furthermore, following the creation of the Giuliano Trust, had Maurice learnt of Papa's decision to advance funds from the foundation to Jersey, he would have known that, under the legislative parlance, the money forwarded from Liechtenstein to Jersey was laundered – the money made from the sale of the soft furnishings business left Italy untaxed, and was essentially converted into legitimate funds by forwarding them to Jersey.

[I.d] Information exchange

Giuliano's hard work had borne fruit in the form of the very profitable Lucca Software SpA in Italy, which develops software for business systems, in particular for Italian banks. Giuliano was advised (be it said: *not* by Maurice Brightman) to use the BVI company for extracting profits from the Italian company via a UK nominee company, which issued inflated invoices to the Italian subsidiary for services rendered by software development consultants employed by the BVI company.

Where transactions within the EU take place to produce a tax saving in a member state, the EU Directive and EC/OECD Convention on Mutual Assistance allow the tax authority of the relevant member state to obtain information in respect of its tax loss. These are particularly used where profits are transferred artificially within group companies. It is believed that the consultants employed by the BVI company charged an excessive fee for their services. The money was extracted from the Italian subsidiary through the use of the UK nominee company. The Italian tax authorities will in all likelihood be very keen to learn about the inflated invoices issued through the UK nominee company. No doubt the Italians will, under the Directive and the Convention, request the UK tax authorities to disclose information obtained from the UK nominee company on the true cost of the consultants' services, to allow them to compare this to the amounts included in the invoices to the Italian subsidiary. In fact, a simple request to furnish the Italian tax authorities with a set of accounts submitted to the UK Inland Revenue would probably reveal that only nominee fees had been included in the profit and loss account. The fees charged to the Italian company may be left out of account since they are held only as nominee for the BVI company.

37. See §5.6.2.

[I.e] Mutual collection of taxes in EU countries

The Mutual Assistance Recovery Directive allows a member state to recover tax, by direct action, that a person owes that state, even though that person might be resident in another member state.

Giuliano is renting a flat in Paris and is spending much of his time in the city while taking care of the French operation of Lucca Software. He decided to maintain the UK property bought by the BVI company. Giuliano's thinking in this respect was that he would rather remain a tax resident of the UK, which means that he would be liable to tax in the UK only, rather than become a tax resident of France. When he asked Maurice about this idea of his, the tax adviser reminded him that since he is spending a substantial part of his time working there, the French tax authorities might be interested in obtaining at least a proportionate part of his income earned while working in France. The French could easily use the Mutual Assistance Recovery Directive to instruct the UK, where Giuliano is hoping to remain a tax resident, to levy the tax due to the French *fiscus*, including interest and penalty charges applicable.

[I.f] Conclusion

The question of legality of the international tax planning is the first hurdle that any advice given has to clear. It is evident that in the trials of the Filipes, it is often easy, on paper, to reduce the tax burden in a particular country, but in practice a fraud on the relevant tax authority has to bear its resulting wrath. The international tax adviser has to keep in mind that although it might seem easy to escape tax liability in a particular country, it is not always so easy to keep within the bounds of the tax laws. Thus, the answer to the question '*Is the advice lawful?*' should always be an unequivocal 'yes'. Ensuring this important fact, in addition to the considerations that any tax advice given should also be commercially viable based on a client's specific circumstances, but complicated by the new role of the tax adviser as whistleblower under the new MLR and the provisions of POCA, makes this aspect of the role of tax adviser rather complex, at the very least.

Chapter 2

Why Are Trusts Useful in Tax Planning?

If there has been one entity that has been extensively used in international tax planning in Anglo-Saxon countries over the last 25 years, it is the offshore discretionary (and, to a lesser extent, life interest) trust,[1, 2] generally with an underlying offshore subsidiary company. This is due to the concept of separation of legal and equitable ownership, something which is generally unknown in civil law jurisdictions. This separation of ownership means that the legal ownership can fall outside an individual's estate for inheritance tax, income tax and capital gains tax purposes (subject to relevant anti-avoidance legislation),[3] while nevertheless being able to be enjoyed by the beneficiary and his family. Surely this is too good to be true? The UK HMRC, the US IRS and tax authorities of many other developed countries think so, and have gradually introduced anti-avoidance legislation to erode the benefits derived from offshore trusts.

Nevertheless, trusts are still very widely used, both for tax and other purposes, such as asset protection, off-balance sheet transactions, charitable and philanthropic

1. A life interest trust may be defined as a kind of fixed interest trust, which is a trust in terms of which the settlor specifically identifies which beneficiaries are to benefit, and expressly stipulates how and when they are to enjoy the trust property in the future. By contrast, a discretionary trust is a trust under which the settlor chooses a class of potential beneficiaries and gives trustees the power to determine how much (if anything) each beneficiary should receive and at what time.
2. Successive interests are created in the trust property when a life interest trust is established. A contingent interest trust, which is another kind of fixed interest trust, is one whereby the beneficiary can obtain access to the trust fund on the occurrence of a certain, specified event. More about specific types of trusts in §2.4 below.
3. Outlined in greater detail in §5.4.

causes and so on. Even if to a large extent the tax benefits have been eroded, trusts still play an important role in pre-immigration tax planning, that is to say they are often used to drop off assets before an individual becomes resident in a new country, or to 'bed and breakfast' assets with latent gains so as to up-lift their base cost.

This chapter illustrates the concept of trusts, and related problems, similarities to other legal concepts and the taxation consequences on settlors and potential beneficiaries in various countries. The interaction between trusts and some tax treaties are outlined, and selected examples of specific types of trusts are given.

2.1 BASIC TRUST CONCEPTS

2.1.1 Background

The trust concept was born out of Anglo-Saxon common law and equity[4] and relies on the distinction between a legal interest in property[5] and an equitable interest.[6] The legal interest vests in the trustee and represents title to the assets giving him the right to manage, administer and transfer those assets. The beneficiaries have an equitable interest in the trust property.

2.1.2 Basic trust mechanism

Generally, a trust is formed when an individual or a corporation (the settlor) transfers cash or assets (the trust fund) to individuals or a corporation (the trustees)[7, 8] on the understanding (expressed in writing in the trust deed) that the trustees will invest, administer and distribute the income and capital of the trust fund for the benefit of specified parties, or a class of persons (the beneficiaries).

2.1.3 The three certainties

In *Knight v. Knight*[9] three 'certainties' were laid down as essential requirements of a valid trust under English law, which have been adapted in all Anglo-Saxon

4. A system of law based on a broad discretion to assist parties who did not have recourse under common law.
5. I.e. an absolute ownership interest.
6. I.e. a personal right, enforceable against the legal owner.
7. The trustee is very often a corporate trustee in order to ensure continuity and provide limited liability status for the trustee.
8. The settlor may have reservations in transferring his assets to trustees with whom he has had no previous relationship. For the trust to succeed, it is generally accepted that he cannot continue to control the assets, otherwise legal ownership will not have passed to the trustees and the purposes for which the trust has been created may not be achieved. The settlor may have a confidant who may not be able to fulfil the role of trustee, but who may be willing to act as a 'protector'. In this respect the trust deed can be drafted in such a way that some of the most important powers of the trustees may only be exercised with the consent of the protector.
9. (1840) 3 Beav.148.

countries that have based their trust law on English law. Without these certainties, the trust will fail. They are as follows:

Certainty of intention

A settlor must have the intention to create a trust, displayed by clear, unambiguous language in the trust instrument. It has to be clear that the settlor intended a binding fiduciary obligation to be imposed on the trustee.

Certainty of subject matter

A trust will not have been created unless the property which the settlor intended the trustee to hold on trust is also certain. If the subject matter is uncertain, the trust will fail. Accordingly, assets to be held in trust have to be described with sufficient precision to ensure that they are identifiable or the assets have to be defined so that they can be ascertained with certainty.

Certainty of objects

In order for a valid trust to have been created, the identity of the beneficiaries must be certain, i.e. the beneficiaries must be either named or else defined so that they can be ascertained with certainty.

2.1.4 Benefits of trusts

The trust is administered in accordance with the intentions of the settlor, and the trust deed, within reason, can include any terms the settlor wishes. In addition, it is usual for the settlor to set out his intentions for the trust in a letter of wishes to or memorandum of understanding by the trustees, indicating how the trust funds are to continue to be administered; these wishes can be varied by the settlor at any time during his lifetime and are non-binding on the trustees. This means that the legal control of assets can be distinctly separated from their economic enjoyment, and in effect the settlor continues to exert a degree of influence over the trust during his lifetime. This ability to have influence over assets in the trust, but not have legal ownership, results in many benefits, examples of which are as follows.

Main uses

For the well-off individual who wants to ensure that his wealth can continue for the benefit of future generations, the trust may be a useful tool. The settlor can effectively lock up the capital of the trust and specify to whom the income and capital should be paid in the years to follow. He can also give the trustees the discretion to pay the income or capital to the beneficiaries if they think it appropriate. For example, the settlor can guard against or provide for the following:

(a) giving a spouse or parent the benefit of the asset for his life but for the children to have the property ultimately, so achieving a result which would not have been obtained if the property were passed directly to the spouse or parent as a gift;

(b) avoiding the dissipation of an outright gift, possibly because the beneficiary of the gift is financially immature or too young;

(c) using the trust for making gifts in the future for providing for children or grandchildren (whether born or not), either equally or unequally depending on the circumstances which prevail at that time: financial need, conduct, health, marriage, success, etc.;

(d) passing assets to individuals with anonymity to provide for individuals or circumstances in a confidential manner;

(e) adding further beneficiaries at any time and changing the terms under which the assets are to be held or dealt with at any time by the settlor issuing a fresh letter of wishes or memorandum of understanding.

One example of wealth preservation would be the case of a family-controlled company which might otherwise become split between many members of a family who might not be directly interested in the business. In a case like this, a trust can be used to preserve continuity of ownership and management while enabling the family as a whole to continue to benefit.

High-risk individuals may need to transfer their assets into a trust in order to protect them against claims by third parties. Following the transfer, the assets are no longer in the legal ownership of the settlor, and provided the transfer was done at a time when no known liabilities existed, the transfer will be valid. If the transfer was done so as to put assets beyond the reach of known or anticipated creditors, the transfer would probably be set aside.[10]

Finally, assets within a trust may fall outside the exchange control laws of the country of which the settlor is resident.

Alternative to a will

The proving and administration of a deceased person's estate can be cumbersome and costly, and they often cause cash-flow difficulties as well as emotional upsets for the dependants of the deceased. Trusts do not require the formalities of probate administration in order to make distributions of income and capital following a death. The trust may therefore own all of the individual's estate and replace his will, or else own a part of it with a view to supporting dependants while the deceased's estate is administered.

10. See also §2.4.2.

The re-writing of wills or drafting of codicils is time-consuming and rigid in formality. A discretionary trust requires only a fresh letter of wishes from the settlor for the trustees to be able to administer the trust in accordance with the settlor's revised intentions.

However, if trusts are to be recognised in European countries, which is currently not the case with a few exceptions,[11] it will be important that they do not contravene any other laws prevailing in that country relating to the disposition of assets. In particular, most European countries have adopted laws on what is known as 'forced heirship', whereby an individual is not free to dispose of all or part of his assets to any individuals other than his spouse or children. If a trust has been created with the specific intention of defeating forced heirship provisions, it will often be considered either by direct provisions or jurisprudence to be invalid, as it is against public policy.[12]

Fiscal benefits

The position will vary from country to country, but trusts formed in most offshore jurisdictions can offer particularly attractive fiscal benefits when assets are placed in separate legal ownership from that of the settlor. Trusts may be used in all aspects of tax planning, but it is the status of the settlor in particular, and to a lesser extent that of the beneficiaries, that will determine whether or not the trust, even if resident in a low- or non-tax jurisdiction, is tax efficient. Simply because the trust is established under the laws of the Isle of Man, for example, does not mean that it is effective in terms of tax mitigation.[13]

Anonymity

Trusts located in certain jurisdictions do not require registration and do not allow production of the trust deed to any authority, unless by injunction or court order. It is also possible to draft the trust deed without the name of the intended parties appearing on the deed itself – in this case the trust is formed by a declaration of trust. In days gone by, such trusts were often used and became colloquially known as 'black hole' trusts, since there was scant information in the deed itself. The settlor was not named, the assets listed in the trust would generally specify the settled sum, often a nominal £100, and the beneficiaries would be the RSPCA, International Red Cross or other such charity. The perceived benefit of this type of trust drafting was limited to secrecy. Anonymity is a benefit of a trust, and is certainly an issue with individuals resident in high-risk regions such as South America, where the risk of kidnap is greater than may be realised. For this type of client, the use of a trust for anonymity is understandable. For the individual who wants to use a trust to 'hide' assets from the tax authorities, such use is misguided.

---

11. Refer to the discussion at §2.2.
12. Compare the discussion under §2.2.2 under France.
13. See discussion of attribution of trust gains and income to the settlor and beneficiaries in §5.4.

2.2 TRUST RECOGNITION

In contrast with the recognition of trusts under Anglo-Saxon common law, the legal and tax treatment of trusts in civil jurisdictions is still uncertain. However, there has been significant movement towards the acceptance of trusts by continental European countries familiar with the Code Napoleon (as opposed to common law). The 1985 Hague Convention on the Law Applicable to Trusts and on their Recognition ('the Convention') accepted the basic concept of trusts as described above. To date, the Convention has only been ratified by two civil law countries: Italy and the Netherlands. Court cases in Belgium, Denmark, France,[14] Switzerland[15] and the Netherlands, among other countries, have established that trusts validly created under Anglo-Saxon law may be upheld in continental courts, particularly if the settlor was resident in an Anglo-Saxon jurisdiction at the time of settling the trust, and if the assets are located outside the jurisdiction of the continental countries.[16]

However, despite the Convention, trusts are often not recognised either from a legal or tax perspective, especially in continental countries where the Code Napoleon does not recognise the difference between legal and equitable ownership. This creates a number of complex problems for the client, both in terms of understanding the arrangement and in terms of the effectiveness of the trust structure.

2.2.1 The Hague Convention

The purpose of the Convention, referred to above, is to give recognition to trusts as separate legal entities in jurisdictions where trusts are not known within domestic jurisprudence. However, ratification of the Convention alone is not enough to overcome the problems created by failure to introduce corresponding concepts in domestic law. Article 5 states that 'the Convention does not apply to the extent that the law specified... does not provide for trusts or the category of trusts involved'. This is the first severe limitation of the Convention and introduces substantial doubt as to whether the Anglo-Saxon trust concept can be introduced at all into civil law systems.[17]

With regard to the recognition of the trust, Article 11 states that a trust *created* in accordance with the applicable law shall be recognised as such. There are minimum, but very important, implications of such recognition relating to the essence of the trust itself:

14. For example, in *Epoux Courtois et autres c. Consorts de Ganay*, 10 January 1970, Revue critique de droit international privé 1971, p. 518, note G.A.L. Droz; *Caron c. Odell* (1986) Revue critique de droit international privé 66; *Zieseniss* Cour de cassation, 20 February 1996, and Cour d'Appel de Paris, No. 91.12837.
15. *G v. C Trust Co (Jersey) Ltd* 4 ITELR 779.
16. More about this under §2.2.2.
17. A problem which Italy, for example, has experienced.

(a) the trust property constitutes a separate fund;

(b) the trustee may sue and be sued in his capacity as a trustee;

(c) the trustee may appear or act as such before a notary or any person acting in an official capacity.

An important practical consequence is that the tax administration will no longer be able to reclassify the trust into a known civil law concept.

Thus, one may conclude that the Convention recognises trusts created under a legal system that authorises their existence, but that it does not go one step further by opening the civil law systems to accept the constitution of a domestic trust.

2.2.2 Trust recognition around the world

In this section, selected aspects of the basic approach taken by the courts towards trusts in various jurisdictions, both common and civil law, is investigated. However, it should be noted that in many civil law countries it might not be possible to distinguish a trend in trust recognition from the cases discussed, since the courts in these countries tend to hold that each case must be decided on its own facts and merits.

Denmark

In a landmark case[18] the Danish special tax court held that an Anglo-Saxon trust may be recognised for Danish tax purposes. Although the local tax administration attempted to ignore the existence of the trust on the basis that it did not comply with the requirements laid down for Danish foundations, the tax court held that this was not a fundamental requirement and that it was only necessary for the trust agreement to comply with the requirements under foreign (in this case, Guernsey) law. Additionally, the trustees showed sufficient integrity and could not therefore be considered as mere puppets of the Danish resident individuals, who were the intended beneficiaries. The court held that a proper gift of the assets had been made irrevocably by the settlor, so that the settlor could not be considered to be the owner of the trust property. It was also held that there were no beneficial owners of the property as it was uncertain which of the beneficiaries would finally become owners of the property due to the discretionary powers of the trustees. Neither the taxpayers (the intended beneficiaries) nor the settlor had been named as a beneficiary with a vested interest so that the assets of the trust could not be held to be theirs. The court held that they should not therefore be subject to Danish wealth tax in respect of the trust's assets.

18. TFS 1994, 605, 11 July 1994.

The decision is a major stride forward in trust recognition in civil law countries, although any decision can only be relied upon to the extent of the facts of the particular case in question; the important elements of this case were that the trust was *irrevocable and discretionary*, and that neither the settlor nor his wife could benefit from the trust.

France

In France the rules relating to 'forced heirship' represent a significant obstacle to the acceptance of trusts. The rules state that a parent is obliged to leave a certain portion of his inheritable estate to his children. Thus, one child is entitled to 50% of his parent's assets, while two children share 66.67% and three or more share 75%. Any legacy or other act that restricts these percentage interests may be declared null and void by the court on application of the children concerned.

These principles are the basis of the French rules of inheritance and, as such, are generally held to be issues of public policy. There is no single definition of this term, but the legal effect is that public policy provisions cannot be set aside by contract, which would include trust deeds. Contractual attempts to defeat public policy provisions will not be supported by the French courts. Consequently, the position taken by the French courts has been to extend a cautious recognition of the effects of trusts, provided that their terms do not seek to set aside the public policy provisions of French inheritance law.

Israel

As part of the ongoing tax reform in Israel, Israeli residents are now taxable on their worldwide income. A committee has been set up by the Israeli tax authorities to consider the effect this will have on Israeli citizens with assets held in onshore and offshore trusts. The basic principles that the committee has decided to follow and which should be passed in the Israeli Parliament within the foreseeable future are:

(a) trusts would be regarded as transparent in circumstances where assets are held in trust for the benefit of Israeli beneficiaries. The tax rate imposed will therefore be the same as would have been imposed had the assets been held by the beneficiaries personally;

(b) the recommendations apply only to irrevocable trusts;

(c) an assessment for the tax due on the trust will be served on the trustees on behalf of the beneficiaries;

(d) trust revenue will be taxed on a current basis, even if it is not distributed to the beneficiaries;

(e) the place of residence of the trustee has no importance in terms of tax liability.

Italy

Italy ratified the Convention in 1985, and provided that a trust is effected under the laws of a country that provides for trusts, such as the UK, Italy will recognise its existence. Provided that the trust is governed by the laws of such a country, it is possible for both the settlor and beneficiaries to be Italian and trust assets to be Italian situs. However, while Italian law recognises the trust concept, Italian tax law makes no references to trusts. Whereas this can create a problem in respect of applying the basic trust concepts, it can also lead to interesting possibilities whereby payments from a trust to Italian resident beneficiaries are not subject to tax since they do not fall within one of the categories of taxable income. However, how long this will continue to be the case is the question.

Norway

The Norwegian Supreme Court had to decide on the ownership of a trust for CFC purposes and during the course of its decision analysed aspects of the trust concept. In reaching its conclusion, the court held that the beneficiaries, resident in Norway, did indeed control the trust, thus negating the distinction between legal and beneficial ownership, and held for the government.[19]

South Africa

In respect of the taxation of trusts, those established or managed and controlled in South Africa are taxed as separate entities, while foreign trusts managed and controlled outside South Africa are subject to attribution rules on the settlor or, failing this, on the beneficiaries upon a distribution from the trust.

Sweden

The Swedish tax authorities had to consider how Swedish law applied to a common law trust. A Swedish citizen who created an Isle of Man discretionary trust while non-resident in Sweden (the beneficiaries being related to the settlor) sought a preliminary ruling from the Tax Panel[20] as to the applicability of Swedish wealth and income taxes on the trust prior to moving back to Sweden. The Tax Panel found that in order to establish how the trust was to be treated under Swedish law, it was first necessary to establish what Swedish entity was analogous to a trust, and in this connection it was held to be the foundation.

19. *State of Norway (Central Office for Large Companies) v. Olsen and Others Re The Ptarmigan Trust* 2 ITELR 482, 5 ITELR 77.
20. *Re an Isle of Man Trust* (1998/99) 1 ITELR.

Points considered of importance were:

(a) the trust had been created by a non-resident of Sweden and in accordance with Manx law, and was administered in the Isle of Man by resident trustees;

(b) the settlor and the beneficiaries had no right to the income of the trust and as such none of them could be assessed to wealth tax on the assets of the trust;

(c) a Swedish resident beneficiary who received lump sums or periodic payments from the trust assets would be liable to Swedish income tax on the amounts received.

It is interesting to note that this ruling has been referred to by other Scandinavian countries in order to ascertain the treatment of common law trusts. The above three factors are therefore considered to be the way in which trusts *should* be considered for tax purposes by civil law countries, provided that the trusts are irrevocable and the trustees have full discretionary powers as to how much of trust income and capital should be paid at any time to the named or unnamed beneficiaries.

Switzerland

The trust concept is unknown to Swiss law and there are therefore no provisions in the statutes dealing directly with the trust. However, the Swiss tax authorities have to deal with trust issues as it is quite common for Swiss residents to be beneficiaries of foreign trusts or for foreigners who have set up trusts to move to Switzerland. Moreover, common law trusts are often administered in Switzerland.

The Swiss tax authorities have in the past applied rules which govern situations resembling trusts. In the case *Harrison v. Credit Suisse*,[21] the Swiss Federal Court found that a trust settlement could be viewed as a combination of various legal concepts recognised by Swiss law, namely the agency (mandate), the fiduciary arrangement, the promise to give, the contract in favour of a third party, and the usufruct.[22]

The Netherlands

With regard to an irrevocable discretionary trust, the Dutch Supreme Court on 18 November 1998[23] held that the transfer of assets by a Dutch resident settlor to an irrevocable discretionary trust was a transfer subject to gift tax. The Supreme

21. RO 96 II 79.
22. Some of these constructions are discussed under §2.6.
23. Four decisions: three concerning a Jersey irrevocable discretionary trust (cases 31756, 31757 and 31758) and one concerning a Cayman Islands irrevocable discretionary trust (number 31759) published in BNB 1999/35 C*, VN 1998/56.23, BNB 1999/36 C* and BNB 1999/37 C*.

Court ruled that the rates were those applicable to unrelated persons.[24] The fact that the trust described above was an irrevocable discretionary trust meant the beneficiaries did not have an enforceable right to payments out of the trust. Whether this means that the beneficiaries will not be taxed with regard to payments out of the trust is unclear, as the judgment did not cover income tax or wealth tax (wealth tax no longer exists, due to the changes in the Dutch Income Tax Act). Furthermore, other trust forms are not covered by the 18 November 1998 decisions. This is no doubt an area that the courts will have to consider again in the future and Dutch law in this respect is by no means concrete. No developments can be noted after the 18 November 1998 Supreme Court decisions.

On the question of whether the transfer of property to a trust can be considered a taxable acquisition by the beneficiaries, a distinction has been made between revocable, irrevocable, discretionary and/or non-discretionary trusts. The above decisions held that the transfer of property to an irrevocable discretionary trust can be considered a taxable acquisition by the trust. It cannot be considered a taxable acquisition by the beneficiary, since the beneficiaries have not yet benefited. The Dutch Supreme Court ruled that the transfer of property by a Dutch resident settlor to an irrevocable discretionary trust is subject to gift tax because three conditions are met: a gift is considered present if (a) the donor impoverishes, (b) it is made out of generosity and (c) it is for the benefit of the receiver. As the irrevocable discretionary trust was regarded as capital for special purposes *(doelvermogen)*, the trust and not the beneficiaries was regarded the receiver. The trustee would therefore be assessed.

In the case of a foundation *(stichting)*,[25] there are some Supreme Court decisions[26] stating that if a Dutch taxpayer uses the property of a foundation as if it were his own, then for income tax purposes, the property will be considered to belong to the taxpayer himself. However, these decisions are heavily debated in professional literature. Perhaps these decisions could be applied to decide on the tax position of a revocable discretionary or a non-discretionary trust, but that remains to be seen.

Having regard to the rights or obligations arising from the different forms of trusts, the wording of the trust deed itself is extremely important. Today, only the tax position of an Anglo-Saxon irrevocable discretionary trust is known insofar as Dutch gift tax is concerned for Dutch settlors.

---

24. Rates for 2004: from 41% to 68%.
25. Compare §2.6.6.
26. 30 October 1985, number 22715, published in BNB 1996/16* and 8 July 1998, number 108057, published in VN 1999/11.14.

2.3 TRUSTS AND DOUBLE TAX TREATIES

Most tax treaties do not expressly mention trusts and the issue of whether trusts are included in the definition of 'persons' to whom a tax treaty may apply is often debated.

2.3.1 General definition of the OECD Model Treaty

Article 3(1)(a) of the OECD Model Treaty, states that the term 'person' comprises an individual, a company and *any other body of persons*, a phrase that could arguably include trusts. However, the Commentary to the Model Treaty does not expressly include trusts within the scope of this phrase[27] and there is some debate as to whether trusts are included within the definition of 'any other body of persons',[28] which, by reason of residence in a particular state, could enjoy tax treaty benefits. It has also been argued[29] that trustees are either individuals or companies, which are 'persons' within the meaning of Article 3(1)(a) of the OECD Model Treaty and amenable to being resident in a particular state under Article 4 of the Model Treaty, and thus enjoying tax treaty benefits.[30]

The above shows that there is some uncertainty surrounding trusts and their ability to benefit from tax treaties. As a result, recent tax treaty developments, outlined below, in which trusts are referred to by name, are significant.

2.3.2 Canada/United Kingdom

The 2003 Protocol to the 1978 Income and Capital Gains Tax Convention between Canada and the United Kingdom, which entered into force in 2004, includes, among other things, in its definition of 'person' a trust. When read together with Article 4 of the said tax treaty, it implies that a trust can be a resident of either states and consequently enjoy tax treaty benefits.[31]

2.3.3 France/United Kingdom

Article 3(1)(e) of the 2004 Income and Capital Gains Tax Convention between France and the United Kingdom, which was signed on 28 January 2004 but is

---

27. See, for example, Philip Baker QC, *The Application of the Convention to Partnerships, Trusts and Other, Non-Corporate Entities*, GITC Review, Vol. II No. I, November 2002.
28. Philip Baker QC at the 1993 ITPA Monte Carlo Meeting, *Treaties and Trusts.*
29. See, for example, Miles Dean, *The Role of Tax Treaties in the Use of the Common Law Trust,* Trimestrale di Approfondimento Scietifico e Professionale, March 2001.
30. The relationship between trustee and the source of the trust fund is of paramount importance, with specific reference to the question whether or not a treaty exists between the country of residence of the trustee and the country in which the trust fund is located (since the trustee as legal and sometimes beneficial owner of the trust income and/or gains).
31. Article I of the Protocol with reference to Article 3 of the 1978 Convention.

yet to enter into force, states, as in most other treaties, that the term 'person' comprises an individual, a company and any other body of persons. The term 'any other body of persons' could arguably include a trust and the various references to 'trusts'[32] within the text of the treaty supports this view.

2.3.4 Double tax treaties and trusts: interaction

The following discussion highlights some of the problems encountered by practitioners in cases where the relationship between trusts and tax treaties exists, as well as examining situations where this relationship may arise. Most practitioners will have experience in dealing with companies and the question of tax treaties, such as Dutch royalty companies for example, and indeed this is a relationship dealt with in some detail by both the 1977 Model Treaty and the Commentaries, not to mention many of the bilateral treaties themselves. However, how is the relationship between a trust and a tax treaty assessed in the absence of any direction from any source? The answer is to establish the basics of trust law and the relationships that exist within a trust and how these may themselves be affected by the existence of a tax treaty. There are ostensibly three relationships that may exist and they are as follows:

(a) between trustee and beneficiary;

(b) between beneficiary and trust asset/source;

(c) between trust asset/source and trustee.

There may be a fourth, that between the settlor and trust assets/source where anti-avoidance legislation imputes income or gains to the settlor, but this is outside the scope of this section.

The above three principal relationships are therefore the fundamental components to a trust. In some cases all three components may be in the same jurisdiction; however more often than not the three components will be situated or resident, if you like, in three separate jurisdictions. Thus, the trustees will often be resident in, say, Jersey, while the beneficiaries may be resident in the US, UK, France and Germany and the trust assets, which give rise to the source of the trust income, may be situated in any number of jurisdictions and comprise many different types of investment such as real estate, shares, bank deposits and so on.

Given the multi-jurisdictional nature of the trust relationship, it may well be that

32. For example in Article 6(5), Article 14(2), and Article 24(1). See also Cussons, Peter and Pascal D'Hont, *Impact of the New UK/France Treaty: Part I,* Tax Planning International Review, February 2004.

a tax treaty exists between all three component states. However, this is unlikely in the majority of cases and indeed this is not a vital ingredient to the successful use of a trust, and of tax treaties in international tax planning. For the trust to be a useful tool, the practitioner will seek a tax treaty between the trustee and the jurisdiction in which the trust asset/source of income is located, since it will be the trustee which will be legally and perhaps beneficially entitled to the trust income and/or gains. In other words, a trust may be a viable tax planning tool as opposed to, say, a standard offshore company where there is no treaty between the source and the beneficiary; to this end the trust may be interposed to take advantage of a tax treaty thus offering protection to gains, income and profits in general.

Can a trust benefit from double tax treaties?[33]

The traditional uses of a trust are as holding vehicle as opposed to being an active undertaking. Trusts are more likely to be used in situations where family wealth is an issue for the preservation of that wealth for future generations. In more recent times the asset protection trust has evolved out of our now litigious society and is a method of protecting assets from vexatious creditors and the like. Certainly the trust, especially the offshore trust, has come in for some negative press but in all these instances the existence of double tax treaties is not a prerequisite, and in some cases may even be detrimental to the cause.

Assuming therefore that a situation arises whereby a practitioner believes a trust may be used to receive income or gains, what steps should be taken to ensure that the treaty will in fact apply to the trust? Certainty, in any business transaction, is the most important aspect and this applies equally to tax planning.

For a trust to be of any use in the treaty context, the relationship between the source of income and the trustee is of paramount importance. For a tax treaty to apply residence is a key factor, thus the first factor to establish is whether the trust falls within the personal scope of the treaty which, if based on the 1977 Model Treaty, will be Article 1. Article 1 states that the treaty will apply to persons who are residents of one or both of the contracting states. The questions, which must therefore be asked, are:

(a) is the trust a person; and

(b) is it a resident of one of the contracting states?

Both questions pose their own difficulties but may be answered by careful examination, again, of the basic principles.

33. This section elaborates on the discussion in §2.3.1.

As far as the trustees of the trust are concerned, they may be either individuals or a trust company. In either case the trustees will ordinarily be resident in the jurisdiction from where the day-to-day management of the trust takes place. This is a prerequisite and should not be overlooked. So, is the trust a person? Philip Baker, in his lecture delivered to an ITPA meeting[34] succinctly came to the conclusion that since Article 3(1)(a) of the 1977 Model Treaty defines a 'person' as including 'an individual, a company and any other body of persons', and despite the fact that a trust is not expressly defined it could nonetheless be pigeon-holed as a body of persons. Even if a different conclusion could be reached, the trustees would either be individuals or companies and thus fall within the definition provided for by Article (3)(1), and so entitled to treaty benefits.

Is the trust a resident of the contracting state? This again is defined in Article 4 as 'any person who, under the laws of that state, is liable to tax therein by reason of his domicile, residence, place of management or any other criterion of a similar nature'. The fact that trustees manage the trust from the jurisdiction in which they are resident is helpful in that establishing trust or trustee residence in the jurisdiction for treaty purposes is not too difficult. Thus, we can safely say that regardless of the fact that the 1977 Model and the Commentaries are by no means conclusive, and despite the lack of academic treatise on the subject, trusts should be able to benefit from double tax treaties.

Much has been written about the interaction between domestic law and double tax treaties and whether the latter are capable of overriding the former and so on. It is not within the scope of this book to discuss this particular subject. However, we must deal with the practical problem we keep coming back to and that is whether a treaty will apply. The first place to look is at the individual treaty and the articles whose benefit are being sought. If this does not provide conclusive proof, in other words if the treaty makes no mention of trusts and whether it will extend to trusts, does the domestic law of the relevant country recognise the trust concept? If domestic law does indeed acknowledge the trust concept or the country in question, while not being a common law jurisdiction and thus not familiar with the laws of equity, and if the country is a signatory to the Hague Convention on the Recognition of Trusts (such as Italy), this is a good indication that the treaty will be applicable.

2.4 TYPES OF TRUST

The basic trust concepts have now been explained, and certain specific types of trust were referred to above, but trusts come in a much wider variety of

34. ITPA Monte Carlo Meeting 1993, *Treaties and Trusts.*

guises. Some more examples, and their outstanding characteristics, are outlined below.

2.4.1 Accumulation and maintenance trusts

Accumulation and maintenance trusts are designed to favour beneficiaries who are minors and relatives of the settlor. The trustee has the discretion to use trust income for the maintenance and educational expenses of the minors. The following preconditions have to be met in order to be recognised as this type of trust:

- one or more of the beneficiaries will, on attaining a specific age, become entitled to possession or absolute title to the trust property;
- the beneficiaries must have a common grandparent;
- any income not used is accumulated;
- the trustees also have the power to distribute capital for the benefit of the beneficiaries.

This type of trust also provides inheritance tax planning opportunities for UK settlors – if it is created under an *inter vivos* settlement for UK inheritance tax purposes, it is a potentially exempt transfer and there may therefore be no further inheritance tax charge.[35]

2.4.2 Asset protection trusts

Generally, asset protection trusts are often used by high net worth individuals who are at risk of claims from their creditors, claims arising under forced heirship laws,[36] governmental claims arising in the taxpayer's home country, or to provide protection against claims made against a beneficiary. Whether the trusts are effective mechanisms against such claims depends on various issues.

For example, in the United States, foreign asset protection trusts (FAPTs) have been aggressively marketed as an effective asset protection tool, but US judges have demonstrated that they dislike FAPTs, based on their aim of defeating creditors, and have been actively working at getting US creditors' judgments satisfied, including sending the settlor to jail. However, the offshore trust's effectiveness as a tool to thwart future creditors will most probably not depend on whether a US court gives credence to the application of foreign trust law when adjudicating a claim against the settlor. Provided that the trust's assets are located offshore, a creditor with a US judgment will still be faced with significant hurdles before actually being able to levy claim on any of the trust's assets.

35. Inheritance Tax Act 1984, Section 3A(1)(c) and Section 71(4).
36. Refer, for example, to §2.2.2 under France.

The best evidence of the practical impediments to enforcing a US judgment against an offshore trust is in the Cook Islands which enacted the world's first asset protection trust legislation in 1989. Notwithstanding the creation of thousands of such trusts since that time, there has only been one reported case in that jurisdiction, *Orange Grove*,[37] which deals with an asset protection trust. Furthermore, although *Orange Grove* is sometimes suggested to be a creditor victory because the trust was restrained and the creditor's claims were allowed to proceed, no Cook Islands judgment was ever entered other than on the procedural issues. This supports the purported result that the creditor ultimately settled his claim for a fraction of the trust's assets. Moreover, since the court's holding was wholly based upon an ambiguity in the governing statute, an ambiguity that was subsequently clarified by statutory amendment, future creditors who get as far as the Cook Islands will not be able to follow in the footsteps of the *Orange Grove* creditors. The attitude of the US court (see the *Anderson*[38] and *Lawrence*[39] decisions) is such that all a creditor needs to do is ask the court to enter a repatriation order against the settlor of an offshore trust. If the settlor does not oblige he is at risk of being incarcerated. The second problem is the adverse tax consequences that such trusts invariably create given the provisions of the Internal Revenue Code.

2.4.3 Bare trusts v. substantive trusts

Under substantive trust arrangements, trustees are given specific powers and duties in respect of management and disposal of trust assets. Conversely, bare trusts may contain powers for the trustees to manage the assets but do not give the trustees any powers over the destination of the funds. Essentially, a bare trust is a nominee arrangement – one party holds assets for another, the latter being absolutely entitled to the entire benefit of the trust assets.

2.4.4 Employee benefit trusts (EBTs)

This type of trust is created for the benefit of employees and is often used for the purpose of acquiring share capital in the employer company. Alternatively, it can be created for the purpose of providing pensions for employees, the trust's money being invested in approved investments. Employee pension fund trusts are usually exempt from tax. EBTs have been a major tax planning tool in the United Kingdom over the past decade, providing up until 2004 a corporate tax deduction for the employer coupled with a tax deferral for the employee. With the ability of the trustees to make loans to employees, individuals may achieve the same cash benefits as direct remuneration without the attendant tax disadvantages.

37. 515 *South Orange Grove Owners Assoc. v. Orange Grove Partners*, 208/94 (Cook Islands 1995).

38. *FTC v. Affordable Media LLC,* F.3d (9th Cir. Case No. 98-16378, June 15, 1999).

39. *In re Stephen Jay Lawrence,* 227 B. R. 907; 41 Collier Bankr. Cas. (MB) 177; 41 Collier Bankr. Cas. 2d (MB) 177.

The UK authorities then announced their crackdown on the uses of EBTs by (a) refusing to allow a corporate tax deduction until a similar tax assessment could be made on the individuals[40] and (b) requiring reporting of the EBT and subsequent loan arrangements to HMRC under the disclosure rules.[41]

However, the use of EBTs for tax planning is far from over. Firstly, foreign employer companies of UK resident employees are unaffected by corporate tax deductions in (a) above although relevant individuals advising in such arrangements, or the employees themselves, may be required to file a report under (b) above. Secondly, HMRC have accepted that the settlor of the EBT is the relevant employer company, so that the attribution rules on settlors described in §5.4 may not apply.

EBTs are by and large uncharted territory in many continental European countries, but their use and tax benefits are nevertheless considerable.

2.4.5 Unapproved pension schemes

Legislation in certain countries provides for unapproved pension schemes.

United Kingdom

Again, taking the UK as an example (since trusts are recognised in the UK as opposed to many other countries), such unapproved schemes are called FURBS, which is the abbreviation for 'Funded Unapproved Retirement Benefits Scheme'. It is an arrangement whereby an employer makes a contribution to a trust for the benefit of the employees to aid the problem of the underfunding of pension schemes.

A FURBS displays the following characteristics:

- Although there is no limit on the contribution which an employer may make to a FURBS, corporation tax relief will only be allowed to the extent that the contribution is made 'wholly and exclusively for the purposes of the company's trade'. This means that the employee's total pay package, including the FURBS contribution, must not be excessive for the duties undertaken.

- The contribution is subject to income tax in the hands of the employee as a benefit in kind. The tax is payable on 31 January following the end of the tax year in which the contribution is paid and thus enables the taxpayers to defer tax for up to 22 months.

40. Finance Act 2003, Schedule 24.
41. These are discussed in §6.2.

- A FURBS is designed to provide a lump sum for an employee on reaching retirement (age 50 at the earliest) with no liability to further tax or national insurance.

- Assets held within an existing FURBS are not part of the employee's estate for inheritance tax purposes, although contributions made after 6 April 2006 will fall within the individual's estate.

- A FURBS pays tax on income and capital gains at the basic rate only. Dividends are taxed at 10% and bank and building society interest is taxed at 20%.

- Capital gains are taxed at the rate applicable to trusts, i.e. 40%. FURBS receive an annual exemption of 50% of that available to an individual.

- Unlike approved pension schemes, there are generally no restrictions on what a FURBS does with its funds. A FURBS can make loans to the employee, for example, provided that a commercial rate of interest is paid.

2.4.6 Grantor trusts

A grantor trust is one whereby the settlor ('grantor') retains control over the income or capital so that the trust income will be deemed to be that of the settlor for taxation purposes. This is also true where another person acting on his instructions retains powers either to subsequently benefit from the trust or to manage and control the investments and eventual distributions of the trust's assets.

In such cases, the transfer of assets to the trust will not be recognised, and indeed no gift tax will be payable, as the 'gift' will be regarded as incomplete. The assets will form part of the grantor's estate on his death, and during his lifetime the grantor must report the trust's income and profits on his personal tax return.

Specifically, a grantor trust will be deemed to exist if:

(a) the grantor has retained or has the power to retain a reversionary interest in the trust fund, or if a third party in any way related to the grantor can determine the beneficial interests of the trust, even if such interests exclude his personal benefit;

(b) the grantor can benefit in any way from the trust through the exercise of certain administrative powers, or if a third party in any way related to the grantor can revoke the trust so that the assets revert to the grantor;

(c) a third party in any way related to the grantor can distribute income to the grantor or his spouse.

Foreign trusts are automatically considered as grantor trusts regardless of the above provisions, unless the grantor can prove that no part of the foreign trust's assets can be paid or accumulated during a taxable year to or for the benefit of any US person. Thus, the grantor of a foreign trust must continue to report the trust's income and profits on his US tax return as his own income and profits. In the event that a foreign trust, which does not fall foul of the grantor trust regulations, is created by a US grantor, gift tax will be payable. Excise tax at 35% may be also imposed on any unrealised gains on the assets transferred into trust, unless the grantor elects to pay US capital gains tax on such unrealised appreciation of assets, or it can be established that tax avoidance is not the principal purpose of the trust's establishment.

2.4.7 Hybrid trusts

A hybrid trust combines elements of both fixed and discretionary trusts.[42] In a hybrid trust, the trustee must pay a certain amount of the trust property to each beneficiary fixed by the settlor. But the trustee has discretion as to how any remaining trust property, once these fixed amounts have been paid out, is to be paid to the beneficiaries.

2.4.8 Cypriot international trusts

The Cypriot international trust was introduced by the International Trusts Law in 1992. It enables a non-resident of Cyprus to create a trust of any property (except immovable property in Cyprus) for the benefit of non-residents (or any charity), with at least one Cypriot-resident trustee. The settlor, any beneficiary or the local trustee (or any combination of those) can be a Cypriot international business company or partnership.

No foreign law relating to inheritance or succession will invalidate the trust or affect any transfer or disposition relating to its creation. It may not be set aside by the settlor's creditors unless it is proved that the trust was set up with intent to defraud those creditors when the property was transferred. The settlor's insolvency after any transfer has no effect. A claim against the trustee(s) must be brought within two years from the date of sale or transfer of property to the trust.

There are no limitations on the investment of trust assets, if the investment powers are exercised with reasonable prudence and diligence and subject to any provisions in the trust instrument.

The proper law of the trust can be changed from or to the law of Cyprus, if the terms of the trust instrument so permit, so long as the new law recognises the

42. Refer to the introduction to this chapter.

validity of the trust and the interests of the beneficiaries. This provision ensures flexibility in the event of a change in tax or other policy.

The Cypriot courts may amend or repeal the terms of the trust or the powers of the trustees, if they are satisfied that the proposed arrangement will be in the interests of the person on whose behalf the application is made, and will not substantially prejudice any other interested party.

The income and profits of an international trust derived from a source outside Cyprus are exempt from taxation in Cyprus, whether in the hands of the trustees or the beneficiaries. International trusts are exempt from any duty of registration, but the trustees are obliged to disclose all documents and information relating to the accounts of a trust to the beneficiaries, and the courts may order the disclosure of documents and information relating to a trust in the event of civil or criminal proceedings.

2.4.9 Purpose trusts

A purpose trust is one established for a particular purpose and has no ascertainable beneficiary who can sue to enforce the trust in the event of a breach. In spite of the fact that a purpose trust does not have beneficiaries, the trust will usually not fail[43] if it has been set up for a specific purpose, and the trust law recognises purpose trusts.[44]

Charitable trusts

In *IRC v. Pemsel*[45] four categories of purpose were outlined which would save an otherwise void pure purpose trust and establish it as a valid charitable trust. The categories are:

- the relief of poverty;
- the advancement of education;
- the advancement of religion;
- any other purpose beneficial to the community.

STAR trusts

The Special Trusts (Alternative Regime) ('STAR') Law of 1997 introduced purpose trusts into Cayman Islands law. Under the STAR law, hybrid purpose trusts are also provided for, i.e. a trust that is a purpose trust during the settlor's lifetime, but a 'normal' trust for the benefit of individual beneficiaries afterwards. Beneficiaries have no standing to enforce a STAR trust, a right which is

43. For lack of a beneficiary – compare §2.1.3 under Certainty of objects.
44. E.g. in the Isle of Man.
45. (1891) AC 521.

exclusively reserved for 'enforcers'.

Isle of Man purpose trusts

The Isle of Man has established purpose trusts as a means of ensuring that a particular set of circumstances occurs, following which (once the purpose is fulfilled), the trust is dissolved. An enforcer may be appointed (similar to a protector) to ensure that the trustees fulfil such purpose. Although there is no appointed beneficiary, any assets in the trust may be appointed to the 'recipient of surplus' who only receives such assets once the purpose of the trust is fulfilled. Little used at the time of writing, it is considered by the writers as a potentially valuable entity to ensure tax deferral for the 'recipient of surplus' without the attribution rules applying as described in §5.4.

2.4.10 Unit trusts and investment trusts

A unit trust is a trust where the beneficiaries (called unit-holders) each possess a certain share (called a unit-holding) and can direct the trustee to pay money to them out of the trust property according to the number of unit-holdings they possess. Unit trusts are primarily used for investment purposes.

2.4.11 VISTA trusts

VISTA trusts have recently been incorporated into British Virgin Islands law by means of the Virgin Islands Special Trusts Act ('VISTA') 10 of 2003. The purpose of VISTA is to make provision for trusts of shares in companies. Before enactment of VISTA, the 'prudent man of business' rule, aimed at preserving the value of trust assets, discouraged use of trusts where the settlor wishes trustees to retain the shares. Under Section 5 of VISTA, the trustee's principal duty is to retain the shares, irrespective of any duty to preserve or enhance the value of the trust fund.

2.5 COMMON TRUST CONCERNS

Trustees play a pivotal role in trust administration, yet breaches of trust regularly occur, albeit unwittingly by the trustees. Examples of this include failing to invest trust funds in an authorised manner, making an unauthorised profit from the trust, failing to distribute trust assets to the correct beneficiaries and in the correct amounts, making unauthorised purchases of property and failing to ensure that trust property is vested in the names of the trustee. From a tax perspective, in spite of, or maybe as a result of, their usefulness, trusts also produce problems in the course of international tax planning. Some of the more common problems arising in this respect are outlined below.

2.5.1 Management and control[46]

The residence of a trust affects the treaty protection it might enjoy,[47] as well as the taxation of any income and gains accruing to the trust. Trust residence, in turn, is determined by where the trust is managed and controlled. The residence of the trustees is one of the determining factors in establishing residence of the trust itself.

UK legislation determining the tax residence of trusts is complex, and differs depending upon the type of tax being considered. For the purposes of income tax, a trust is considered resident in the UK if all the trustees are resident in the UK; if all the trustees are non-resident, then the trust is non-resident, and the distinction between worldwide and UK-source income shall apply. In the case of mixed-resident trustees, one must look to the resident status of the settlor, in accordance with Finance Act 1989, Section 110: if the settlor is resident, ordinarily resident or domiciled in the UK, either on the creation of the trust or on any addition of property to the trust, then the trust is a UK-resident trust. In other words, any link whatsoever of the settlor to the UK shall establish the UK residence of the trust.

The position is quite different for capital gains tax purposes. A trust will be treated as resident in the UK *unless:*

(a) the general administration of the trust is ordinarily carried on outside the UK; and

(b) the trustees, or a majority of them, are not resident and not ordinarily resident in the UK.

However, where the trustee is a professional trustee (for example a trust company, bank, solicitor or accountant), the professional trustee is treated as being not resident in the UK if the trust property was provided by a person who is neither domiciled, resident nor ordinarily resident in the UK at the time of provision of the assets to the trust.[48] If the majority of trustees are non-resident in the UK, then the general administration of the trust shall be treated as being carried on outside the UK.

It may therefore be possible for a non-UK settlor to create an English trust, with UK resident trustees, but for the trust to avoid liability to UK capital gains tax on any gains made.

46. For management and control issues in respect of residence of companies, refer to §5.1.2.
47. See §2.3
48. TCGA 1992, Section 69.

2.5.2 Settlor-directed trusts

This type of trust contains a clause that reserves to the settlor or some third party an ability to direct the trustee as to the acquisition, retention or disposal of investment assets. However, reserving power in such manner may lead to negative consequences, as the case below illustrates.

Any settlor who envisages that a trust arrangement merely allows him to remove assets from his estate without actually giving up control over those assets is likely to face the accusation that the trust is simply a sham. It is not always the tax authorities who seek to set aside a trust in this manner. In the case of *Rahman*[49] it was in fact the settlor's wife who sought to set aside the trust.[50]

Rahman, the settlor, was a life tenant of a Jersey trust who retained considerable powers over the trust assets, including the power to take much of the capital back and a power of appointment over capital. The trustees also needed to obtain the settlor's permission to exercise important powers such as those concerning management, investment and distribution of the assets. The court decided that the trust was a sham as the settlor was effectively in control of the assets, and the settlor had continued to treat the assets as though they were still his own.

Further to this case it is clear that a trust must have substance and that the trustees must not simply act as agents of the settlor. The trustees must have real control of the assets and must exercise this at their own discretion. If an individual wishes to retain control over his assets, a trust is not a suitable vehicle with which to structure his tax planning. The trustees themselves are under a duty to act in a way which benefits all of the beneficiaries and so must not simply act on the whim of the settlor.

2.5.3 'True' sham trusts

Reserving powers for the settlor as in *Rahman* is indicative that there is a lack of any true intention to create a trust at all. Conversely, the test for existence of a 'true' sham trust involves establishing whether a valid trust was created for legal purposes and then establishing whether this was a sham trust for income tax purposes.[51]

In the United States, the court[52] considered four factors to establish whether a trust is a sham trust:

49. *Rahman v. Chase Bank* [1991] JLR 103.
50. There have also been other cases in the past where individuals who would have benefited under forced heirship rules have challenged a trust arrangement.
51. Compare Robert L. Sommers, Sham Trust Analysis, 2000, www.taxprophet.com.
52. *Buckmaster v. CM* TC Memo 1997-236.

- Did the taxpayer's relationship, as settlor, to the property differ materially before and after the trust's formation? This question seeks to investigate whether the taxpayer transferred the assets to the trust, continued to use the assets and received income from the assets.

- Did the trust have an independent trustee? This question seeks to establish whether there was a meaningful restriction on the taxpayer's use of the trust property for his own purposes.

- Did an economic benefit pass to the other beneficiaries of the trust? The question here is whether the taxpayer transferred an economic interest to a third party when he transferred the assets, i.e. did he transfer all his legal and beneficial interests in his assets?

- Did the taxpayer feel bound by any restrictions imposed by the trust deed itself or the law of trusts? The question that needs to be answered here is whether the actions of the taxpayer are limited by restrictions imposed by the trust deed or the law of trusts in respect of the transferred property. The crux is whether the taxpayer had unrestricted use and control over the property without fiduciary limitations imposed on trustees.

When a court, following the analysis carried out in *Buckmaster,* finds that a trust is a sham trust, the settlor is taxed directly on the income as though the trust did not exist at all.

2.6 ALTERNATIVES TO TRUSTS

Some structures appear similar to trusts but are different in their basic construction. Although the following concepts show similarities with trusts, care should be taken not to confuse them with trusts.

2.6.1 Agency

Agency is a common law construction whereby an agent represents his principal in a manner that can be similar to the way in which a trustee is responsible to the beneficiary. Further, a principal in an agency agreement has similar remedies against his agent as the beneficiary has against his trustee. However, there are essential differences:

(a) the relationship between a principal and his agent are governed by an agreement between them. There is normally no agreement between a beneficiary and the applicable trustee;

(b) an agent represents his principal and binds the principal into a contractual relationship with third parties. In contrast, the trustee does not represent his beneficiary and cannot bind him into contractual relationships with third parties;

(c) an agent need not have any control over property belonging to a principal. In contrast, every trust requires the existence of trust property;

(d) an agent is subject to control by his principal. By contrast, a trustee is not controlled by the settlor or by any beneficiary who can only compel him to fulfil the terms of the trust.

2.6.2 Bailment

This is a common law concept whereby one person (the bailor) delivers goods to another (the bailee) on condition that they should be delivered either back to the bailor or in accordance with the bailor's instructions on the terms of the bailment being carried out.

While there are certain similarities between a bailment and a trust, a bailment is in fact a much more limited concept than a trust:

(a) the bailee has no title to the goods but only a special property interest in them, while a trustee has absolute legal title to the trust property;

(b) only goods, not land, can be subject to a bailment, while any kind of property can be the subject of a trust.

2.6.3 Contract

This is another common law concept – a bargain between parties giving each some advantage. It bears some similarity to a trust in that until the property that is the subject of the contract has been transferred, the person who has contracted to dispose of the property owes a duty and obligation to the person who has contracted to buy the property.

However, there are fundamental differences between a contract and a trust:

(a) in English law, for example, a contract must be enforced by consideration before the courts will enforce it. By contrast, in a trust, a beneficiary has provided no consideration and there is no need for such for the Equity Court to enforce it;

(b) a contract is only enforceable by the parties to it (this relationship is called privity of contract). By contrast, a trust may be enforced by the beneficiaries who normally are not parties to the trust agreement.

2.6.4 Fiduciary arrangement

The fiduciary arrangement is one where the ownership of an asset is passed from one person to another (the fiduciary), who is to hold them in his name but on behalf of and at the exclusive risk of the first party. As far as tax law is concerned, beneficial ownership of the asset has not passed and as such wealth and income tax would be assessed on the beneficial owner to the exclusion of the fiduciary. The fiduciary is only taxed on the fiduciary commission he charges. Furthermore, the fiduciary is required to maintain separate books regarding the fiduciary assets, since these are clearly not his assets.

2.6.5 *Fidei commissum*

Under a *fidei commissum*, a person (the fiduciary) occupies a position of power with regard to the property of another (the fidei commissary) of such extreme intimacy and confidence that the law imposes upon him the duty to act solely in the interest of the person he represents.

2.6.6 Foundations

The main difference between trusts and foundations is the leeway permitted to enable the founder/settlor to continue to control foundation assets during his lifetime, unlike the strict legal position with trusts. To the US IRS, for example, a foundation is regarded as a transparent structure.

A foundation is an autonomous legal entity, unlike a trust which is at its simplest a relationship between three parties: settlor, trustee and beneficiary. A foundation holds assets in its own name for the benefit of the beneficiary(ies) as specified by the founder.

The main difference between a trust and a foundation is that there is no separation of legal and beneficial ownership. This means that foundations are much more commonly used by individuals resident in a civil law country: the Code Napoleon does not distinguish between legal and beneficial ownership as is the case with common law. The effect of this is that trusts are often alien to the tax laws of civil countries and are often mistrusted by individuals who have no concept of splitting an asset in two. A foundation allows the founder (analogous with the trust settlor) an element of control without risking a 'sham' argument, although the concept of management and control is never too far away.

The foundation assets are managed independently according to the wishes of the founder in pursuit of the stated aims of the foundation. The beneficiaries of a foundation can be decided by the founder and may include children, partners, extended family, charities and the founder himself.

2.6.7 Life assurance

Life assurance may be an alternative to a traditional holding vehicle such as a trust. Insurance is the purchase by one individual or company of an undertaking from another to indemnify him in the event that certain risks occur, making it a universally accepted concept that does not generally suffer from the recognition pitfalls of trusts. The participants in this arrangement are similar to settlor, trustee and beneficiary in a trust arrangement. Thus, the investor enters into a contract with the life assurance company to provide benefits for his family, for example, in the event of his death.

The life of an individual is insured ('the life assured'), generally the policy-holder, through life insurance. On the occurrence of the insured event, i.e. the death of the life assured, the policy matures and a sum of money becomes payable to the beneficiaries named under the terms of the contract. The premium paid by the policy-holder is used by the insurance company to provide the beneficiaries with a specified sum in the event of the death of the life assured. Depending on the life cover required, the life company may need to reinsure the risk by using an element of the premium to buy additional cover, which may in any event be necessary to establish that the life policy is in fact a commercial arrangement and not simply a sham.

The investments made by the insurance company under the policy form part of the insurance company's long-term business fund. The company finds available investments to meet commitments due to policy-holders, and investments may be segregated from other policies written by the insurance company. The investor is therefore guaranteed a great degree of security and asset protection. Assuming that the local insurance law has been complied with, it is necessary to determine whether the fiscal authorities of the country in which the client is taxed will recognise the life assurance policy as such, or will seek to classify it as an investment. Care is therefore required in the contractual drafting of standard life assurance products to achieve the desired planning goal.

The premium paid by the policy-holder may be single or multiple payments of cash, or it may simply be an existing investment portfolio that the policy-holder has with his bankers. In this case, the portfolio is transferred into the name of the insurance company which avoids losses by having to liquidate the individual investment within the portfolio, and the bank becomes the custodian of the assets. The main benefit here for all parties is that the general relationship with the bank remains unchanged: the bank does not lose the client to another competitor, and the client's relationship with the bank which may have developed over a number of years remains the same.

The policy-holder owns a right in contract against the life company but does not have direct ownership in the portfolio of investments contained within this policy. Ownership of assets is clearly separated from the policy-holder, which are both legally and beneficially owned by the life company. The assets are not held on behalf of a third party or policy-holder. The insurance company will invest the premium in accordance with the instructions of the nominated investment adviser and pay the sum assured upon the death of the life assured.

Certain forms of life policy, known in the UK as personal portfolio bonds (PPBs), allow the policy to be used as a 'wrapper' for general or specific assets. The owner (or connected persons) of a PPB can choose the underlying investment which may include a wide range of assets such as securities quoted on any recognised stock exchange, unlisted shares and offshore funds, cash/deposit funds, government bonds, unit trusts, investment trusts and open-ended investment companies (OEICs). The life assurance element allows sums insured to be paid out under the insurance contract to the beneficiaries named by the purchaser, which can be an international trust. PPBs are taxed in a unique way: in the first year the bond is deemed to have made a notional gain of 15% of the total premiums paid, while in subsequent years the gain is increased on a cumulative basis; in each year after the first policy anniversary, the gain will be charged at a rate of 15% of the premium paid for the bond, plus compound interest per annum for each of the previous years during the existence of the bond. The deemed gain is purely notional and the policy-holder is then taxed at their individual rate.

A number of advantages arise due to the unique nature of the relationship between the life company, the individual and the contents of the life policy. As a result, this structure can be used beneficially in a wide range of circumstances. This is particularly so for continental Europe where concepts such as *fraus legis* and *abus de droit* mean that substance is a vital component of any structure if it is to succeed. These can often serve to undermine trusts solely in existence to provide a tax-exempt holding vehicle. However, the fact that an individual wishes to take out a life assurance contract on his life in order to provide for his family in the event of his death is very unlikely to be challenged on public policy grounds. The concept of insurance is universally recognised and is similar to concepts found in a trust relationship; the 'umbrella' is not, however, a trust deed, but a life insurance contract.

United States: variable life insurance policies

In the US, variable life policies are available to individuals who want to take out an insurance policy that is not fixed or guaranteed by the insurance company, but is a variable policy with a dedicated separate portfolio account. Thus, the insured gets the entire benefit from the growth in the portfolio, rather than the insurance company, where general portfolios are grouped together. Although the legal owner of the assets is the insurance company, these assets are not available for general creditor claims against the insurance company. Thus, excellent asset protection is afforded where the insurance company is the legal owner but only to support the policy taken out by the insured.

In a variable life insurance policy, a tax-free roll-up of income is permitted, with the capital passing on death being tax free to the family of the insured. In order to qualify as a life policy and benefit from the advantageous tax treatment, certain conditions must be met. These relate to actuarial and premium requirements and also diversification.

Diversification

Variable life insurance policies have to be structured to comply with requirements of Section 7702 of the Internal Revenue Code (IRC) for this to be characterised as 'life insurance' for US tax purposes. In addition, Section 817(h) IRC requires the segregated asset account of variable life policies to meet certain minimum 'diversification' requirements in order to qualify as a 'life insurance contract' for US income tax purposes. The general diversification requirements are as follows:

(a) no more than 55% of the aggregate value of the policy investment account can be invested in any single asset;

(b) no more than 70% of the total value in any two investments;

(c) no more than 80% in three investments;

(d) no more than 90% in any four investments.

This 'diversification' requirement is tested at the end of each calendar quarter over the life of the policy, but does not apply during the first year the policy is in effect.[53] The diversification requirement must be satisfied on the last day of the calendar quarter or within 30 days thereafter.

As a basic premise for a variable life insurance contract to qualify for tax deferral, the assets in the segregated asset account supporting the variable contract must be owned by the insurance company and not by the variable contract owner. The IRS has ruled, albeit mainly in relation to annuities, that certain acts of 'ownership' by the contract owner, such as the ability to select and control specific investments in a segregated account, will cause the contract owner to be treated as the owner of the assets for tax purposes. The 'investor control' position of the IRS is primarily based on the theory that the policy-owner has 'constructive receipt' of the earnings within the policy segregated account.

To reduce exposure to these issues, insurance companies generally require the appointment of an independent investment adviser who will control and direct all investments made within the segregated account.[54] This investment adviser

53. See Treas. Reg. Sec. 1.817-5(c)(1) & (2)(i).

54. Section 817(h)(5) expressly provides that 'Nothing in this subsection shall be construed as prohibiting the use of independent investment advisers'.

may be a US or non-US person, although it is generally preferred to use an offshore investment adviser who is familiar with this type of planning and related issues. The policy-owner retains the ability to remove and replace this investment adviser throughout the life of the policy.

The first step is to ensure that the policy qualifies as a 'life insurance policy' under the US IRC. If so, income and gains earned within the policy and the death benefit on its maturity is exempt from US tax.

Once this first step has been met, the policy can fall into one of two categories, each having their distinct tax treatment. The two types of variable life policy are the non-modified endowment contract ('non-MEC') and modified endowment contract ('MEC').

Whether a policy is a non-MEC or MEC policy depends upon the timing and amount of premiums paid in relation to the death benefit provided under the policy.

Non-MEC policies

For a policy to be treated as a non-MEC, it must satisfy the so-called 'seven-pay' test. This requires the premiums to be paid into the policy over a period of several years (rather than in a single premium). Although the seven-pay test purports to be based on theoretical level payments over seven years, the test can typically be satisfied if payments are made over a period of only five years. A non-MEC is required where it is anticipated that withdrawals will be taken from the structure during the lifetime of the insured. This is because loans from the policy are generally tax-free and will not be considered as constructive distributions subject to US taxation. Upon a complete surrender of the policy, or if benefits are paid before the policy matures, the amount paid out is taxable as ordinary income to the extent that it exceeds the total investment in the policy. The disadvantage of a non-MEC is that it generally has lower mortality costs.

MEC policies

A MEC is a policy which fails the seven-pay test, i.e. is paid by a single premium policy. If the policy is a MEC, the following tax rules will apply:

(a) all distributions, including those under surrender of the policy, are treated as ordinary income subject to tax up to the amount equal to the excess (if any) of the policy value immediately before the distribution over the investment in the policy at that time;

(b) loans taken from or secured by the policy value, as well as accrued but unpaid interest thereon, are treated as distributions from the policy and taxed accordingly;

(c) a 10% additional income tax is imposed on the portion of any distribution or loan taken from or secured by the policy that is includable as income, where such distribution is taken before the taxpayer reaches the age of $59^{1}/_{2}$.

Notwithstanding the above, a MEC is still attractive from a tax point of view since income and gains roll up tax-free within the policy.

2.6.8 Quasi trusts

A hybrid company,[55] which can be structured to have the characteristics of a trust, is used to benefit residents of civil law countries where trusts are not legally recognised.[56] In this way, assets can be placed in a vehicle which operates as a company, can trade as a company and has protection of its assets. In the hybrid company trust structure, the instructions from the 'settlor' are given to incorporate the company. However, directors and shareholders control the company and a protector may be appointed.[57]

It is the distinction between a shareholding member and a guarantee member that enables the structure to function as a trust. Guarantee members who have limited obligations in respect of contributions at insolvency of the company, who are eligible to receive dividends yet have very restricted voting rights, are 'passive' beneficiaries of a hybrid corporation, which makes it similar to a trust.

2.6.9 Usufruct

Under the concept of usufruct a party is granted the exclusive right during his lifetime to use an asset, although the ownership rights of that asset remain with the other party. Income tax and wealth tax in respect of the assets subject to usufruct will usually be assessed on that party who has the use. The party who has the ownership rights becomes taxable at the time the right of use is extinguished, i.e. when he assumes full enjoyment of the object.

2.6.10 SIPPs

An anticipated driving factor in Guernsey is the change to the UK legislation relating to Self-Invested Personal Pension Schemes (SIPPs) from 6 April 2006. Over the past few years, SIPPs have been very widely used to hold commercial property investments, a strategy which has been expressly encouraged by the SIPPs regulations. Under the new regulations, SIPPs will be able to invest in a much wider

55. A company limited by guarantee and having a share capital. Such a company has two types of participants – shareholders, who are entitled to capital, and members, who are entitled to dividends.
56. Compare §2.2.
57. Compare §2.1.2.

range of properties, as opposed to just commercial properties, thereby improving their popularity and use. An important point is that at present, SIPPs can gear up to invest in commercial property by borrowing up to 75% of the purchase price of a property. From April 2006, SIPPs will only be able to borrow up to 50% of the value of the entire fund. However, SIPPs will be able to freely invest in the shares of companies listed on the Channel Islands Stock Exchange, which in turn can be established with the express capacity to borrow with a higher level of gearing than will be possible for direct property investments made by SIPPs after that date. SIPPs coupled with Protected Cell Companies (PCCs) listed on the Channel Islands Stock Exchange may therefore become an alternative to direct investment routes.

[II.] CASE STUDY 2

This chapter has explained the theoretical, tax and legal framework relating to trusts and trust-like structures, and how trusts might be used for international tax planning purposes. The question of whether trusts or similar entities can be usefully employed in international tax planning seems to be one that the Filipes have already thoroughly explored, as will be seen below:

(a) the creation of the Filipe Foundation on the sale of Lucca Furnishings (Diagram 2);
(b) the creation of the Giuliano Trust to own the Lucca Software business (Diagram 4);
(c) life assurance policy for Renata's income (Diagram 9).

How did the Filipes utilise trust-like structures and did the plan reduce their overall tax burden?

Diagram 2

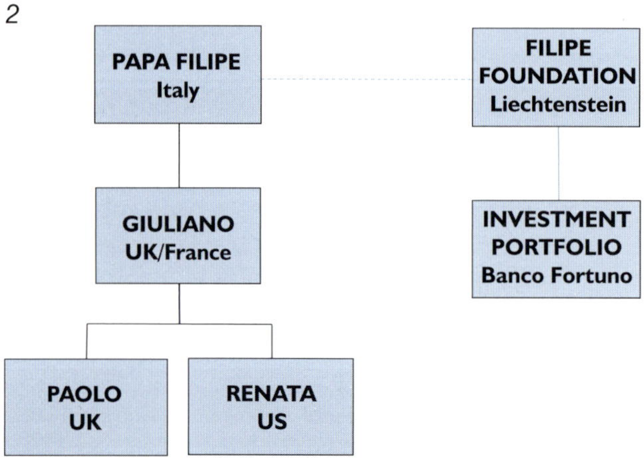

Diagram 4

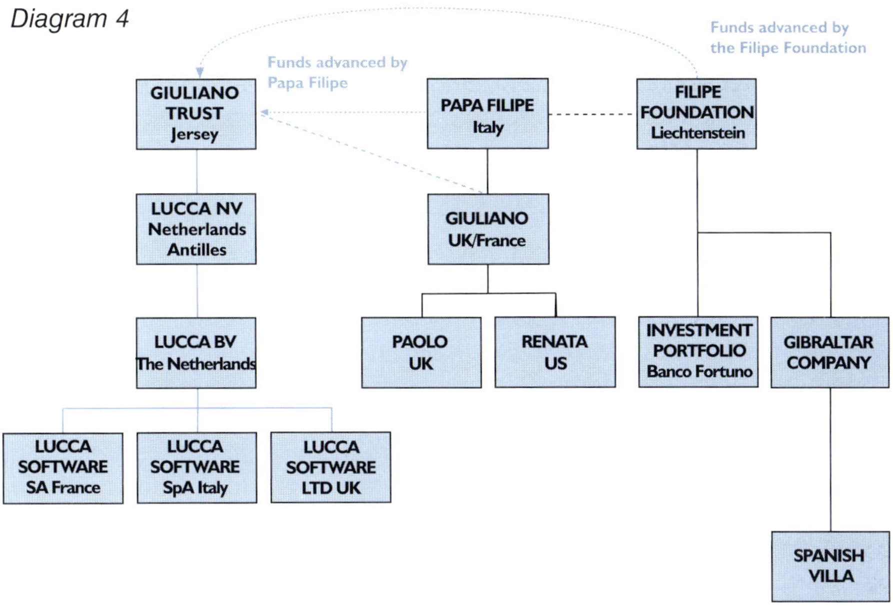

Diagram 9

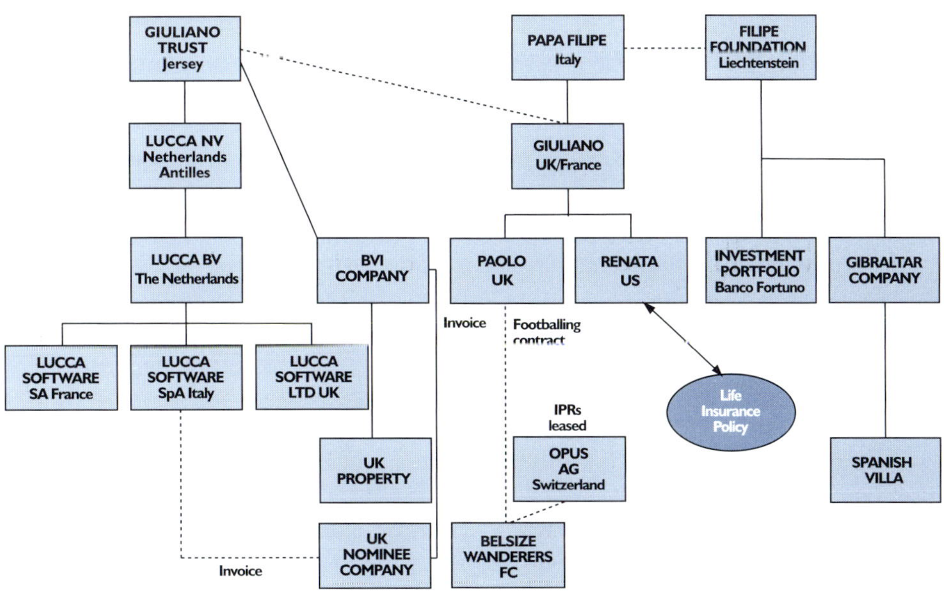

[II.a] Creating the Filipe Foundation

When Papa Filipe sold the soft furnishing business in Lucca, much of the sale proceeds were directed to the Filipe Foundation, which had been established in Liechtenstein in 1980 at the time of the sale. By executing a foundation deed and transferring the money from his personal account to the foundation's account in Liechtenstein, Papa Filipe effectively became the settlor in a trust-like arrangement. The bankers at Banco Fortuno, who are now looking after the substantial investment portfolio, became the foundation's fund managers, and the money transferred became the foundation fund. Papa Filipe effectively became the beneficiary, although the Giuliano Trust was later added as beneficiary when funds were transferred from the foundation to the trust as stipulated in a letter of wishes executed by Papa Filipe. However, unlike the case of the trust, the legal ownership had not been separated into two parts: the management of the foundation fund now vests in the bankers, but the legal and the beneficial ownership still in reality belongs to Papa Filipe through ownership of the foundation's founder share.

Papa Filipe failed to report his gains from the soft furnishing business on his Italian income tax return. He did this after consultation with one of his business contacts, who advised Papa that creating a foundation effectively removes the legal ownership rights of the foundation fund from the settlor, namely Papa Filipe, and that, as a result, he need not report his gains. However, this is not the legal consequence of the creation of a foundation if Papa Filipe retains the founder share in his personal ownership for control purposes.

It was indeed only to prevent the Italian tax authorities from getting their hands on the sale proceeds that Papa Filipe created the foundation. Although Papa Filipe found the foundation a useful tool for removing the sale proceeds from the attention of the Italian tax authorities, he did not keep in mind that the Italian tax authorities might not recognise the existence of the foundation and might, as a result, require inclusion of the sale proceeds in his annual Italian income tax return. Papa's actions essentially had the character of money laundering. Fortunately for Papa Filipe, and many papas like Filipe, the Italian tax amnesty of 2001/2002 gave Papa Filipe the possibility of dissolving the foundation and bringing the undeclared funds back to Italy upon payment of as little as 2.5% of the value of the funds. However, being so long in the tooth and very suspicious of the motives behind the Italian tax amnesty, Papa Filipe decided to maintain the foundation and risk discovery at a time when he had probably thrown off his mortal coil. Again, Maurice was catapulted into the situation where he knew he had to report his client to the NCIS.

[i.] The Filipe (near-)sham trust

Papa Filipe, who had heard from Giuliano that the latter was thinking of setting up a trust for his part of the business, thought that this seemed like a fine idea.

Papa had heard that trusts are very beneficial tax planning tools and contemplated setting up a trust for the villa the foundation had bought for Maria. As a result, the foundation would become the settlor of the trust, Maria the beneficiary, and the villa the trust fund. But although Papa was very fond of Maria, he was less fond of her son from her first marriage, Alfonzo, whom he had met only once but whom he decided on the spot he did not trust. (It should be noted that when Giuliano asked Papa about his suspicions, Papa could not give any clearer explanation than that he did not trust Alfonzo because 'he smells of garlic sausages'.) So, Papa wanted the villa in trust for Maria but did not want Alfonzo to obtain any rights in, or control over it. Papa's idea to surmount the problem was to act as trustee himself; in this way he would remain in charge and could 'keep an eye on the garlic sausage son'.

Maurice Brightman, the Filipes' tax planning adviser, was less than pleased when he heard about this – he knew that if Papa went through with the plan, no trust would have been created. It would simply be a sham trust. Maurice drafted an email to Papa containing the following warning:

To: PapaFilipe@Lucca.com
Cc: GiulianoFilipe@LuccaNet.com
Subject: Filipe Trust

Dear Papa,

Earlier this week you and Giuliano mentioned that you and were thinking of establishing a trust to hold the villa you own in Mijas, Costa del Sol. You also mentioned that for personal reasons you would prefer to be the trustee to be able to keep an eye on matters.

I pointed out during our conversation, but I feel it is worth reminding you in writing, that a 'trust' such as the one you envisage may constitute a sham trust. If your relationship to the property in 'trust' does not change after it has been put into trust (i.e. you do not relinquish your control of it) and if the 'trust' does not have an independent trustee, no trust would have been created. I realise that the foundation could formally be the settlor, but in view of your ownership of the founder share in the foundation, most tax authorities would take the point of view that what you have created is a sham trust for tax purposes, even if the structure met the legal threshold of a trust. The tax consequence of this would be that any gains in respect of the villa may be attributed to you on a current basis, but also the trust fund should be subject to personal wealth tax on an annual basis.

If you wish to discuss the above in further detail, or have any other concerns, particularly potential money laundering issues that I have pointed out to you on previous occasions but which you indicated you would prefer to discuss at a later opportunity, you are very welcome to contact me.

With kind regards
MB

After drafting the email, Maurice changed his mind and asked his PA to copy and paste the contents into his firm's letterhead and post it by recorded delivery – information like the above is best not distributed via the ether.

Following receipt of Maurice's letter Papa realised that creating a trust to hold the villa was hardly worth the trouble if he wanted to retain control over it, and this he definitely wanted.

[II.b] Creating the Giuliano Trust

[i.] Validity of the trust

During the time that Giuliano was contemplating the creation of the Giuliano Trust, he contacted Maurice to find out what needed to be done in respect of setting up a trust. Although Maurice is not a lawyer and does not practise as one,[58] he had enough experience in the field to advise Giuliano on the *essentialia* of a legally valid trust. The following is a transcript of their telephone conversation:

Giuliano: Maurice, you probably recall the conversation we had last month about creating a trust to act as holding entity for my part of the business?

Maurice: Yes, of course I do. You said that your father is willing to provide the initial funding for the setting up of the trust and also its underlying subsidiaries.

Giuliano: That's right. I've decided this is the best way forward, but I need to know what we have to do to get the ball rolling.

Maurice: Oh, good. I'm glad to hear you've made a decision on that. We are working closely with reliable trust companies who would be able to help you set up. Basically, they'll have to draft a trust deed showing your clear intention to create a trust. This is the first thing. You have to show that you are willing to relinquish power over the trust assets to the trustees.

58. He is actually a chartered accountant by profession and practises as an international tax adviser.

Giuliano: I see. I'm fine with that. Anything else?

Maurice: Well, there two other essential requirements that should be shown in the trust deed. The first is a clear indication of the property you are designating to be put on trust. In your case, it's quite simple since we are only talking about a sum of money from your father, which will be utilised to capitalise the Netherlands Antilles ultimate holding company, Lucca NV. Sometimes it gets more complicated if the assets are scattered all over the world and they are all sorts of possessions; you get sailing ships and gold coins and all that sometimes ... it gets a bit messy, you know. And you have to be certain who the beneficiaries will be ...

Giuliano: I'm certain about that – the beneficiary will be me.

Maurice: Sure. We'll have that written into the trust deed, but you need to consider what happens if you are no longer here. Wouldn't you like your children to benefit as well?

Giuliano: Yes, certainly I would, but not their mother. She's not going to get her hands on any of my money.

Maurice: I quite understand. Would you like me to put you in touch with the High Fidelity Trust Company in Jersey? They know what they're doing and...

Giuliano: Brilliant. Email me their contact details and the person there I should talk to. I want to get this off the ground ASAP.

In the conversation, Maurice summarised the essential elements of a legally valid trust: certainty of intention (Giuliano was sure that he wanted to put the money from his father in trust for trustees to administer as fiduciaries), certainty of subject matter (Giuliano decided that it was money from his father that would create the initial trust fund), and certainty of objects (Giuliano was certain that he would be the beneficiary of the trust, and had been persuaded to think also in terms of future generation planning).

[ii.] A settlor-directed Giuliano Trust

Giuliano had a very positive experience setting up the trust with the help of the Jersey-based trustees and created the Giuliano Trust in Jersey to act as a holding entity for the Lucca Group. During their first conversation, Maurice had advised Giuliano that by creating this kind of entity, the legal ownership and the beneficial ownership of the trust assets would be separated. The legal ownership would be with the trustees, whereas the beneficial ownership would be with Giuliano. This meant that dividend income received by the Giuliano Trust from Lucca NV did not become Giuliano's personal property, but formed part of the assets of the Giuliano Trust. The trustees were to administer the trust in accordance with the trust deed for the potential benefit of Giuliano, or his children, should Giuliano die. Furthermore, Giuliano also executed a letter of wishes, requesting the trustees to purchase the house near London through the BVI company.

However, Maurice had been concerned about Giuliano's habit of instructing the trustees of the Giuliano Trust in respect of their actions relating to the trust. Giuliano often required them to involve him in important decisions relating to the management of the trust's assets. He also executed a letter of wishes retaining the power to withdraw a part of the initial funding that the trust received from Papa Filipe's personal funds and later from the Filipe Foundation. In 1991, Maurice became aware of the *Rahman* court decision. He phoned Giuliano and told him that this decision in Jersey had held that where a settlor of a trust, which Giuliano in fact was, retained significant powers over the trust assets or had power over the decisions made by the trustees, the court could rule that such a trust was a sham. The reason for this was that the settlor continued to treat the assets as if they belonged to him. Giuliano took heed of Maurice's advice and revoked all his letters of wishes in which he required the trustees to involve him in significant decisions relating to the trust fund, and also those in which he reserved the power to withdraw much of the capital of the trust.

[II.c] Giuliano's asset protection trust

Giuliano had a substantial sum of money which he had inherited from his late mother, Mama Filipe. No Italian inheritance tax was paid on the sum at the time of transfer to Giuliano.[59] Giuliano wanted to ring-fence this amount from the Italian tax authorities and decided to transfer it to a Cook Islands asset protection trust. Giuliano learned from a business contact that although the Italian tax authorities, similar to tax authorities in other developed countries, are not fond of this kind of trust and its function of protecting the trust assets from creditors' claims, it is relatively difficult for creditors to enforce their claims against such trusts. Giuliano, fearing that Maurice would take his usual taxation moral high ground, did not inform the tax adviser of this trust.

[II.d] Renata's life assurance policy

Although Giuliano expressly refused to provide for the woman he divorced, Renata had other plans and once her career had taken off, she decided to use some of

59. Inheritance and gift taxes in Italy have been abolished by Law No. 383/2001, and accordingly this was the correct tax treatment in respect of the money inherited by Giuliano. Law No. 383/2001 provides that in the case of a gift to spouses, direct ascendants or descendants and relatives up to the fourth degree no registration tax applies, which explains the fact that no such tax was paid on the money inherited from his mother by Giuliano. However, in the case of a gift to persons other than the aforementioned, such as to an offshore discretionary trust, registration tax (rates between 1% and 15%) applies on the amount of the asset (other than cash and securities) attributed to each beneficiary exceeding €180,759.91.

the Giuliano Trust funds, which had been given to her by the trustees using their discretionary powers, to benefit her mother. Renata took out a life assurance policy to provide for her mother in the event of Renata's untimely death. At first, Renata considered establishing a trust in Italy, but Maurice cautioned her that trust arrangements were not recognised in Italy. Although it is true that Italy ratified the Hague Convention, the consequence of this is only that Italy will recognise foreign trusts if established validly under the laws of another country; this does not mean that Italian law provides for a trust structure. Renata thus decided that a life assurance policy was a better way to provide for her mother. The arrangement was quite similar to a trust, in that Renata paid a one-off premium, based on which the life insurance company would provide a specified sum to Renata's mother if Renata died. The life insurance company would use the premium for investment purposes, and Maurice asked to review the life insurance policy to check that the wording made it clear that the investment was not Renata's but that of the life insurance company. Consequently, although the structure of the parties and the cash flow in the life assurance policy arrangement resembled that of a trust, the tax risks related to a trust in a country where trusts were not recognised were avoided.

[II.e] Conclusion

Trust structures have been very useful in international tax structuring for many years because they allow a taxpayer, with careful planning, to defer and sometimes avoid altogether paying capital gains tax for many years, as well as providing an escape route from income and inheritance tax. For this reason, they have been and still are used extensively in common law jurisdictions such as the UK, US, Australia and Canada. However, tax planning using trusts has become more complex with the evolution of sophisticated anti-avoidance legislation and case law. In some jurisdictions, trusts may even still be employed successfully in international tax planning; however, careful analysis of local laws is required, not least an appreciation of how entity classification rules will apply to a trust. The creation of a trust may trigger certain reporting obligations for both the settlor and beneficiary with non-disclosure often incurring stringent penalties.

Chapter 3
What Is the Importance of Source Compared to Residence?

In this and the following two chapters, the three principal questions that tax planners always need to address when considering any international tax structure will be looked at, namely:

- Will foreign tax be levied if one has a foreign source of income or capital?[1]
- Can one reduce that foreign tax through double tax treaty arrangements or other conduit structures?[2]
- Will one have to pay domestic tax because of one's residence, even if one does not remit the income or capital?[3]

These three questions are applicable to both individuals and companies, and indeed extend to trusts and other forms of legal entities.

1. Issues relating to this topic are discussed in this chapter.
2. Issues relating to this topic are discussed in Chapter 4.
3. Issues relating to this topic are discussed in Chapter 5.

The first of these questions relates to the source of income and capital and the rights of a foreign country to impose taxation as a result of any profits derived from that source.

3.1 SOURCE AND *SITUS*

The income of an individual, whether earned or otherwise, and wherever he may be resident,[4] will often be subject to tax in the state in which it is sourced. Examples of this are as follows:

All US-source income, for example, is subject to personal income taxation, whether earned by a US citizen, resident alien or non-resident alien. Thus, remuneration from any work performed in the US is basically subject to tax, unless an applicable double tax treaty exempts a non-resident from tax.[5] The nature of the tax will depend on the laws of the particular state exercising its taxing rights.

In France, for example, all non-residents including French nationals who have no ordinary residence in France are taxed on French-source income only, and their tax payable is the higher of:

(a) tax on a lump sum per annum equal to three times the market rental value of their property in France; or

(b) tax on their French-source income.

Unusually among high-tax countries, non-UK-source income earned by a UK resident but non-domiciled individual is only taxable on that portion of income remitted to the UK. This is one of the reasons why many have claimed that the UK is a 'tax haven for non-domiciled individuals'.

Similarly, in respect of capital gains, the country in which assets are situated may continue to lay claim to taxing rights on them. However, there is scope for double taxation in circumstances where the state of residence also lays claim to these. For example, French residents are taxed on all their assets, including those located outside France, although this is subject to double tax treaty provisions, which may exempt foreign *situs* assets from French wealth tax.

In the UK, an individual who is non-resident and not ordinarily resident will generally not be subject to capital gains on UK *situs* assets unless these arise through a trade, profession or vocation carried on in the UK (or a UK branch

4. Compare the more detailed discussion in Chapter 5.
5. As discussed in Chapter 4.

or agency), or unless they are realised during a temporary period only of non-residence. The non-domiciled resident of the UK is also afforded substantial benefits in terms of capital gains tax, and Section 12 of the TCGA 1992 exempts from capital gains tax the gains made by a non-domiciled UK resident on the disposal of assets situated outside the UK to the extent that they are not remitted to the UK. Thus, the remittance basis applies to capital gains as for income.

A US citizen or resident is subject to estate tax on his worldwide assets, subject to a credit for foreign death duties on foreign *situs* property.

3.2 EU DIRECTIVES

Several EU Directives that to some extent affect the taxation at source of certain items of income have been issued by the European Council over the past few years. Some of the most important Directives, for the purposes of this book, are discussed below.

3.2.1 EU Savings Tax Directive

As regards portfolio investments and taxation based on *situs* (where dividends and interest are paid from), general agreement was reached on the EU Savings Tax Directive in 2003.[6] However, Austria, Belgium and Luxembourg have managed to protect their banking secrecy by postponing their entry into information exchange, the price of which is the requirement to levy withholding taxes starting at 15%, but increasing to 20% in 2008, before rising to 35% in 2011. Switzerland together with a host of other smaller nations such as Andorra, Liechtenstein and Monaco have also signed up to the Directive on the same terms.

The Directive is due to be implemented into the national laws of participating states and applied from 1 July 2005. Under the terms of the Directive, signatory EU member states will automatically exchange information on cross-border payments of interest sourced in their respective states. Meanwhile it appears, for Austria, Belgium and Luxembourg, that the automatic exchange of information will commence if and when the EU reaches agreement with Switzerland, Liechtenstein, Andorra, Monaco and San Marino to exchange information on request as set out in the OECD Agreement on Exchange of Information in Tax Matters 2002, and the US also enters into exchange of information on request as defined in the OECD Agreement. However, Jersey, Guernsey and the Isle of Man may now follow Luxembourg and others into implementing withholding taxes rather than introducing the information exchange regime.

6. See also §1.4.3.

The Directive is part of a package of measures introduced to reduce 'harmful tax competition'. The provisions also include the EU Code of Conduct on Business Taxation[7] and the EU Directive on Interest and Royalties.[8]

3.2.2 EU Interest and Royalty Directive

The Interest and Royalty Directive exempts certain interest and royalty payments from local source taxation, where they are paid between related enterprises (and permanent establishments of such enterprises) resident in different member states. Thus local source withholding taxes and tax assessments in the member states in which those payments arise will be avoided. To benefit from the Interest and Royalty Directive, both companies must have a type of legal form that is listed in the annex to the Directive, be resident in the EU for tax purposes and be subject to corporate taxation without being exempt. The exemption is only granted if one company has a minimum direct 25% share in the registered capital of the other company or a third company has a minimum direct 25% share in the registered capital of both paying and receiving companies. The member states need not apply the Directive if the share has not been held for a minimum two-year period and this has been proven at the time of payment. The provisions of the Directive had to be implemented by the EU member states by 1 January 2004, although certain concessions or transitional arrangements exist for Greece, Portugal, Spain and certain of the states that joined the EU on 1 May 2004.

3.2.3 EU Parent/Subsidiary Directive

Under the provisions of the EU Parent/Subsidiary Directive[9] dividends from substantial shareholdings (in excess of 20%[10]) in other EU-resident companies may be exempted from tax, i.e. again the state where the local source of profits is derived gives up its taxing rights on local source dividends to EU parent companies. Moreover, if an EU-resident parent company holds at least 20% of the paid-up capital of a subsidiary resident in another EU member state, the participation exemption will apply even if the investment is of a portfolio or passive nature provided that the following conditions are met:

(a) the parent company and the subsidiary are legal entities as mentioned in the annex to the Directive and not considered to be resident for tax purposes outside the EU under the provisions of a double tax treaty concluded with a third state; and

7. 98/C2/01.
8. Council Directive 2003/49/EC.
9. 90/435/EEC.
10. Reduced to 15% for 2007–8 and 10% for 2009.

(b) the subsidiary is subject to tax in the other EU member state without the possibility of an option, exemption or application of any special tax regime.

However, no reference has yet been made to whether capital gains derived will also be tax free if the interests are passive, as capital gains are not covered under the Directive. Certainly, capital gains derived on non-passive investments fall directly within the provisions of most countries' participation exemptions.

3.3 REAL ESTATE TAXATION

The issue of acquiring real estate in a second country has long revolved around the mitigation of local taxes. This is particularly so in countries where a wealth tax[11] is levied, where forced heirship rules apply and where the 'special tax' of 3% applies in the absence of declaration of beneficial ownership of real estate, such as France and Spain. Also, registration tax is a major issue in many countries.

Belgium

The purchase of real estate located in Belgium triggers the payment of a registration tax which is due at the rate of 12.5% on the transfer price or the fair market value, whichever is the higher. If the purchaser is a real estate merchant, that is, an entity or an individual whose activity consists of buying and reselling real estate, registration tax is restricted to 5%.

In order to avoid the application of the 12.5% registration tax, it is common practice for the real estate to be contributed to a company (which triggers a 0.5% contribution tax on the value of the contribution to the Belgium company), and then the shares are issued in consideration for such contribution. The shares themselves are then sold rather than the underlying real estate. However, this structure has been criticised by the Belgian tax authorities under the 'substance over form' doctrine, especially in cases where the shares of the company have been sold simultaneously and where the real estate has been recently contributed in exchange for the capital of the company.

The Belgian tax authorities take into consideration the existence of a pre-contractual agreement between the seller and the purchaser before the contribution of the real estate to the capital of the company. New legislation attacks such structures where residential real estate is involved, primarily to avoid properties being parked in so-called 'villa companies' to avoid

11. An annual tax levied on the net estate of an individual and applied at graduated rates.

inheritance tax. Instead of the 0.5% capital duty as above, contributions of Belgian *situs* residential real estate to a company may incur the full 12.5% registration tax, but transfers of commercial property may still be made to companies in exchange for shares at the lower 0.5% capital duty cost.

France

In order to alleviate exposure to wealth tax, individuals wishing to purchase property in France were advised to acquire the real estate through an offshore company, e.g. in Gibraltar or Jersey, which was not subject to wealth tax and whose shares, as movables, were not subject to the provisions of French inheritance tax nor capital gains tax legislation. In many cases the shares of the company were owned by an offshore trust, further distancing the ownership of the real estate from the individual concerned.

This route was challenged following the introduction of anti-avoidance legislation in France in 1983 (followed thereafter by similar legislation in Spain, Portugal and Greece), whereby an annual tax was levied at 3% of the market value of real estate held by such an offshore company. Even onshore companies would be similarly liable in the absence of full declaration of beneficial ownership of the company's shares. To avoid the special 3% tax in France, French property is now often purchased through a fiscally transparent *société civile immobilière* or SCI. Although a fiscally transparent SCI means that the foreign investor is treated as if he had made the investment directly, so that there are no immediate tax advantages, the investor now has movable assets (the shares of the SCI), which may fall outside French inheritance law (but not inheritance tax itself).

3.3.1 Mitigation of income and capital gains tax

The mitigation of income and capital taxes needs to be considered when tax planning for the cross-border acquisition of real estate. In this respect, taxes on the capital gains on the disposal of the property are often of principal concern. It is commonly postulated that property can be acquired by an offshore entity. The purpose of such an acquisition, wealth tax, special taxes and forced heirship rules aside, is to allow the shares of the company holding the property to be sold rather than the property itself. The company is often based in a low-tax jurisdiction, thus creating no liability to capital gains tax on the sale of the shares. The immediate problem is that someone, somewhere must own the shares of the company. In circumstances where the shares are held by an individual resident in a country with a developed tax system, it is likely that tax will be due on the sale of the shares at the rates applied to domestic gains in his country of residence or domicile. It is therefore usual for the ownership of property to be vested in an offshore company, the shares of which are held by an offshore trust.

Such an arrangement may often be fraught with difficulties. For example, the taxation authorities of a particular state may, as in the UK, try to infer that the individual occupying the property is a shadow director of the offshore company owning it, and as such is receiving a benefit in kind which is subject to income tax in the UK at the individual's marginal rates.[12] Any gain arising under the arrangement may be attributed to the settlor or the beneficiaries. The use of such structures, together with their cost, should be considered carefully before they are recommended.

As regards rental income, this is usually taxed in the source state irrespective of double tax treaties and thus the fact that the owner is based in a low-tax jurisdiction is generally not important. The technicalities of the tax-efficient acquisition are very important and must also be considered. In this respect it is common to acquire real estate by means of a loan arrangement, thereby allowing interest payable on the loan to be set off against the rental income received. Moreover, any surplus of interest over rental income may be carried forward to be offset against subsequent capital gains. Any anti-avoidance rules relating to connected parties, and to the limitation as to the amount of interest that may be deductible, must be considered. In circumstances where the loan is between connected parties it is usual that the rate that may be deducted is limited to the market rate of interest at that time. For this purpose, the country in question may impose a set rate to apply for that particular year. Furthermore, there may be issues over a hidden distribution of profits equating the interest payable to a constructive dividend. Finally, any interest paid to a non-resident company may also be subject to withholding tax, thus increasing the overall tax expense of the structure.

The taxation treatment of the above will obviously depend upon the jurisdiction in which the property is located. For example, in the Netherlands, if the real estate is rented out as part of a portfolio investment, the rental income is not taxed and no deductions can be made.

Generally, it is beneficial to avoid capital gains taxing rights being in the source country, but this is rarely possible (the UK being a notable exception). Where gains are related to the conduct of a trade or business, a different tax treatment may apply. In such circumstances, it may be preferable to create separate sources of profits. For example, a care home business may split ownership of the relevant real estate and the trading activities between two separate legal entities.

---

12. See, for example, the cases of *R v. Dimsey* [2001] UKHL 46 and *R v. Allen* [1999] STC 846. Both defendants were convicted of failing to disclose benefits received in the form of living accommodation from offshore companies. They were found to be 'shadow directors' of the companies and assessed on the cash value of the benefit under Section 154 ICTA 1988. The Inland Revenue stated that shadow directors are liable to charges under Sections 145 and 146 ICTA 1988 in the same way as if the individual had held a formal appointment as director. The ICTA provisions have in the meanwhile been replaced by relevant provisions in the Income Tax (Earnings and Pensions) Act ('ITEPA') 2003.

Canada

It is generally considered that, subject to the proposal to tax indirect foreign interests in Canadian real estate, direct investment (rather than using a Canadian-formed corporation) provides a basis for minimising overall Canadian taxes, including income taxes on rents and sale proceeds, and provincial taxes on capital and taxes at death. An important aspect of the overall comparison is the greater flexibility to structure-related or third-party financing (interest) charges which are deductible to the owning entity, but at the same time free from Canadian withholding taxes to the financing party or entity. Such effects flow from the following rules:

(a) interest is normally deductible in computing taxable Canadian income;

(b) interest paid by one non-resident person to another would only be subject to withholding tax where the payor is deemed to be resident. Such deemed residence (of the payor) is avoided in the context of financing Canadian real estate where the loan is not secured by Canadian real estate *and* the owning entity is not considered to be carrying on a business (principally in Canada) in respect of or by reason of the investment.

3.4 EMPLOYMENT AND CONSULTANCY INCOME

Generally, employment performed for remuneration creates a source of income within that country for any individual working there. Such employment income would therefore be subject to local wage tax and social security contributions. In an effort to change the source from employment income to business income of a company, an individual could consider the use of a so-called personal service company which attempts to reflect business income derived from a foreign source (where the company is resident) rather than local source (in the absence of a local permanent establishment of the company[13]).

In a simple manner, a change of source could be achieved by creating a domestic company to contract for an individual's services so that the individual receives predominantly dividend income taxed in a more beneficial manner than employment income. The growth in the use of personal service companies by entertainers and sportsmen, and also more recently by IT contractors, led to the introduction of anti-avoidance legislation in many developed countries.

13. See discussion in §7.3

3.4.1 United Kingdom

The clearest example of this anti-avoidance tactic was the introduction of HMRC's set of rules on 'Countering Avoidance in the Provision of Personal Services' (commonly referred to as IR 35), which outlines the distinction between employment and self-employment.[14] IR 35 was aimed at tackling the advantages of personal service companies: payment via dividends rather than salary is more attractive, since the tax rate is lower; perhaps of equal importance, social security contributions can be limited to the amount actually received as a salary by the individual and not on the 'dividend' amount.

The proposals contained in IR 35 came into effect on 1 April 2000. Basically, the provisions cover situations where services are provided through an intermediary company, often by the majority shareholder (or a person connected with him), in circumstances where if the individual had provided his or her services directly, the payment would have been treated as arising from employment. The exemptions that are available are where:

(a) the client is an individual and not in business (although this was amended by the 2003 budget to include personal service companies used by domestic staff), and

(b) the worker receives income only in the form of wages or salary and has no significant right to dividend income.

The provisions contained in the legislation have the effect of deeming any income arising from a relevant engagement to a personal service company,

14. IR 35 lists the following factors which, among others, are taken into account in determining whether an individual is employed or self-employed:
    - Employment involves a 'contract of service', whereas self-employment involves a 'contract for services'.
    - An employer exercises 'control' over an employee, whereas a self-employed person is not under the control of the person who contracts for the self-employed person's services.
    - A self-employed worker usually provides the equipment needed to do the job, whereas a worker who is, for example, provided with equipment and/or office space is usually employed.
    - An individual who risks his own money in respect of his employment is almost certainly self-employed.
    - Employees tend to be paid a fixed wage, whereas independent contractors are usually paid for completing a particular job.
    - A person who becomes 'part and parcel' of the organisation is usually an employee.
    - An employer has the right to terminate an employment relationship, whereas a contract for services is usually terminated upon completion of the job (or breach of the contract).
    - Substance over form is important – if the intention of the parties is to create an employment relationship, calling it something else will not be taken into account.

that would have been treated as arising from employment, as being a salary paid at the end of the tax year. In other words, the general effect of IR 35 is to disregard the existence of the personal service company if the income arising to the company could be classified as being from employment had the services been provided directly. Where the provisions apply, Pay As You Earn (PAYE) and social security contributions are due in the normal way, and once the deemed payment has been made (with PAYE and social security contributions accounted for), no further tax is due when the individual or employee receives payments from the company as dividends.

The use of a personal service company arrangement before the IT boom generally focused on loan-out companies. A loan-out company is one organised for the purposes of supplying the services of an entertainer or an athlete to third parties, which is often owned by the individual and whose sole employee is usually the individual. These entities were commonly used by entertainers working in a foreign country as a means of diverting earnings away from them and into a third party. Loan-out companies are now recognised by many developed tax jurisdictions with the effect that payments to such a company will be taxed in any event.

Nevertheless, genuine employment arrangements through third-party owned service companies (non-personal service companies) may be very beneficial. Such companies often assist in reducing the level of social security costs as well as direct taxation of salaries, allow deferral of tax liabilities to occur, maximise contributions to pension arrangements without limitations that would otherwise be made, and permit stock options to be held in an advantageous manner through employee benefit trusts. 'Rabbi trusts' in the US have been commonly used as a recognised means of tax deferral, although their uses are to be curtailed according to current announcements.

A non-personal service company may also enable individuals to be employed under split contracts of employment, one for local services and one for worldwide services outside the particular country of residence. Such contracts are very useful for non-domiciled UK residents,[15] where income for foreign services are not subject to UK tax if not remitted to the UK.[16] Windows

15. See Chapter 5.

16. Note that HMRC has recently announced in Tax Bulletin 76 that it will change its emphasis in respect of dual contracts of employment. Under such arrangements, resident but non-domiciled individuals can benefit from having separate contracts of employment for UK duties performed, which are taxed in the UK, and non-UK duties, which are not taxed in the UK provided that the relevant income is not remitted. HMRC has clarified that it will investigate the fact relating to such arrangements more closely, and consider whether there is in fact a single employment in spite of the fact that two separate employment agreements were entered into. If it is found that duties performed under dual employment contracts benefit the employer in the

Continued overleaf...

of opportunity may arise where individuals transfer their residence, allowing previously deferred income to be paid as 'Golden Hellos', for example, without being subject to tax in the new country of residence.

3.5 TAXATION OF ENTERTAINERS AND SPORTSMEN

Foreign entertainers and sportsmen are considered a separate category, and double tax treaty provisions acknowledge this. Thus, in the OECD Model Convention with respect to Taxes on Income and Capital 2003, Article 17(1) states that notwithstanding the provisions of the treaty relating to dependent and independent personal services, income derived by a resident of one state as an entertainer (such as a theatre, motion picture, radio or television artiste, or a musician) or as a sportsman (which will include footballers, golfers, jockeys, cricketers, tennis players, racing car drivers), from his personal activities *as such* exercised in the other state may be taxed in the other state. The words 'as such' are important to understand in relation to income from non-performing activities contracted by the entertainers and sportsmen, such as endorsement and merchandising contracts.

Article 17(2) extends the right of the local tax administration not only to tax income paid directly to the above individuals, but also to tax such income even if it is received by companies or indeed any other entity, which of course is directed primarily to loan-out companies.

The source rules are thus again relevant for Article 17, in that clearly performance income has its source where the performance is undertaken, and therefore should be taxed in the source state. Other income which is derived from performance activity, such as receiving income for wearing a company's logo whilst playing tennis also has a source where the performance is undertaken (the *André Agassi* case did not deny this basic concept).[17]

However, merchandising income may not *necessarily* be related to where a performance takes place, although CDs sold at a venue where a performance is taking place may have a local source. General sponsorship income is normally unrelated to a local source and would most likely be taxed where the individual is resident for tax purposes.

16. *...continued from previous page*
UK, the employee will be assessed in the UK for duties performed outside the country. Also, in a case where there is a 'real' dual agreement but the employee performs substantive duties for the overseas employer in the UK, the employee will be taxed in the UK on all earnings resulting from the overseas agreement.

17. Compare §3.5.1.

3.5.1 Relevant types of income

Training income

Many sportsmen receive income during a period of intensive training for a particular tournament, which would normally be taxed in their country of residence. However, they may decide to train in another country, which has, for example, better facilities than their home country. In the absence of a double tax treaty, they may find themselves subject to considerably higher income taxes than would be applicable in their country of residence, where they may be entitled to certain concessions, or to reduce their taxable base by deductible expenses, especially pension contributions or tax shelter possibilities. Double tax treaties normally address this problem so that the country of residence only retains the taxing rights.

Income from endorsement contracts

Where an entertainer or sportsman contracts with the manufacturer of a particular product to allow his name, logo or likeness to be used by the manufacturer to endorse his product, this should be treated as a grant of a licence, and therefore a royalty receipt. Endorsement contracts entered into by a company may minimise or avoid the withholding tax that would normally be levied upon payment of such a royalty directly to the individual. Ancillary obligations under the contracts, such as television appearances, may again not be personal service income for the performance of their services *as such*, but again treated as royalty income. This is not, however, clear under the OECD Model Treaty where such income is not expressly covered within the royalty article, and this should be looked at on a case-by-case basis.[18]

18. The UK High Court in a recent decision involving André Agassi seemed to depart from the general understanding that income earned by a sportsperson for playing in the UK (e.g. prize winnings) is taxable in the UK (compare the discussion above of the wording 'as such' of Article 17(1) of the OECD Model Treaty and also §4.3.2). Conversely, endorsement income paid to a loan out company with all the parties being UK non-resident is not taxable there. Agassi, a UK non-resident individual, entered into endorsement contracts with Nike Inc. and Head Sports AG, neither of which have a tax presence in the UK. Agassi would then occasionally play in tournaments in the UK, including Wimbledon, with Nike and Head paying endorsement fees to Agassi Enterprises Inc, Agassi's loan-out company. The High Court held that such endorsement payments would be taxable at least in part, under Section 556 ICTA 1988, in the hands of Agassi via his loan-out company. However, the Court of Appeal decided in favour of Mr Agassi, with the Appeal judges deciding that on the basis that the offshore company had no UK tax presence it was as such not subject to tax in the UK under the relevant UK tax laws. *André Agassi v. S Robinson* (HM Inspector of Taxes) [2004] EWHC 487 (Ch).

Income from sponsorship contracts

Payments under these contracts are not necessarily for the performing activities of entertainers and sportsmen as such, and therefore may not be subject to local withholding taxes. However, where, say, a tennis player wears a T-shirt with the manufacturer's name emblazoned on it, while playing tennis in a tournament, then the fee under the sponsorship contract will be taxable in the particular country as discussed above. Where there is one fee under the contract covering a period in which the player performs in several countries, then the fee must be apportioned in the most acceptable manner for each relevant taxing jurisdiction, perhaps on the number of performances in one country compared to the entire number of performances during the period of the contract.

It becomes more difficult where the tennis player wears the T-shirt on, say, a television quiz programme, where the income should not be taxed, while also performing in public in it, and such allocation problems need to be thought out in advance when preparing the relevant contracts. Bonuses under the contracts for winning tournaments would normally be taxed in the country where the performances are taking place.

Income from merchandising contracts

Merchandising contracts will probably be entered into with specialist merchandising companies, as may a sponsorship contract. It may be helpful to design a special logo when reproducing the artiste's name or picture, so that this can be separately licensed for a royalty payment (such as a shirt number for a renowned footballer). This is one of the areas in which sportsmen can definitely receive copyright royalties for the use of their name coupled with a specially designed logo for copyright purposes, and even payments under an endorsement contract where the artiste's name and logo is attached to the endorsed article may fall under the category of royalties rather than personal services. This would normally be more advantageous for tax purposes, since the receipt of such royalties may be free of local source withholding tax while income from personal services may be subject to local tax as explained above.

Royalty payments would normally require two factors to be present, the first being the use of some proprietorial right (which is why the creation of logos for entertainers and sportsmen is so valuable), and the second being that the payment is based on usage of that right. It is therefore essential when preparing such contracts that these factors are reflected in the contractual arrangements.

Income from creative services contracts

The greatest scope for international tax planning, in particular for music entertainers, is to differentiate their income between performance fees and creative services. Creative services typically fall under the heading of copyright royalties, and can include literary copyrights for writing music or other material, recordings of music, and other artistic works covering paintings, drawings, photography and designing costumes, lighting, sound and so on.

Take, for example, a pop group about to embark on a world tour using their own music. Besides the performance contracts, contracts should be drawn up for recording the music, publishing and composition, as well as merchandising contracts, sponsorship contracts and possibly film and video contracts. The recording contract may require a lump sum advance together with royalty percentages, and will need to state the commitment of the group to recording a certain number of tracks within the period of the recording contract. The publishing contract should preferably retain copyright for the artistes but will license the records for a fee based on amounts collected.

Another contract could cover the creative input of the tour itself, allowing for a royalty to be paid based on gross box office receipts for bringing a fully rehearsed show to the promoter. The royalty income will cover the costs of designing the set, costumes, lighting, sound systems, photographic material etc., and is often sufficient to achieve considerable profits depending upon the number of times the show can be performed in any one country.

Certain countries may have considerably more income potential than others, e.g. the US for pop musicians, and one may need to vary the terms of similar contractual arrangements with different promoters. Although it is always useful to be able to submit to any tax administration similar contracts that have been entered into with promoters in other jurisdictions, fine-tuning is possible by, for example, limiting the rights to a particular territory or extending them beyond the frontiers of the relevant country, limiting duration of the contract with extensions permitted only on more advantageous terms, or negotiating a profit entitlement as opposed to straight royalties (although this could have tax consequences as deemed partnership income rather than royalty income), or requesting a lump-sum advance payment (often desirable in any event and sometimes enabling withholding taxes to be avoided).

3.5.2 United Kingdom

In the UK, tax at the basic rate (currently 22%) has to be deducted from any payments made to entertainers or sportsmen, even if they are capital (e.g. loans) rather than income payments. Regulations provide for a nil or reduced rate of withholding tax in particular cases and a *de minimis* limit of £1,000. Although the withholding tax is supposed to be a payment on account of a foreign individual's total UK tax liability, arising from a deemed trade in the UK, in many cases the withholding tax will be accepted as a final payment.

In the event that payments are made to third parties in connection with the activities of an entertainer and sportsman, the payment will be considered a net amount equivalent to a gross sum less the withholding tax liability; the withholding tax liability will therefore be much higher than may be initially realised (i.e. 22% of 100/78 x payment, so that a payment of, say, £10,000 has a tax liability attributed to it of 22/78, i.e. £2,820 or 28.2% of the net). This is one of the more contentious areas, since it includes payments for hotel accommodation, as well as subsistence, transport, *per diems*, etc. It should also be noted that the income of a foreign entertainer or sportsman is not only the fees that he receives for his actual appearances, plus other payments related to his appearance as above, but also any other income which may be associated with the appearances, e.g. from advertising, sponsorship, public appearances or endorsements. However, receipts from activities like these may be exempt under double tax treaty provisions described above in Article 17, which override domestic provisions in conflict. In particular, if the income is not from his personal activities *as such*, i.e. as an entertainer or sportsmen, but from intellectual property rights, for example, that he owns, then no withholding tax may be applicable.

Connected payments that are not actually made to the entertainer or sportsman will only be subject to withholding tax if made to a company, individual or other entity:

(a) who is under the control of the entertainer; or

(b) who is not resident in the UK and is liable to a rate of tax of less than 22%; or

(c) which is a trust of which the entertainer is a settlor; or

(d) who enters into an arrangement with the entertainer or sportsman by which it is reasonable to suppose that the latter will become entitled to receive amounts in cash or otherwise which are not substantially less than the amounts of connected payments received from the UK promoter.

Other countries have similar rules, and perhaps the US is the most developed of these. Here, the withholding tax is as high as 30%, and the provisions against diversion of income to third parties are extensive – the so-called 'Rent-a-Star' provisions.

3.5.3 United States

All US-source income is subject to personal income taxation unless the individual is present in the US for less than 90 days in a year and his income is less than $3,000. Although double tax treaties may generally improve the position for non-resident aliens having US-source income, if they are artistes or athletes, Article 17 of the OECD Model Treaty permits the US to impose US taxation in respect of income derived from performances rendered in the US.

Even if the payments are not made direct to the individuals but to a company, whether owned as a slave company or otherwise, salaries paid to the individuals by the company will be subject to US taxation.

There have been several Revenue Rulings issued by the IRS relating to transactions involving independent agents, particularly with regard to foreign entertainers, and whether the presence of such entertainers in the US constitutes a permanent establishment in itself, or whether their income is effectively connected with a trade or business in the US.

3.5.4 France

In France, both French and foreign entertainers and sportsmen are required to file a tax return and pay income tax together with the employer's share of social security assessments (about 35%) and the employee's share of 15%. This social security charge is only assessed on a limited amount of salary, although approximately 18% relating to medical insurance is imposed on all compensation, without any ceiling. The social security charges may not be imposed on EU-resident entertainers and sportsmen who are not residents of France and who pay social security charges in another EU member state, or who are resident in those countries with a totalisation agreement with France in respect of social security charges.

In order to be sure that such tax assessments are collected, a withholding tax of 15% is due on gross receipts paid to a non-resident entertainer or sportsman. The individuals would still have to file a French tax return, but the 15% of gross receipts would then be creditable against the individual French income tax due; however, any excess of withholding tax over personal tax due is not reimbursed unless the withholding tax has been applied without justification. Therefore, it may be more beneficial to become French tax resident to avoid the 15% withholding tax regime, since if the payments are characterised as salaries, they will be entitled to standard deductions available to employees together with additional deductions for professional expenses granted to most entertainers; the resultant tax liability may often be less than the 15% withholding tax that would otherwise be due.

The French tax administration will consider most remuneration paid to entertainers or athletes as payments in respect of an employment, even if the payments may be in respect of royalties and copyrights. Deeming provisions will ignore the existence of a loan-out company if: (a) the company is located in a low-tax regime, and (b) the entertainer or sportsman controls the company directly or indirectly, and (c) the company has no other business than the rendering of services such as the performances of artistes. In cases where the loan-out company is in a high-tax country with which France has entered into a double tax treaty, the French tax administration may argue that the treaty is inapplicable since the relevant treaty, if any, should be between France and the country in which the entertainer or sportsman is resident, an argument which does not seem to curry favour with most international tax professionals. However, if royalties are paid which are clearly related to activities exercised outside France which: (a) do not require the physical presence of the artiste in France, and (b) are based on the results of exploitation, then the French tax administration may accept that the normal withholding tax regime applicable to royalties applies, subject to the provisions of any double tax treaties. Licensing companies established in tax treaty jurisdictions may therefore enable such royalties to be paid gross, leaving the individuals to sign separate service contracts for performances in France direct with the French promoter.

Where a film producer in, say, the US employs a UK film star to feature in a film made in France, the taxing rights of the various countries become more confused. Although the UK individual should be subject to French tax, there is no withholding mechanism, since the producer is a non-resident of France. This is similar in many countries such as Italy, Australia and Spain, where although there is an obligation, there is no withholding mechanism. In the US, the problem is somewhat resolved by the need for the actor to obtain a so-called 'sailing permit', which will confirm to the exit authorities that all relevant taxes have been paid.

3.5.5 The Netherlands

Foreign artistes and athletes performing in the Netherlands are treated as employees of the Dutch promoter and therefore subject to individual income tax. Normally, a wage tax should be withheld which will be credited against their income tax liability, but if the individuals perform in the Netherlands for a short time only (not exceeding three months), a fixed rate of tax at 20% may be considered as the final tax in respect of their income tax liability.

The Netherlands' double tax treaties normally incorporate a clause preventing the avoidance of individual income tax liability by the creation of offshore slave companies to which the services of the individual are contracted. However, even without such a clause, a Supreme Court case dated 23 November 1983[19] held that for purposes of the wage tax, musicians employed by a Swiss company hired by a Dutch promoter were deemed to be employed by that promoter who was then responsible for the withholding of wage tax. Under the new legislation that came into force on 1 January 2001, Dutch artistes will be treated in the same way as foreign artistes. International professional sportsmen playing in the Netherlands will also be subject to 20% withholding tax on income from 1 June 2000.

Non-resident individuals who are resident in a tax treaty country that does not contain a specific entertainers and sportsmen clause would only be subject to

19. Case No. 21818, published in BNB 1984/33.

Dutch taxation if they fall within the employment provisions requiring a presence in excess of 183 days, or employment by a Dutch company or permanent establishment, or the fixed base provision relating to professional services. If foreign artistes perform via their own legal entities, it appears that tax cannot be withheld, as such legal entities only become taxable in the Netherlands if they have a permanent establishment in the Netherlands. Also, if the artistes are independent, they will only become taxable if they create a permanent establishment in the Netherlands, which would be extremely rare.

3.6 WITHHOLDING TAX ON ACCOUNT OF INCOME TAX

Withholding tax is a preliminary tax imposed at source and is widely applied in respect of interest, dividends, royalties and similar payments. Wages and salaries, discussed above, may also represent the underlying taxable payment and a wage tax may be levied in the form of a withholding tax. A withholding tax may be either final or, in the case of certain kinds of income, will be taken into account for the purpose of calculating the amount of annual income tax payable by a taxpayer. It is not a separate tax, but a tax withheld at source to ensure collection of the ultimate income tax liability due.

3.6.1 Interest

The OECD Model Convention with respect to Taxes on Income and Capital of 2003 states in Article 11(3) that 'interest' means income from debt-claims of every kind, whether or not secured by mortgage and whether or not carrying a right to participate in the debtor's profits, and in particular, income from government securities and income from bonds or debentures. Interest paid to a foreign recipient will often be subject to withholding tax in the source country. The rate at which tax will be withheld is usually determined by domestic law, but it may also be reduced under tax treaty provisions, if applicable, or under a multilateral agreement such as the EU Interest and Royalty Directive.[20]

3.6.2 Dividends – holding company regimes

The concept of 'dividends' usually relates to income from shares, but could also relate to income from other corporate rights, which is subjected to the same taxation treatment as income from shares by the laws of the state of which the distributing company is resident.[21]

One of the best-known entities used in international tax planning is the holding company. Perhaps because the balance sheet of the holding

20. See §3.2.2.
21. OECD Model Treaty 2003, Article 10(3).

company is generally the sum of the individual participations, and with an overriding tendency towards the concept that 'size matters', holding companies have become revered by entrepreneurs, advisers and perhaps even tax administrations themselves.

Because of the importance of holding companies in international tax structures, the following pages compare the holding company jurisdictions of Austria, Cyprus, Denmark, Ireland, Luxembourg, Singapore, the Netherlands and the United Kingdom. The analysis and comparison is useful in understanding three of the basic requirements for any holding company:

(a) mitigation or exemption from foreign withholding taxes in respect of local source income passed on as dividends to the holding company, and capital gains;

(b) minimal or no corporate taxes in the holding company jurisdiction on receipt of the income and capital gains; and

(c) minimal or no withholding taxes on the onward distribution of income and capital gains to the ultimate beneficial shareholders.[22]

In each of the jurisdictions reviewed, the basis of the planning starts at minimising local source withholding taxes on dividend distributions. This generally requires suitable double tax treaty provisions between the local source country and the relevant holding company regime.

Choice of the holding company regime is then based on an absence of tax on dividends or capital gains derived from holding the shares in the local companies. This may well depend on the tax characteristics in the local source country (rate of tax being comparable) as well as the nature of the activities of the subsidiary (business or passive income). The combination of such local characteristics with those of the specific holding company regime will determine the appropriate structure.

Since this is a book about principles as opposed to a reference book on the specific tax laws of each country, the holding company regimes are illustrated by reference to the concepts one needs to consider for each holding company structure. At the outset, it should be realised that there are two major distinctions in the treatment of dividends received from subsidiary companies: the first is to exempt such dividends from tax in the holding company jurisdiction ('the participation exemption'), and the second is to

22. The characteristics outlined in this section and in the country analysis below do not constitute an exhaustive list but provide general guidance as to the main points to consider when deciding on a holding company jurisdiction.

allow a credit for foreign tax against the domestic tax liability on such dividends ('the credit method').

Low-tax regime of subsidiary

If the holding company regime operates a credit method, such as the UK and Ireland, then unless the tax incurred by the subsidiary (on its profits as well as any withholding tax on dividends distributed) is equal to or exceeds the UK or Irish domestic tax rate, an additional tax burden will be levied in the holding company on receipt of dividends from such subsidiaries, whereas where it is desired to locate a subsidiary in a low-tax regime, countries such as Austria, Cyprus, Denmark, Luxembourg, Singapore and the Netherlands may be more appropriate jurisdictions since they offer a participation exemption for dividends received, subject to certain conditions being met. However, some of these countries recognise that they would be party to wholesale tax avoidance unless they impose a minimum tax requirement in the subsidiary company before the participation exemption is granted. Thus in Austria, the foreign company should be comparable to an Austrian company or meet the requirements of Article 2 of the EU Parent/Subsidiary Directive.[23] Thus the participation exemption will be restricted by an anti-avoidance provision which requires a subsidiary's tax burden, calculated according to Austrian tax principles, to be 15% or more, unless there are specific tax concessions (such as a tax holiday) in the country of residence of the subsidiary.

Similarly, Luxembourg requires a non-resident subsidiary to be subject to 'normal taxation', which is accepted as a rate of at least 15% on profits, out of which the distributions are made, but if there is an applicable double tax treaty between Luxembourg and a country or residence of the subsidiary, this minimum tax rate may not be relevant.

The Netherlands has one of the most advantageous participation exemption regimes, as well as one of the oldest, and exempts from Dutch tax even those dividends emanating from low-tax subsidiaries, as long as the subsidiary is actually subject to taxation at any level (even a 1% tax rate would suffice for this purpose). Moreover, as with Austria, the Dutch tax administration accepts that a temporary exemption from income tax due to investment or other incentives will not affect the qualification for participation exemption, as long as the country concerned operates a normal system of taxation based on profits.

In 1999, Denmark introduced a holding company regime, which for a short period made Denmark a very attractive jurisdiction in which to locate a holding company. As regards the subject to tax requirement, this is only relevant where the business of the subsidiary is of a financial (passive) nature,

23. Which provides a list of entities to which the Directive will apply.

in which case the foreign tax should not be less than 75% of what the Danish taxation would have been (at the standard Danish corporate income tax rate of 28%, this means a 21% level of taxation, but only for passive companies).

An even more recent holding company regime was established in Cyprus as a result of the 2003 tax reform provision.

The Singapore system is a combination of the participation exemption and credit method. Under the foreign income exemption (FIE), foreign-source dividends, among others, received by a Singapore-resident company will be tax exempt if the following conditions are met:

(a) in the year the income is received in Singapore, the corporate tax rate of the relevant jurisdiction is at least 15%;

(b) the specified foreign income received in Singapore has been subject to tax in the foreign jurisdiction;

(c) the Singapore Revenue is satisfied that the tax exemption would be beneficial to the Singapore company.

Where the FIE is not available, for foreign income received in Singapore from a country with which Singapore has a double taxation agreement, or within the list of countries for which Singapore grants unilateral relief, or a Commonwealth country for which Singapore grants Commonwealth relief, the foreign tax suffered may be allowed as a claim against the income brought into Singapore, restricting the maximum relief to the Singapore tax which would have been suffered on the income but for the double tax relief.

Also, where the FIE is not available, for foreign income received in Singapore from a country with which Singapore has no double taxation agreement a unilateral tax credit for foreign tax incurred is allowed. In addition, where the Singapore company owns at least 25% of the shares of the foreign company, the unilateral tax credit will also cover the underlying corporate tax on the profits out of which the foreign dividend is paid. The Minister of Finance is empowered to waive the 25% shareholding requirement on a case-by-case basis.

For active trading companies in tax regimes where the rate of tax is less than 15%, and where dividends are required to be distributed up to the holding company and from there to the ultimate shareholders, the participation exemption regimes in the Netherlands, Denmark and Cyprus appear to be the most favourable. However, where dividends are not required to be distributed to the holding company, but the investment is primarily made for capital growth and profits are reinvested within the subsidiary company, the subject to tax requirement may not be relevant unless the holding company regime operates the controlled foreign company provisions below.

Controlled foreign company laws

The concept of holding subsidiaries for capital growth but refraining from dividend distributions from low-tax subsidiaries may be an appealing one for tax deferral purposes. For example, an active trading company in Hong Kong is taxed at 17.5%, and an active trading company in Cyprus is taxed at 10%, both of which are substantially below the tax rate that would apply if a UK company were to conduct such trading activities. It would therefore seem logical for the UK company to form subsidiaries in either Hong Kong or Cyprus to provide tax deferral on such profits until distributed back to the UK company.

To compact this obvious means of tax deferral, controlled foreign company (CFC) legislation has been introduced in most high-tax jurisdictions (whether renowned for their holding company regimes or not). The effect of the CFC provisions is to attribute the profits earned in the underlying trading subsidiary to the UK parent, regardless of any dividend distribution policies.[24]

A review of CFC provisions as they relate to passive investment companies is covered in the next subsection, this section dealing with CFC provisions as they relate to active trading companies. Among the holding company regimes reviewed, only the UK has significant CFC provisions preventing tax deferral in active trading subsidiaries, but there are some exemptions which may apply for those trading subsidiaries who satisfy the 'exempt activities test' (requiring commercial substance with limited intercompany activities which could generate artificial profits through transfer pricing mechanisms). Thus any of the other regimes could provide holding companies for low-taxed, active subsidiaries for the purposes of tax deferral on income, but the problem arises if the capital growth is significant and a sale of the subsidiary is envisaged in the future. Unless the subsidiary qualifies for the participation exemption (for most countries other than Cyprus, this requires a minimum subject to tax level), capital gains may be subject to full local taxation without exemption. In this connection, the substantial shareholders' exemption in the UK may be an alternative to Cyprus in providing capital gains tax exemption, subject to the ability to retain tax-deferred profits in a low-tax subsidiary which qualifies for the exempt activities test or one of the other tests within the UK CFC legislation.

Passive activities of subsidiary

Although many of the holding company regimes do not have CFC legislation for active subsidiaries, they may well deny the participation exemption for income and capital gains derived from passive subsidiaries. This is true in Austria where the company's business should not primarily consist of

24. See §5.3 for a more extensive review of CFC legislation in various countries.

generating passive income, although it is accepted that dividend income from, say, a sub-holding company from operating companies in the same or other territories would not be considered passive income. Cyprus's CFC rules extend only to non-resident companies whose activities result directly or indirectly in investment income, but even dividend income from these companies will be exempt from Cyprus taxation if the foreign tax burden is not substantially lower than the tax burden of the Cypriot resident company (where the tax rate is 10%).

The Danish rules require dividends from subsidiaries who conduct mainly financial activities to be fully subject to Danish corporate income tax, and Danish CFC legislation extends to such foreign companies if:

- the Danish holding company controls the foreign company;
- the business of the foreign company is of a financial nature;
- the foreign company is subject to low tax.

The control requirement will be met if the Danish holding company directly or indirectly owns at least 25% of the share capital or controls more than 50% of the voting rights. Share capital and voting rights held by Danish or foreign group companies are taken into account. The financial nature requirement will be met if at least 33% of the company's gross income is financial income or insurance premiums. The low-tax requirement will be met if in any year the foreign tax on the subsidiary is less than 75% of what the Danish taxation would have been.

CFC taxation implies that the Danish holding company must add the financial income of the CFC to its taxable income in Denmark on a current basis. Income from business activities other than financial activities are exempt from CFC taxation. The financial income is taxed at 28% but a foreign tax credit is granted for underlying corporate tax.

Neither Luxembourg nor Singapore has CFC legislation, even for passive companies, but the subject to tax requirement of 15% in each jurisdiction must be borne in mind if the income is to be distributed to the ultimate shareholders through the holding company, as opposed to being accumulated within the subsidiary for tax deferral purposes.

The Dutch tax code restricts the participation exemption (*deelnemingsvrijstelling*) to active foreign subsidiaries as opposed to passive ones. Moreover, shares in subsidiary companies, even domestic ones, cannot be held as 'inventory'. On 23 February 2000 the Supreme Court[25] stipulated that shares are considered to be held as inventory if:

25. Case number 34775, published in BNB 2000/215.

- the shares are part of the working capital of the holding company and are held for purposes of selling; and
- the subsidiary does not run a substantive business; and
- the subsidiary does not (or practically not) have any other assets than liquid assets and/or assets which can immediately be transferred into liquid assets without substantial losses.

In principle, shares are considered inventory in case of trading in dormant and cash box companies.

For foreign subsidiaries, the holding of shares must not be considered to be a portfolio holding or passive investment. A Dutch portfolio holding company pays full Dutch corporate income tax on the net dividends received; however, tax relief on the basis of a double tax treaty or unilateral rules may be available in order to prevent double taxation. This requirement may be waived as regards 25% plus interests in EU-resident companies.[26]

Generally speaking, however, either passive investment subsidiaries would be regarded as CFCs and their income attributed to the holding company on a current basis, as in the UK and Denmark, or dividends and capital gains received or derived from the passive subsidiaries would not fall within the participation exemption provisions of the holding company jurisdiction. Provided the tax rate of the passive company exceeds 15%, Singapore would appear to be a beneficial jurisdiction for holding shares in passive investment companies, since there is no CFC legislation in Singapore to assess the annual profits to Singapore tax, and the participation exemption provisions appear to apply even to passive income provided that the underlying corporate tax rate is at least 15%.

Shareholding requirement in subsidiary

Most jurisdictions require a minimum shareholding requirement for both the participation exemption and the credit methods to apply. In the UK, the tax credit for underlying corporate tax paid (as opposed to foreign withholding tax on dividends received) requires a minimum direct or indirect shareholding in at least 10% of the share capital of the subsidiary company – or indeed, underlying subsidiaries where the 10% level is relevant throughout a chain of companies. The 10% level is also required in Austria,[27] as well as in Luxembourg, although there is an alternative of a minimum investment amount of €1.2 million if the 10% level is not met.

Lower levels of investment are acceptable for the participation exemption or credit method to apply in Ireland and the Netherlands where the participation

26. Compare the provisions of the EU Parent/Subsidiary Directive in §3.2.3.
27. Section 10(2) of the Austrian Corporate Income Tax Act.

must be at least 5%, although in the Netherlands, a lower participation may be acceptable if the shareholding is in the normal course of a Dutch company's business or if the acquisition serves the general interest of the public. Cyprus has the lowest participation requirement, where it is just necessary to own more than 1% of a foreign company for the participation exemption to apply.

Besides the actual percentage ownership, certain countries require the ownership to be held for a minimum period of time. This is to prevent companies being brought into a holding company regime specifically with the intention of stripping out dividends with the minimum amount of local source withholding tax, and therefore an anti-abuse provision imposed within holding company jurisdictions. Thus in Austria, shares need to have been held for a minimum period of one year, and this is the same in Denmark (where the percentage ownership in fact must be at least 20%) with effect from 1 January 2002 to benefit from the Danish participation exemption. Luxembourg has a similar 12-month holding period, or at least the holding company must permit itself to hold such shares for a period of 12 months, but there is no minimum holding requirement in the other holding company jurisdictions including Ireland, UK and Cyprus.

Beneficial double tax treaty network

As stated at the outset of this review, one of the most important elements in structuring holding companies is to benefit from low or zero rates of withholding tax on dividend distributions from subsidiaries, either because the country imposes no withholding tax on dividends under its unilateral tax law (e.g. Australia) or according to the provisions of double tax treaties or multilateral treaties such as the EU Parent/Subsidiary Directive. Most of the holding company jurisdictions reviewed in this section have an extensive network of double tax treaties, and Austria, Cyprus, Denmark, Ireland, Luxembourg, the Netherlands and the UK are able to benefit from the EU Parent/Subsidiary Directive so that all dividends receivable from European Union subsidiary companies are exempt from local source withholding tax. In respect of dividends emanating from non-EU subsidiaries, generally speaking the Netherlands and the UK have the most beneficial and extensive double tax treaty network reducing foreign withholding taxes to a minimum, but as treaties have become renegotiated and updated, the discrepancy between local source withholding taxes payable to one country as opposed to another has been significantly reduced. It is noteworthy that at a time when the Cold War froze relations between East and West, Cyprus developed an extensive network of double tax treaties with Soviet Union countries, which maintain their relevance and advantages today. Coupled with the new holding regime in Cyprus, the benefits derived from such treaties are now bearing fruit for those ultimate shareholders establishing Cyprus holding companies for such structures.

Corporate tax on dividends received and capital gains

Having obtained dividends from subsidiary companies with the lowest possible local source withholding tax, the income should either be tax exempt under the participation exemption, assuming this is applicable, or subject to limited taxation in the holding company jurisdiction as a result of the credit method. The above analyses have described the requirements for the participation exemption, and why CFC legislation may prevent tax deferral on annual profits.

What is equally important is to ensure that a future sale of the subsidiary companies will not be subject to capital gains tax in the holding company jurisdiction. Even if a sale is unlikely in the short term, restructuring possibilities often require a disposal of all or part of the shares owned by a specific holding company within a group, either because another holding company jurisdiction is more beneficial, or existing shares need to be made available to minority interests, or for any other good commercial reasons such as employee incentives. The requirements of most of the participation exemptions apply equally to dividend income as to capital gains, thus the Austrian requirements as described above, although an Austrian holding company may elect to include capital gains and losses from an international participation in its tax base; such irrevocable election must be made when filing the tax return for the business year during which the participation has been purchased. The Luxembourg rules for capital gains exemption are similar to those for dividend exemption except that whereas the 10% investment level can be ignored if the investment exceeds €1.2 million, the investment has to exceed €6 million for similar capital gains tax exemption.

The position in Singapore and Cyprus is more beneficial under unilateral law, in that neither country imposes capital gains tax on sale by a holding company of its shares in foreign subsidiaries. Thus, provided there are no CFC concerns, Singaporean and Cyprus holding companies may be more advantageous than relying on the participation exemption rules in Western European holding regimes, which are sometimes unclear as to their application.

In Ireland, a capital gains tax exemption has been provided for by the 2004 Finance Act for certain disposals by an investor company of shares in the company it holds. This exemption applies where at the time of the disposal the investee company is resident in the EU or in a country with which Ireland has concluded a tax treaty. Further, the investor must have held for a period of at least 12 months ending in the previous 24 months at least 10% of the investee company where the holding had a value of €15 million or at least 5% of the investee company that had a holding value of €50 million. Also, there is a requirement that at the time of the disposal the investee company was carrying on a trade.

This 'substantial shareholding' provision in Ireland is similar to the one introduced in the UK by the 2002 Finance Act. The effect of the substantial shareholding provisions is that a company disposing of all or part of a substantial shareholding, which has been confirmed as being 10% of the ordinary shares of the company invested in, which has been held for a period of at least 12 months in the two years before the sale of the shares, will be exempt from capital gains tax on gains realised thereon. It should be noted that while gains will be tax exempt, losses realised will not be allowable to be set off against gains.

The main condition of the exemption, other than the 10% requirement, is that the company disposing of the shares, i.e. the investing company, has been a sole trading company or a member of a 'qualifying group'[28] prior to the sale of the shares, as well as immediately afterwards. It is also necessary for the company invested in to be a trading company. It is the requirement for the holding company to meet the conditions of still being a trading company or a member of a trading company after the disposal which may cause potential issues in the future, and it seems this has been included so as to limit the applicability of the new legislation and thus avoid possible conflict with the EU.

A 'trading group' is defined as meaning a group where:

(a) one or more of whose members carry on trading activities; and

(b) the activities of whose members, taken together, do not include to a substantial extent activities other than trading activities.[29]

Thus a one-off investment in a trading company would mean that a sale of the only asset of the holding company would leave the company without its means of being part of a trading group.

Furthermore, the sale by a holding company of one of its five subsidiaries, for example, may give rise to capital gains, the size of which dwarfs the value of its remaining trading activities. As outlined above, 'trading company' is defined[30] as one whose activities do not include to a substantial extent activities other than trading activities. Presumably, the investment of the gains would be substantial enough to take the company out of the category of a trading company for these purposes. It may be that the holding company also trades –

28. Which basically means a trading group, TCGA 1992 Schedule 7AC.
29. The Inland Revenue seems to be relaxing this requirement – significant trading companies even if they have substantial cash reserves or hold a considerable amount of investment property are still likely to qualify.
30. Section 21(1), TCGA 1992.

it may, for example, have management activities, in which case no issues arise. However, if the size of the gain could potentially threaten the trading status of the group, it may be advisable for the holding company, prior to the sale, to create a new subsidiary which it capitalises with the proceeds of sale with a view to commencing a new trade.

Clearly, the legislation has been drafted so as to satisfy the European Commission and equally clearly, the intention is not to make the UK a holding company regime *per se*, or one which encourages investment in tax haven or low-taxed entities. This is apparent from the retention of a tax credit system for dividends receivable, as well as the continued impact of the controlled foreign company legislation. Nevertheless, the ability to realise capital gains tax free is very attractive, especially so given that the UK imposes no withholding tax on dividends paid by a UK company, irrespective of the residence of the recipient.

Interest deductibility in holding company

At first sight this may not seem the most vital of tax requirements, since if the dividends receivable and capital gains are not taxable, there is no need to worry about deductibility of interest in respect of, say, loans secured for particular investments. However, where the holding company has trading subsidiaries in the same tax jurisdiction and is able to file consolidated returns, interest deductibility on such loans is vital in order to reduce the taxable profits derived through the consolidated trading subsidiaries.

This possibility is unavailable in the Netherlands, which specifically prohibits the deductibility of interest on loans incurred to finance acquisitions in foreign companies for which the qualifying participation exemption is relevant. However, it may still be preferable to structure the finance of a Dutch holding company through loans rather than equity, partly to reduce the Dutch capital duty, provided that the acceptable 85:15 debt-to-equity ratio is observed, and partly to avoid Dutch withholding tax on redistribution of dividends from subsidiaries to the ultimate shareholders. Instead of a withholding tax on dividends to the ultimate shareholders (see below), interest payments may be made which carry no withholding tax under Dutch unilateral law. However, an even better arrangement could be achieved in, say, Luxembourg and Belgium where costs relating to a participation in a subsidiary (including interest costs) may be deducted against other Luxembourg or Belgian source income. Again, no withholding tax is levied on the payment of interest to non-residents, and therefore this is more beneficial than paying dividends to shareholders, again subject to observance of debt-to-equity ratios. Austria, like the Netherlands, does not allow such interest deduction. Cyprus, on the other hand, does permit interest deductions, and since the Cyprus holding company may also trade subject to a 10% corporate tax rate on profits, the payment of interest to finance acquisitions of subsidiaries may reduce the actual tax payable in Cyprus even further.

Absence of withholding tax to ultimate shareholders

Having worked one's way through the myriad of considerations when deciding upon the relevant holding company structures, the last leg is to ensure that dividends can be remitted to the ultimate shareholders without withholding tax at the holding company level. Of the jurisdictions reviewed, Singapore, Cyprus and the United Kingdom impose no withholding tax on outgoing dividends under unilateral law. Otherwise, a general withholding tax on dividends payable of 25% in Austria, 28% in Denmark and 20% in Ireland will be levied if the recipient is located in a country which is neither a member of the EU nor has a double tax treaty with the relevant holding company jurisdiction.

Summary

There are so many commercial factors to be taken into account when advising on a corporate structure that by concentrating on the tax issues, it is all too easy to fall into the trap of 'letting the tail wag the dog'. However, choosing a holding company jurisdiction is perhaps more tax-based than choosing other entities within a corporate structure, and the specific jurisdiction will depend upon many of the factors described above.

From a general review, it would appear that both Cyprus and Singapore can generally provide significant benefits where subsidiaries are located in the specific double tax treaty jurisdictions with which Cyprus and Singapore have each negotiated favourable treaties; with Cyprus's concentration on Eastern European jurisdictions (although not exclusively so) and Singapore's concentration on Asian countries, the particular holding company will be primarily determined according to the most favourable treaty jurisdiction. In this connection, it should not be overlooked that the UK has probably the most extensive double tax treaty network, often with more favourable, reciprocal tax rates than are afforded to other jurisdictions. Coupled with the reputation of the UK and the substantial shareholders' exemption for capital gains, the UK may be one of the most favourable holding company regimes for holding subsidiaries located in countries where the local tax rate is the same or higher than the standard 30% UK tax rate. The participation exemptions in the more established holding company jurisdictions in Luxembourg and the Netherlands have been the most favoured over the past two decades of international tax planning. The clear absence of tax on income and capital gains under the relevant participation exemptions have, however, become muddied by the uncertain application of the exemptions in specific circumstances – this uncertainty has not been alleviated by the withdrawal of tax rulings available from local tax administrations. Moreover, there is a general withholding tax on dividend distributions to ultimate shareholders, which may be relevant. In Luxembourg, assuming that neither double tax treaties nor EU Directives can reduced the standard withholding tax rate, a Luxembourg holding company can be liquidated without the application of withholding tax on the liquidation proceeds, but this may appear to be a short-lived use of a holding company, which may be required to have some degree of longevity.

As regards the Netherlands, the traditional route of distributing dividends from the Netherlands to the ultimate shareholders (if double tax treaties or EU directives are unavailable) is by holding the Dutch company through a Netherlands Antilles parent company. However, since 1997, the benefits of the tax treaty between the Netherlands and the Netherlands Antilles have been gradually eroded, so that the initial zero rate of withholding tax in the Netherlands was increased firstly to 5% provided that the tax rate in the Netherlands Antilles was 5.5% minimum, and then to a composite rate of 8.3%. Tax practitioners are now advising the use of a Cyprus company to own the shares of a Dutch holding company so that the EU Parent/Subsidiary Directive may apply to exempt dividends paid by the Dutch holding company from Dutch withholding tax. However, this begs the question as to why the Dutch holding company is required at all, and this would only be the case if the specific circumstances of the underlying investments favour the use of the Netherlands rather than Cyprus as the direct holding company.

Denmark and Austria have always been holding company jurisdictions on the fringe of international tax structures, although the Danish holding company rules introduced in 1999 made Denmark a very attractive jurisdiction for a short period of time; this was because the legislation provided that no withholding tax was to be levied in Denmark on dividend re-distributions to ultimate shareholders, even if they were located in tax havens. However, this was considered a 'harmful distortion' to the community at large, and under pressure from the European Union, Denmark changed its legislation on 1 January 2002 to require the ultimate shareholders to be resident in a tax treaty jurisdiction with Denmark, or any EU member state if dividends were payable without a 20% withholding tax supply.

3.6.3 Royalties

The OECD Model Treaty 2003 states in Article 12(2) that 'royalties' can be defined as payments of any kind received as a consideration for the use of, or the right to use, any copyright of literary, artistic or scientific work including cinematograph films, any patent, trademark, design or model, plan, secret formula or process, or for information concerning industrial, commercial or scientific experience.

In the tax laws and tax treaties of many countries similar definitions may apply, delineating the taxability of such payments, particularly when paid to non-residents, as well as providing the applicable rate of tax (either by assessment or withholding) on such payments.

[III.] CASE STUDY 3

The fundamental question asked in this chapter is: what is the importance of source in an international tax planning context? Source refers to the origin or deemed origin of a particular item of income, and the definition varies from country to country based on legislation, case law or tax treaty provisions. In all events, source often triggers withholding tax, a preliminary tax the rate of which may be reduced in accordance with tax treaty provisions. The Filipes, either applying their very own 'expertise' or requesting Maurice Brightman's professional tax services, very much like the idea of reducing their tax burdens.

This chapter has explained in some detail various aspects of holding companies. The Filipes, too, have heard of the usefulness of holding companies, and, on Maurice's recommendation, have inserted two of these, Lucca NV in the Netherlands Antilles, and Lucca BV in the Netherlands, into their business structures.

The following diagrams are relevant when investigating how the Filipes have managed to escape taxation, where applicable:

(a) the use of the Filipe Foundation to hold the portfolio investment in Switzerland (Diagram 2);
(b) the use of the Gibraltar company to own the Spanish villa (Diagram 3);
(c) the use of Lucca NV and Lucca BV as holding companies (Diagram 4);
(d) the use of the BVI company to acquire a house in London for Giuliano (Diagram 5);
(e) the use of the BVI company to employ Giuliano (Diagram 6);
(f) the use of the Swiss company, Opus AG, to lease Paolo's merchandising rights (Diagram 8).

Diagram 2

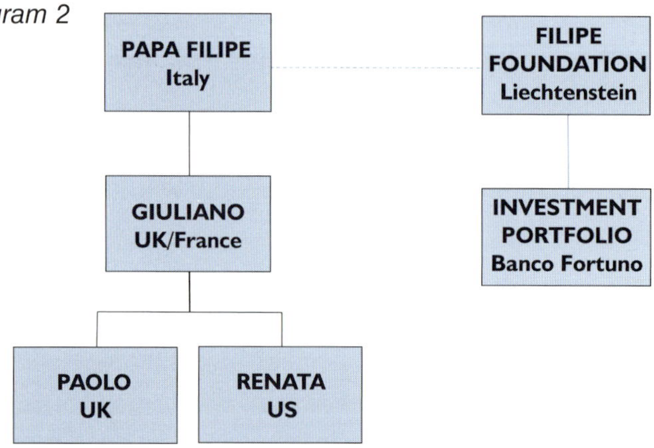

Diagram 3

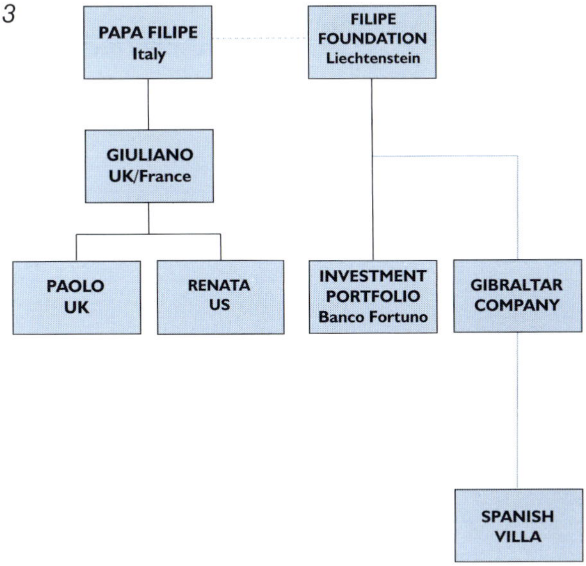

Diagram 4

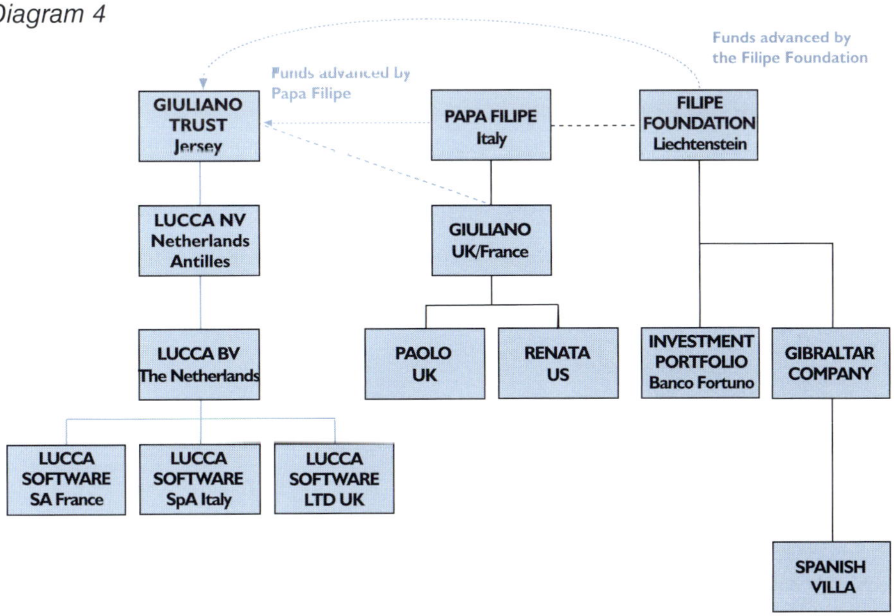

Diagram 5

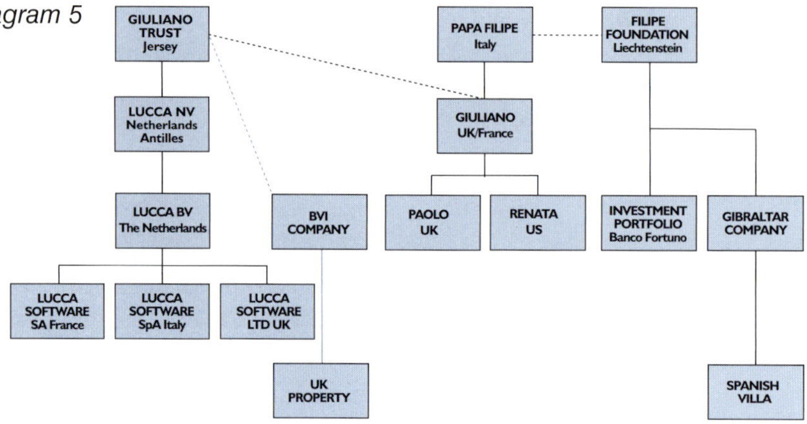

Diagram 6

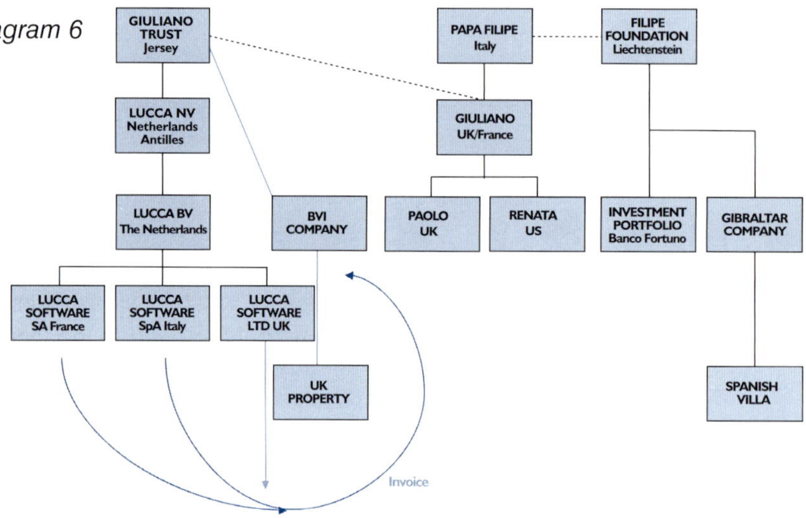

Diagram 8

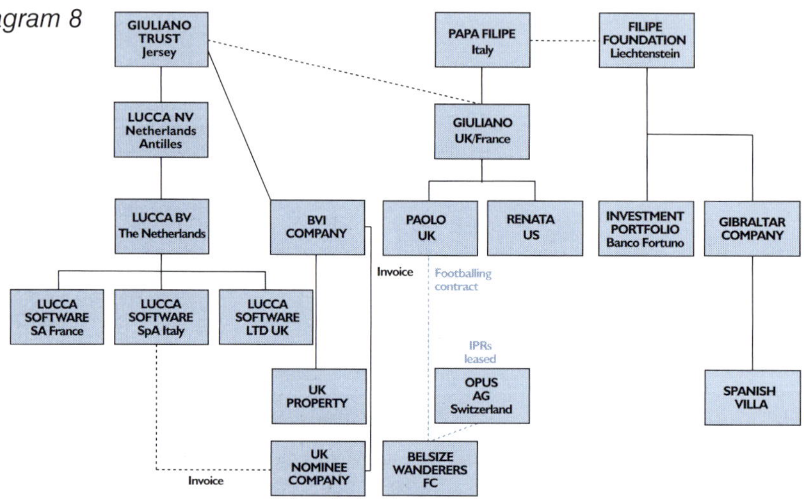

[III.a] Portfolio investment in Switzerland

From funds originally emanating from the sale of Lucca Software, the Filipe Foundation has created a substantial investment portfolio expertly looked after by Banco Fortuno in Switzerland. When Papa Filipe created this structure, he called it an 'ingenious international tax structure' – he knew that no information would be leaked from his Swiss bank to the Italian authorities about his rather sizeable interest income. Papa Filipe simply chose not to include this interest income on his annual Italian income tax return, and *voila!*, a huge tax saving was created.

When Maurice, during a casual conversation over a pint of warm British bitter, told Papa about the new EU Savings Directive that will be applied within the EU, the oldest Filipe was quite unhappy. As Maurice explained more, Papa was concerned that his 'ingenious international tax structure' had rather lost its ingenuity, and that Papa was about to lose some serious money. Maurice told Papa that all EU member states will automatically exchange information on cross-border payments of interest paid in the respective states. However, not being part of the EU, Switzerland has not agreed to apply similar treatment to interest paid by its banks. Instead, Switzerland, has agreed to withhold tax from interest payments made from this country. Initially, Papa feared that he would now receive his interest payments minus a sizeable chunk, which would be collected by the Swiss tax authorities. However, when Papa voiced his unhappiness, Maurice explained that the Directive only applied to individuals, so that ownership of portfolios by trusts and foundations would not be caught under Exchange of Information or Withholding Tax provisions. However, Maurice explained that although Papa's 'ingenious international tax structure' might withstand the Savings Directive, it may fall at the first hurdle under other concerns previously voiced by Maurice.

[III.b] Gibraltar company owning Spanish villa

On selling the soft furnishing business, Papa Filipe bought, as he had promised, a dream villa on the Costa del Sol for the use of his long-time sweetheart, Maria Rodriguez. Although Papa is a generous man, signified by this gesture of affection to the beautiful Spanish lady, he is also a man who likes to save a penny or two when he can, especially if these pennies could otherwise become the taxman's. Although Maria was never let in on Papa's international tax 'secrets' surrounding the acquisition of the Spanish villa, Papa knew that he could save on wealth tax that would otherwise be due on his net estate, i.e. the villa, should he acquire it directly as an individual in Spain. By purchasing the villa through the Gibraltar company, the company itself would not become subject to this tax in Spain. By using the Filipe Foundation as the entity owning the Gibraltar company, further distance is put between Papa and the villa itself, making it harder for the Spanish tax authorities to link Papa to the villa and impose the wealth tax on his estate.

Maurice, who knew about this plan, could not help but feel sorry for Papa when he had to tell Papa three years later that the Spanish tax authorities had seen through schemes like Papa's and had decided to impose an annual 3% special tax on the market value on all real estate held by offshore companies, such as the one holding the villa.

Although Papa was cross about being liable for 3% of the market value of a quite expensive property, he consoled himself by thinking about Maria and that the expense was, after all, really worth it. He nevertheless found out that he could avoid the 3% tax through a redomiciliation of the Gibraltar company to a jurisdiction with which Spain has an appropriate double tax treaty. The catch, however, is that he must disclose himself as the beneficial owner of the redomiciled company. On reflection, therefore, he decided, like so many before him, to pay the 3% annual tax charge.

[III.c] BVI company acquiring house for Giuliano

The trustees of the Giuliano Trust used a BVI company to acquire a house in London for Giuliano's anticipated move to the UK to expand the Lucca empire. The underlying tax-saving plan, this time Giuliano's, was to have the BVI company own the UK property, so that the asset would fall outside the UK's inheritance tax net. As a non-domiciled individual, Giuliano knew that he would only be subject to UK inheritance tax on UK situs assets. Maurice had previously informed him that on Giuliano's death, it would be shares in the BVI company (not UK *situs*) as opposed to the underlying property, which would form part of Giuliano's estate for inheritance tax purposes.

Maurice suggested that Giuliano firstly ensures that directors of the BVI company are competent individuals who really manage the company irrespective of Giuliano's indirect shareholding interest, and secondly that Giuliano enters into a licence agreement whereby he pays rent to the BVI company. Alternatively, if the property needed substantial renovations, he could agree to maintain and improve the property under the licence agreement without necessarily paying out to the BVI company, on which UK withholding tax would apply (share rental income has a source where property is located). However, Giuliano had to admit to Maurice that the directors of the BVI company had never seen the UK house, nor dealt with the financial institution which had arranged a mortgage on the property but had simply signed the relevant contracts when presented to them. Maurice had to inform Giuliano that clearly, he was the *de facto* director of the BVI company which had the following consequences. As a *de facto* director, he would be considered an officer of the company and therefore an employee under UK employment tax legislation. As an employee, he is living in the property tax free, and this creates a significant benefit in kind. Based on a property valuation of £1 million, the benefit could be quantified as in excess of £75,000 and subject to UK tax accordingly. Giuliano's non-domiciled status would not help him here as the benefit has been constructively remitted to him in the UK by virtue of his rent-free occupation.

[III.d] Dutch holding company

Maurice advised Giuliano on creating a holding company structure for his software empire. The structure involved creating a holding company in the Netherlands to own the French, Italian and UK entities of the Lucca Group. Maurice is comfortable with the Netherlands company being the first tier holding company of the group – the country has a reputable business climate and tax regime, and at that time it was reasonable to expect advance rulings from the Dutch tax authorities. Maurice knows very well that by having the Dutch holding company in place, Giuliano's group can save a significant amount of taxes through use of the relevant tax treaties the Netherlands has in place. When any of the existing Lucca Software Europe companies distribute dividends to Lucca BV, no withholding tax will apply to the dividends distributed from any of the companies under the EU Parent/Subsidiary Directive. Moreover, should Giuliano at some time in the future wish to expand the Lucca empire to beyond the borders of the EU, the comprehensive Dutch tax treaty network may surely help to reduce the withholding tax amounts payable in the countries where the Lucca subsidiaries are located.

One of the benefits of interposing a Dutch holding company is that corporate shareholders in the Netherlands, who can claim a participation exemption in a foreign subsidiary, are exempt from Dutch corporate income tax on dividends received from the subsidiary, and also on capital gains realised on the disposal of shares in the subsidiary. The crucial question is: what constitutes a participation exemption? Lucca BV and its three subsidiaries, Lucca Software SA (France), Lucca Software SpA (Italy), and Lucca Software Ltd (UK) illustrate the requirements that need to be met for the participation exemption to apply.

(a) *Lucca BV must own at least 5% of the issued and paid-up share capital of its respective subsidiaries for the participation exemption to apply in respect of each of the subsidiaries.*

Lucca BV owns 100% of each of its subsidiaries, and since the three subsidiaries are each engaging in business in France, Italy and the UK, respectively, the holdings are not mere portfolio investments. Thus, the first requirement is met.

(b) *The capital of Lucca Software SA, Lucca Software SpA and Lucca Software Ltd has to be divided into shares.*

Each of the subsidiaries is a registered stock company in the applicable jurisdiction where each is incorporated, with capital divided into shares. Thus the second requirement is met.

(c) Lucca BV cannot hold the shares in its three subsidiaries as mere inventory; in other words, the shares are intended for selling and the shares are effectively part of the working capital of Lucca BV, as opposed to fixed asset investments.

Lucca BV does not hold the shares of its three subsidiaries only for the purpose of selling; in fact, Lucca BV wants to hold on to the shares for an indefinite period of time. The shares do not form part of Lucca BV's working capital – Lucca BV is sufficiently capitalised through cash injections from Papa Filipe via the Giuliano Trust, and later by the Filipe Foundation via the trust. Furthermore, the three subsidiaries each hold a significant number of assets, including office and software manufacturing equipment. Thus the third requirement is met.

(d) Lucca BV's holding of the subsidiaries' shares may not be a mere portfolio holding or passive investment.

This aspect was already touched upon in requirement (a) above, but the holdings are not mere passive investments since each of the three subsidiaries is actively engaged in business. Furthermore, Lucca BV is actively involved in the activities of each of its subsidiaries – for example, Giuliano, as one of the directors of Lucca BV, is actively involved in the management of the three subsidiaries from Lucca BV's office in Amsterdam, and the staff of Lucca BV are involved in providing administrative and, to some extent, technical assistance to the three subsidiaries. Thus the fourth requirement is met.

(e) Lucca Software SA, Lucca Software SpA and Lucca Software Ltd must be subject to tax in France, Italy and the UK, respectively.

Whether Giuliano likes it or not, the subsidiaries are taxed at full corporate tax rates on their profits in the respective countries. Thus the fifth requirement is met.

[III.e] Lucca NV

Lucca NV was interposed as the ultimate holding company in respect of the Lucca Group,[31] essentially making an intermediate holding company of Lucca BV in the Netherlands. In the past this meant that, in addition to the beneficial treatment in the Netherlands of dividends remitted by Lucca BV's three subsidiaries, the dividends would also leave the Netherlands withholding tax-free according to the Dutch tax treaty with the Netherlands Antilles. However, a withholding tax initially of 5% and then increased to 8.3% applies to dividend remittances from Lucca BV to Lucca NV – this was news that Giuliano was rather disappointed to learn.

31. With the Giuliano Trust as the group's ultimate holding entity.

[III.f] BVI company employing Giuliano

Giuliano initially arranged for the BVI company to charge the Italian, French and UK entities of the Lucca Group for his salary. Giuliano then thought he could save a bit of tax by acquiring a shareholding in Lucca Software UK and allowing the entity to distribute dividends to him in the UK. As a result, he hoped, he would not be liable for social security contributions on the amount now paid as dividends as opposed to salary. Maurice was, as is the case so often, much less enthusiastic about this plan, since IR 35 in the UK had just come into force. For Giuliano, the implications were that the dividend income received from Lucca Software UK might be deemed by the UK tax authorities as employment income for his services rendered to the company, which would have to be included in his annual UK income tax return as salary. Moreover, social security contributions would be due on the amount equivalent to the dividends received from Lucca Software UK.

[III.g] Swiss company leasing Paolo's merchandising rights

Turning to the third generation's tax planning possibilities, Paolo, Papa's grandson, is a football star who just moved from Athletico Roamer to Belsize Wanderers, currently top of the Premiership in the UK. Due to Paolo's fame and the popularity of his No. 11 shirt, Belsize Wanderers (or the Armadillos, as they are more affectionately known) entered into two separate agreements: the first, with Paolo for Paolo's football performances; the second with a Swiss company, Opus AG, for Paolo's image and merchandising rights.

Under Article 17(1) of the OECD Model Treaty, a sportsman like Paolo is taxable on his sports performance in the country where the performance takes places. Thus, when he plays for the Armadillos in the UK, the money he earns from such a game will be taxed in the UK, but if he plays in Italy, Italy could have the taxing right on his income relating to that game. Article 17(1), however, relates to the sportsman's sports performance only; where the sportsman's income relates to other sources, such as merchandising rights, he will be taxed according to the laws of his country of residence. Thus Opus AG could avoid Paolo's income resulting from the merchandising rights being taxed in the UK. The rights to Paolo's No. 11 shirt that the Armadillos held originally were transferred to Opus AG, who then leased the rights to manufacture and sell the shirts to other parties. Opus AG now receives the income from these licensees and royalty income is accumulated for Paolo in Switzerland. The royalty income might, depending on the country from which it is paid, be subject to no or a low rate of withholding tax under the relevant double tax treaty.[32] The source of any income paid by Opus to Paolo would now be Switzerland, emanating as it does from an employment arrangement; provided such income is not remitted to the UK, Paolo is not taxed thereon under the laws of the UK relating to non-domiciled individuals.

32. But refer to the provisions of the 1999 amendment to the 1962 Swiss Federal Decree in §4.4.3.

[III.h] Conclusion

From the above it can be seen that there are quite a number of ways to reduce a client's foreign tax burden. However, since no tax authority of any high-tax country is keen to let revenue that, according to the provisions of domestic law or of a relevant double tax treaty that it concluded, belongs to that country go untaxed, the Filipes and other international tax planners should ensure that they are well aware of any anti-avoidance legislation that such countries apply to plans to reduce the relevant tax burden.

As to holding companies, these have been successfully, and profitably, employed in international tax planning for a considerable amount of time. This situation is likely to continue; however, the general free-for-all is gradually being shut under pressure from OECD and EU member countries. Nonetheless, the international tax adviser who is up to date with rules and requirements applicable in traditional holding company jurisdictions will still be able to advise his clients on how to use holding company structures as efficiently as possible, and in what jurisdictions.

Chapter 4

How Can Tax Treaty Provisions Help?

Having realised that foreign *situs* income and capital is likely to attract foreign taxes, irrespective of the residence status of the owner, the international tax consultant will want to consider how such taxes can be mitigated.[1] Although local advisers may insist that the income or capital has a local *situs*, and is therefore taxed locally, they may not understand that there may be a superior law which is applicable; that superior law may be a relevant double tax treaty that has been signed between the local country and the country of residence of the owner of the income and capital. If the terms of the double tax treaty state that local taxes will not actually be incurred, or will be reduced below their standard levels, then this will be the case. However, if the treaty allows for a higher rate of taxation than is levied at local level, then it is the local level that is applicable, since the treaty cannot impose a higher burden of taxation.

Thus, if an individual is considered tax resident in two countries, a relevant double tax treaty needs to be reviewed to determine which country has the overriding right to tax that individual; however, if the local law of one country does not regard the individual as tax resident there, then the treaty article is not applicable. Equally, if dividends are not subject to a withholding tax at source in a local country, the fact that the double tax treaty allows the relevant countries to impose a 10% withholding tax, for example, will be irrelevant.

---

1. It might be useful for the reader to recall the fundamental questions asked at the beginning of Chapter 3, and particularly 'Can one reduce foreign tax through double tax treaty arrangements or other conduit structures?', which is the main question relevant to this chapter.

An understanding of double tax treaty arrangements is therefore critical in determining whether, in fact, local taxation is due, notwithstanding the rules considered in Chapter 3 that the income and capital has a local *situs*. The international tax consultant often utilises specific treaties to prevent local taxes from applying, even if such treaties would not normally be applicable to the owner of the income and capital (because they are not resident in that treaty country). This might be referred to as treaty shopping and is further discussed below.

Thus double tax treaty planning is an integral component of the international tax consultant's intellectual library. To an amateur consultant the main articles appear to be the dividend, interest and royalty articles, which minimise local withholding taxes; the more experienced adviser will realise that the entire treaty is relevant, specifically as regards the personal scope and definitions articles to determine whether subsequent provisions are applicable. Moreover, care should be taken to ensure that there are no protocols to the treaty, which may affect the conclusions reached by studying the treaty itself.

4.1 FUNCTIONS OF DOUBLE TAX TREATIES

Double tax treaties are viewed as beneficial by most states because they allow business to be transacted with a degree of certainty both on the part of individuals, partnerships or corporate entities and the government of the state in which the business entity operates. The basic functions of double tax treaties can be summarised as follows.

4.1.1 Clarification of taxing rights of each state

Double tax treaties allow clarification of taxation rights between contracting states. The taxing rights under the treaty only apply to residents of a particular country (and some partnerships, for example, may not be covered), and only in respect of taxes stated within the treaty. There may also be some items of income or capital which are not covered by the treaty, in which case, without a general article, one falls back again to domestic law.

4.1.2 Avoidance of double international juridical taxation

International juridical double taxation is where the same profits are taxed in two or more states on the same person (corporate or individual); this compares with economic double taxation where the same state may tax the same profits to two or more persons (e.g. dividends representing taxed corporate profits are taxed again in the individual's hands, namely the classical system of taxation).[2]

2. As compared to the imputation system.

4.1.3 Prevention of fiscal evasion with anti-avoidance provisions

The exchange of information provision should enable countries to obtain information in order to ensure their taxing rights are preserved. The various articles then individually legislate wherever possible to prevent tax avoidance in clarifying what would be considered business profits, acceptable interest deductions etc., and the views of each state may differ significantly in practice on such subjective issues. The mutual agreement article attempts to provide for such eventualities, but the willingness of the competent authorities to agree these issues are currently left to discussion rather than specific legislation.

4.2 COUNTRIES WHICH ARE PARTIES TO DOUBLE TAX TREATIES

High-tax countries have no reason to enter into double tax treaties with low-tax countries such as Bermuda, British Virgin Islands and Anguilla, which do not levy or only levy low tax on profits. Indeed certain countries such as Hong Kong, with a source system of taxation, may equally have no reason to worry about international juridical double taxation since non-local source profits are exempt from tax in any event. However, where their residents are actively engaged in business abroad, countries would wish to conclude treaties to clarify taxing rights and prevent fiscal evasion.

Low-tax countries that offer certain concessions (e.g. the Channel Islands, Liechtenstein, Malta and Cyprus), may have double tax treaties. However, they are either very few in number (e.g. the Channel Islands with the UK only, Liechtenstein with Austria only), or the countries with whom they negotiate treaties may wish to impose limitations within the treaties (e.g. exclusion of offshore companies). Cyprus is one of the few countries that has generally been able to negotiate a wide range of treaties without such limitations; the limitations that do exist in certain treaties (treaties with the UK and the US, for example) are no longer relevant following the addition of Cyprus offshore companies in 2003.

High-tax countries need the widest range of double tax treaties to limit international juridical double taxation; their residents require clarification of what profits will be taxed where. Countries will often permit certain activities to be either exempt from tax or suffer a reduced rate of local tax in an effort to stimulate their international trade. Equally, such countries will desire anti-avoidance provisions to enable them to secure their tax revenue.

Double tax treaties have become more standardised pursuant to the work of the OECD. Although the OECD Model Tax Convention on Income and Capital, with the 2003 updated version being the most recent, and its Commentary are an invaluable starting point in negotiating and subsequently interpreting double tax treaties, they are only guidelines and the provisions of the individual treaties as they are implemented in local law are the only relevant determining factors.[3] These specific provisions are negotiated according to the fiscal requirements of each country; once ratified and the treaty enters into force, it is not surprising that the relevant provisions take precedence over unilateral law, certainly that which was in existence at the date of negotiating the treaty.

4.3 ARRANGEMENT OF THE OECD MODEL TREATY

The OECD Model Treaty is commonly adopted in full or in part by most countries when designing their double tax treaties. The following sections give consideration to the articles of the Treaty.

4.3.1 Articles to clarify application of the Treaty[4]

Article 1 – Personal Scope

Article 1 limits the benefit of the treaty to persons who are residents of the contracting states, as defined in Articles 3 and 4.[5]

Article 2 – Taxes Covered

Article 2 limits the taxes covered by the treaty to direct taxes on income and capital of the relevant persons, so does not, for example, cover inheritance taxes, VAT or other indirect taxes.

Article 3 – General Definitions

Most contracts or agreements contain a general definition clause and the OECD Model Treaty is no different. The purpose of Article 3 is to define terms or expressions used elsewhere within the treaty and enable readers and those seeking to rely on the treaty to understand its terms and scope. It should be noted that Article 3 does not provide a definitive guide to the terms contained within a treaty and many definitions are contained within the individual articles. If not specifically defined in the treaty, the terms are as defined under national laws of the country concerned.

The standard OECD definition of a 'person' includes an individual, a company and any other body of persons.[6] It is this last – 'other body of persons' – that has

---

3. Other model treaties include the United Nations Model Double Taxation Convention between Developed and Developing Countries 2001 and its Commentary and also the United States Model Income Tax Convention 1996 and its Technical Explanation. These model treaties are not discussed in detail in this book.
4. This section is organised in accordance with the topic of the most important articles of the Model Treaty.
5. See, for example, §2.3 for a relevant discussion.
6. Compare §2.3.

been the subject of the greatest intellectual debate. Thus, transparent entities such as partnerships may not be included, but semi-transparent entities such as the French *groupement d'intérêt économique* (GIE) may be considered a person and therefore its foreign members may be subject to local tax under the treaty.[7]

The position as regards trusts is particularly contentious and was discussed in Chapter 2.[8]

The greatest modification and use of Article 3 is made by recently negotiated US double tax treaties. The US has decided to use the article as an extra means by which to place limitation on benefits on those who are able to benefit from its treaties. In this vein we have witnessed the inclusion of the term 'conduit arrangement' in its renegotiated treaty with the UK.[9]

Many treaties extend this general definition clause to other items. The definition of terms is not limited to this article. Indeed, Article 4 defines residence, Article 5 a permanent establishment, Article 6 immovable property, Article 10 dividends, Article 11 interest, Article 12 royalties, and Article 14 professional services. Again it seems that that the US has been most innovative here and treaties negotiated over the past ten years or so often include a new 'limitation on benefits' article which is discussed in greater detail below.[10] However, the article provides further opportunity for draftsmen to include even more definitions, for example, the term 'qualified person' is defined in Article 26 of the Netherlands/US double tax treaty.[11]

7. Compare the *Société Kingroup* case, before the French Conseil d'Etat and dated 4 April 1997. In *Société Kingroup* a Canadian company (Kingroup) was a partner in a French GIE, which derived the majority of its income from the granting of licences to French companies. It was assessed to French tax on its proportion of profits arising to the partnership, and although prior to the assessment Kingroup had submitted a Canadian tax return declaring its share of the profits, the French authorities took the view that French tax should be levied. Under French law, foreign partners of a French partnership are assessed to French tax not because a permanent establishment has been created, but because the income is deemed to accrue to the French enterprise. This therefore permitted the authorities the benefit of not having first to ascertain that a permanent establishment does exist before assessing the partner in question to French tax. Under Article 7 of the France/Canada tax treaty, a contracting state may only subject a resident of the other state to tax if there exists a permanent establishment in the first state, and it was Article 7 of the treaty that Kingroup relied upon in its defence to the assessment. The court held, however, that the terms of the tax treaty only applied if the Canadian company had received the income directly and not via a French partnership; it was the fact that the income had travelled through the partnership, which had caused it to change character, thus taking it outside the scope of the treaty. In addition to Article 7 Kingroup also invoked Article 10; however, the court also rejected this on the grounds that the distribution of the profits of the partnership were not dividends.
8. Compare §2.3.
9. Signed 24 July 2001.
10. In §4.4.
11. Signed 18 December 1992.

Article 4 – Residence[12]

Article 4 provides that a person's residence should firstly be determined by reference to the domestic laws of each contracting state. In circumstances where a person would be resident in both states on such basis, it establishes a mechanism for determining in which state that person should be regarded as being resident for the purposes of the treaty. The article also provides that a person will not be resident in a particular state merely because income is sourced there. The mechanism by which individuals may determine which state has the right to tax by reason of residence is known as the 'tie-breaker' clause. This states, in order of priority, that a person will be resident where he has a permanent home available to him or if he has such a home in both states, the state with which his economic and social ties are closer (the 'centre of vital interests' test). If the aforementioned is unclear, his residence will be determined by reason of the place where he has his habitual abode. If he does not have a habitual abode in either of the states, he will be deemed resident in the state of which he is a national. If he is not a national of either states, the tax authorities of the applicable states will agree on where he is resident.

It should be realised that the 'tie-breaker' provisions only apply (a) if both countries consider a person is resident of that state by virtue of the unilateral residence laws of that state and (b) to income covered by the other treaty provisions.

Article 5 – Permanent Establishment

The 'permanent establishment' article is very important because it is designed to encourage international trade by providing clarity as to the level of presence required for an entity to be taxable on trading profits arising within a state. The article works in conjunction with Article 7 to define the element of the enterprise's profits that are taxable in the state in question. If Article 5 did not exist, then an enterprise based in one state but wishing to undertake business transactions in another would face uncertainty as to how and where its profits would be taxed.[13]

Article 29 – Entry into Force

The stages of a treaty are:

(a) signature;

(b) ratification by each state;

12. Compare §5.1.1 for more on this topic.
13. Article 5 is discussed in further detail in §7.3.

(c) exchange of the ratification instruments; and

(d) implementation into domestic law.

The provisions of the treaty enter into force according to this article within a stated time of the exchange of ratification instruments, but not all provisions may be effective as from the same date; transitional reliefs are often allowed.

Article 30 – Termination

This provision allows the treaty to be terminated by either state giving the appropriate notice, generally six months before the end of a calendar year.

4.3.2 Articles to avoid double international juridical taxation

Article 6 – Income from Immovable Property

Article 6 provides that income from immovable property, generally real estate, although the definition given to immovable property under domestic law is the relevant definition, will be taxed in the state in which the property is located.

Article 7 – Business Profits

Article 7 is an extension of the permanent establishment article, which clarifies the profits on which local taxes may be levied. Under paragraph 1 'The profits of an enterprise of a Contracting State shall be taxable only in that State unless the enterprise carries on business in the other Contracting State through a permanent establishment situated therein'. Therefore, it is clear that the profits of an enterprise carrying on business in, say, France will only be taxable in, say, Germany, if the French enterprise actually has a permanent establishment in Germany (assuming that the OECD Model Treaty is applied). If there is no permanent establishment, no tax would be due on the French company's profits. If a permanent establishment does exist, the profits of the French enterprise may be taxed in Germany 'but only so much of them as is attributable to that permanent establishment'. The right of the German authorities to tax the French enterprise is therefore restricted to profits attributable to the permanent establishment in Germany. If profits arise to the French company from a source in Germany which is not connected to the permanent establishment, then these will not be subject to tax in Germany under the provisions of this article. However, it may be noted that this article is not always interpreted in a strict manner and it may be that a state which utilises the OECD Model Treaty does not agree with the commentary described.

It is also worth highlighting that the profits subject to tax, that is the profits attributed to the permanent establishment, will be the profits that the permanent establishment would have made in circumstances where it was a standalone entity. The permanent establishment is therefore treated as if it were operating on an arm's-length basis.

Article 8 – Shipping, Inland Waterways Transport and Air Transport

There is clearly a great deal of scope for confusion and double taxation in circumstances where ships and aeroplanes constantly move around the world. Article 8 therefore provides that such an enterprise will be assessed in accordance with its place of effective management.

Articles 10, 11 and 12 – Dividends, Interest and Royalties

Articles 10, 11 and 12 define the scope of payments of dividends, interest or royalties and must be read with care (in particular Article 12 as the definition of royalties frequently varies in treaties negotiated between contracting states). The purpose of these articles is to limit the tax that may be withheld at source on dividend, interest or royalty payments by a person resident in one contracting state, to a person resident in the other, thereby reducing or eliminating double taxation. It should be noted that the reduced withholding taxes may only apply if the recipient is the beneficial owner of the income. Thus nominee or agency arrangements sometimes may not permit the beneficial owner to claim treaty benefits unless the owner is resident in the relevant treaty jurisdiction.

For the past few years, restrictive 'limitation on benefits' articles have been added to, for example, every new US treaty to place restrictions on treaty shopping, i.e. the ability of third-country residents to enjoy tax treaty benefits by using a company formed in a jurisdiction having a favourable treaty with, say, the US. These 'limitation on benefits' articles are relevant where it is envisaged that dividends, interest and royalties will be paid out by the treaty entity to a third country, since it is particularly in this context that the ability to treaty shop[14] for beneficial withholding tax rates is relevant.

Thus, under Article 10 (relating to dividends), many countries levy a withholding tax, but there are some very notable exceptions where profits have been subject to primary tax, such as Australia and the UK. Also, capital distributions may not attract withholding tax, as for example liquidation distributions in the US or Luxembourg.

Article 10 generally limits the withholding tax that may be charged, provided that the recipient is beneficially entitled to the dividends. Such limitation is often to a nil or 5% rate where a substantial interest of, say, 10% or 25% is held in the payor company, and in other cases the withholding tax rate is limited to

14. Compare §4.4.

15%. But each treaty may be different, depending upon the effect of local primary tax coupled with this secondary tax.

If countries have entered into a double tax treaty but then have subsequently entered into a multilateral treaty which has supremacy over the double tax treaty, such as the EU Parent/Subsidiary Directive which eliminates withholding taxes on dividends to recipient companies owning more than 20% of the payor, then the provisions of the double tax treaty may still be relevant if the Directive's provisions are not fulfilled.

As with all articles, the purpose of a double tax treaty is never to create a tax liability where none exists under domestic law. Thus, whatever the treaty rate permitted, if a lower rate exists under domestic law, it is the lower rate which is adopted. There may be anti-avoidance provisions to prevent treaty abuse, such as in the Netherlands/Switzerland treaty discussed below.[15]

Interest payments to non-residents may also attract a local withholding tax, which is generally reduced according to treaties to 10% under the OECD Model Treaty, but often to nil. Under certain treaties, the requirement for the recipient to be the beneficial owner is notable for its absence, especially the older ones.

There are anti-avoidance provisions in the interest and royalty articles where excessive payments are made which the payor's country of residence may treat instead as constructive dividends; however, if they do not fall within the definition of dividends under the dividend article, they may not be subject to the dividend withholding tax permitted under the treaty.

Royalties are covered under Article 12, and are often exempt from withholding tax, as they are under the OECD Model Treaty. Again, excessive royalties may be treated as constructive dividends, and there may also be anti-avoidance provisions where licensing structures have been created merely for the purpose of obtaining withholding tax exemption, such as Article 12(5) of the Netherlands/UK treaty. Each treaty contains the definition of royalties covered under the article, and there may be different rates or exemptions applicable to patent royalties as compared, for example, with copyright royalties or film royalties.

It is also necessary to understand the distinction between licensing activities, which may be covered under this article, and trading activities covered under Article 7, even if they are items which may also be licensed under different contractual arrangements e.g. software packages or franchise arrangements. Also, lease rentals of, say, containers or other equipment need to be differentiated from licensing agreements for such equipment.

15. See §4.4.1.

Article 13 – Capital Gains

Capital gains derived from real estate are covered under Article 13, and generally capital gains on direct interests in real estate (and often on indirect interests through real estate-owning companies) are subject to tax where the real estate is situated. Gains on any other property which may be similar to having business interests locally, such as movable property attached to a permanent establishment, as well as the permanent establishment itself, may be subject to local tax, but the article generally grants the right to tax all other gains only to the state where the alienator is resident. Nevertheless, there may be a period of, say, five years during which the state where an individual was previously resident continues to have the right to tax such gains which are not specifically covered under this article; this is an anti-avoidance article to prevent individuals moving from one country to another to obtain treaty exemption from the local tax that would otherwise be payable.

The *Lamesa*[16] case in Australia determined that indirect interests in real estate through a chain of companies did not constitute immovable property, even if this means that capital gains derived thereon may escape taxation altogether, which, it should be noted, is not one of the objectives of a double tax treaty. Paragraph 21 of the Commentary to Article 13 of the Model Treaty suggests that if a particular country is concerned about such tax avoidance, it should incorporate within the relevant article look-through provisions for such indirect interests in immovable property.

Article 14 – Independent Personal Services

Similar to Article 7 but applicable to individuals rather than companies, the article provides that independent personal services (such as those of accountants, lawyers and architects) will only be taxable where the individuals are resident, unless they operate in the other state through a fixed base there.

16. (1997/1998) 1OFLR 179. The court dismissed the Commissioner's application on the grounds that the treaty should be interpreted literally; the fact that a company lower down the chain did own assets which would have been within the definition of real property for the treaty was irrelevant. The question considered by the court in coming to its decision was the meaning of the word 'direct'. Einfeld J, in giving his judgment, reaffirmed the fact that a tax treaty overrides domestic law, in this case the Income Tax Assessment Act. Article 7 of the Australia/Netherlands double tax treaty, which Lamesa invoked as its defence to the assessment, provides that profits of a Dutch company may only be subject to Australian tax where the Dutch company carries on a business in Australia through a permanent establishment, i.e. Article 7 of the treaty provides protection unless Article 13 applies. This was emphatically not the case; the only property Lamesa had in Australia was the shares in the underlying company. Einfeld J went on to say that 'wholly owned subsidiary companies are separate legal entities and independent from their parent company' and if the court were to attribute the assets of a far removed company to the parent, as was the hope of the Commissioners, this would result in the lifting of the corporate veil, something the court would not do.

Article 15 – Dependent Personal Services

Article 15 deals with income from employment other than that covered elsewhere in the treaty (such as the specific articles concerning directors' fees, pensions or income from government services) and provides that employment income will generally be taxed only where the individual is resident in the relevant country. Thus, if the individual exercises his employment in two countries, the right to tax will remain in the state of the individual's residence unless the employee is physically present in the other state for more than 183 days in any 12-month period, and the remuneration is paid by an employer resident there, or recharged to a permanent establishment there of a foreign employer.

Article 16 – Directors' Fees

Directors' fees are generally subject to tax where the company is resident.

Article 17 – Artistes and Sportsmen

The income of entertainers and sportsmen may be of such magnitude that countries where they are performing are reluctant to release their taxing rights to the country where the entertainer or sportsman is resident, simply because they do not exceed the proscribed limit of days required to establish residence in the country of performance. One may say that the country does not have the right to impose taxes on such individuals who do not receive any social or other benefits from that country, but the prospect of significant taxes becomes an overriding motivation for Article 17.

Article 17(1) states that income derived by a resident of one state as an entertainer (such as a theatre, motion picture, radio or television artiste, or a musician) or as a sportsman (which will include, for example, footballers, golfers, jockeys, cricketers, tennis players, racing car drivers) or a participant in public entertainment (such as snooker, chess or bridge players), from his personal activities as such exercised in the other state may be taxed in the other state. The words 'as such' are important to understand in relation to income from non-performing activities contracted by the entertainers and sportsmen, such as endorsement and merchandising contracts.

Article 17(2) extends the right of the local tax administration not only to tax income paid direct to the above individuals, but also to tax such income even if it is received by companies or indeed any other entity. Very few treaties still exist which afford protection to loan-out companies from local taxation.[17]

17. See §3.5 for a detailed review of the taxation of entertainers and sportsmen.

Article 18 – Pensions

Double tax treaties normally confer the taxing rights on the state where the individual has now taken up tax residence.

Article 21 – Other Income

Income not dealt with elsewhere within the treaty will generally be taxed where the recipient is resident. However, many treaties do not have this general 'mop-up' article, so that items of income and capital not covered under the other provisions of a double tax treaty fall to be taxed solely under the domestic law of the relevant country.

Article 23 – Methods for Elimination of Double Taxation

Article 23 allows for the credit[18] of foreign tax paid or the exemption of foreign income (on which tax has been paid) from tax in the state in which the individual is resident.

4.3.3 Articles to prevent tax avoidance/evasion

Article 9 – Associated Enterprises

Article 9 concerns profit shifting between related parties in different states and provides that the state that has suffered a tax disadvantage may adjust taxable profits of the entity in question.

Article 26 – Exchange of Information

As discussed in Chapter 1, the 'exchange of information' article of a double tax treaty can be a very effective tool in the war against tax evasion.[19]

18. The foreign tax credit system allows that tax paid in a foreign country may be deducted from any domestic tax due in the country of the recipient. Foreign tax credits are generally granted against income tax and corporate tax, wealth tax and capital gains tax. The amount of foreign tax credit is usually limited to the amount that would have been chargeable under the domestic country's (i.e. that of the recipient) tax rules.

    Relief in respect of foreign tax may also be given in the form of tax exemptions, i.e. exempting income from domestic tax. Under a variant of the aforementioned, i.e. exemption with progression, domestic countries providing for an exemption retain the right to take foreign income or gains into account when determining the tax rate applied to the rest of the income or gains.
19. For example, in early 2004 Belgium and the Netherlands signed an exchange of information agreement on the basis of the EC Directive on Mutual Assistance, the OECD Convention on Mutual Administrative Assistance (see also §1.4.1 for a more detailed discussion) and Articles 29 and 31 of the new Belgium/Netherlands tax treaty. Under the exchange of information agreement, the automatic exchange of information will take place in respect of salaries, directors' fees, pensions, income from real estate, business profits, etc. The spontaneous exchange of information will take place in respect of, *inter alia*, commission fees, credit invoices and VAT registration numbers.

4.3.4 Miscellaneous provisions

Article 24 – Non-discrimination

This article prevents nationals of a contracting state (as opposed to residents as for all other treaty provisions) from being treated in a more unfair way in the other state than nationals of that state. Moreover, the typical non-discrimination clause applies to taxes of every kind imposed by the other state, not just those mentioned in the treaty.

Article 25 – Mutual Agreement Procedure

This article provides the basis on which disputes between taxpayer and revenue authorities may be settled by agreement between the competent authorities of each state, generally either the relevant Ministry of Finance or the tax administration.

Article 28 – Territorial Extension

Territories of either state may be included under the double tax treaty if the state has responsibility for its international relations.

4.4 LIMITATION ON BENEFITS CONCEPT IN DOUBLE TAX TREATIES

'Treaty shopping' involves the use of the protection offered under a particular treaty by interposing a person who can claim treaty protection that would have otherwise been unavailable. The use of, for example, Dutch holding companies to own shares in subsidiary companies to minimise income or capital gains tax is an example of treaty shopping; or licensing companies to license intellectual property rights to minimise tax on royalties; or indeed personal service companies for specific purposes.

Following the growth of such planning arrangements, it became clear to the signatories of tax treaties that their interests were not being protected by treaties which allow income such as dividends or royalties to be routed through a conduit based in a second treaty country and through to another non-treaty state with a low rate of tax. Treaties generally restrict their application to residents of the contracting states. With regard to persons other than individuals, treaties increasingly incorporate the term 'beneficially owned' by a resident of a contracting state, but this does not really rule out the use of conduit companies, merely nominee or agency companies. The objective of most countries, which has now been incorporated into more recently concluded treaties, is to prevent the abuse of treaties by companies without substance.

4.4.1 US 'limitation on benefits' (LOB) provision

As a general point, it should be noted that the principle that a double tax treaty overrides domestic law was amended in the US in 1988 as follows:

> *For purposes of determining the relationship between a provision of a treaty and any law of the United States affecting revenue, neither the treaty nor the law shall have preferential status by reason of its being a treaty or law.*[20]

To the extent that the provisions of US treaties do apply, the following is important to note.

US Model Treaty

The US 'limitation on benefits' clauses are probably the broadest in terms of application and effect. The contentious article of the US Model Treaty[21] is Article 22, which was introduced into the US Model Treaty in 1981. Generally, the provision limits treaty benefits to corporations that are owned by local residents. Thus, recent US treaties state that the recipient of income must be the beneficial owner if the treaty benefits are to apply, and that the recipient may enjoy the benefits only if the ultimate beneficial owners would also have been able to enjoy the same benefits if income had been paid direct to them.

The US Model Treaty provides for two tests in terms of which a foreign entity may be treated as a qualified resident as a prerequisite for claiming benefits under any US double tax treaty. A foreign entity will only be deemed to be a 'qualified resident' of a treaty country if:

(a) under a stock ownership test, at least 50% of the value of the foreign entity is directly or indirectly owned by individuals who are residents of that country, or by US citizens or US residents;

(b) under the base erosion test, 50% or more of the foreign entity's income is not either directly or indirectly utilised to meet obligations to non-residents of that country.

In the event of the income of an entity resident in a treaty partner state being subject to a tax which is significantly lower than that which is imposed on similar types of income derived by residents of the country from domestic sources, then such entities shall not be entitled to take advantage of the benefits granted by the US under a relevant double tax treaty.

This is very much a limited summary of the definition of qualified resident. For example, a publicly quoted company listed on a recognised stock exchange may automatically qualify, as may a government-owned entity. But generally,

20. US Internal Revenue Code, Section 7852(d).
21. See footnote 3 above.

LOB provisions prevent companies owned by non-residents, or those which pay out the major part of their treaty-protected income, from benefiting from the treaty in entirety; not only are the dividend, interest and royalty articles inapplicable, but all of the other articles (residence, permanent establishment, business profits etc) are inapplicable as well.

Netherlands/United States 1992 Tax Treaty and 2004 Protocol

The first time such a provision appeared in a tax treaty that the US concluded was in its 1992 treaty with the Netherlands (the 1992 Treaty). In respect of the Netherlands/US tax treaty, the 2004 Protocol replaces the complex LOB provision of the 1992 Treaty. The provision contained in Article 26 of the Protocol is simpler and now in line with LOB provisions in other recent US tax treaties. Generally, a US or Dutch resident may be eligible for tax treaty benefits if he is: (a) an individual; (b) a governmental entity; (c) a company (including a subsidiary of it) that is listed and regularly traded[22] on a recognised stock exchange; (d) a pension or not-for-profit entity described in the new provision; (e) an entity that is controlled by publicly traded entities and satisfies a base erosion test;[23] (f) an entity that is owned or controlled by seven or fewer equivalent beneficiaries and satisfies a base erosion test; (g) engaged in a trade or business in the other country and the income at issue arises in connection with that trade or business; (h) a headquarters company for a multinational group of companies; (i) a shipping or air transport company that satisfies the alternative rules applicable to those companies; or (j) in receipt of a ruling from the competent authority of the source state.

The new LOB provision expands on the former LOB provision in that it adds a *substantial presence requirement* to the *publicly traded test.* This test states that a company will fail the publicly traded test if: (a) it is not managed and controlled in the country in which it is a resident; and (b) its stock is not primarily traded on a stock exchange within the company's 'primary economic zone' (for Dutch companies this means the EU and the EEA and for US companies it means NAFTA countries).[24]

United Kingdom/United States 2003 Tax Treaty

The limitation on benefits provision in Article 23 of the UK/US double tax treaty restricts the application of the treaty to a 'qualified person', as defined by that article. This sets a series of tests which must be passed if an entity is to benefit from the terms of the treaty. For example, a company will only be considered to be a qualified intermediary in circumstances where either:

22. This is opposed to the provision of 'substantially and regularly' traded of the 1992 Treaty.
23. See above (under US Model Treaty) for a description of the base erosion test.
24. This addition might have negative implications for Dutch quoted companies who are relying upon the stock exchange test but who do not meet the substantial presence criteria.

(i) the principal class of its shares is listed or admitted to dealings on a recognized stock exchange ... and is regularly traded on one or more recognized stock exchanges, or

(ii) shares representing at least 50 per cent. of the aggregate voting power and value of the company are owned directly or indirectly by five or fewer companies entitled to benefits under clause (i) of this sub-paragraph, provided that, in the case of indirect ownership, each intermediate owner is a resident of either Contracting State ...

Companies failing to fulfil the requirement of being a 'qualified individual' may still benefit from the treaty under other paragraphs of Article 23, but again there are numerous restrictions placed on such companies.

Other anti-avoidance provisions in treaties

Many US treaties provide that not more than 25% of the gross income of a US paying corporation should be derived from interest and dividends, other than interest and dividends received from its own subsidiary corporations, thus preventing passive income from being routed via treaties for tax avoidance purposes. The Netherlands/UK double tax treaty contains under Article 12(5) a provision that the reductions in withholding tax on royalties will only be relevant if the licence has not been assigned to the recipient for the purpose of obtaining the treaty benefits. The Netherlands/Switzerland double tax treaty contains under Article 9(2)(a) an anti-avoidance provision denying withholding tax exemption on dividend payments to parent companies if the parent has been incorporated primarily for the purpose of obtaining the withholding tax exemption.

4.4.2 Certain treaties exclude offshore companies

Several countries have specific legislation designed to promote their offshore financial services industry, such as Switzerland with its domiciliary companies, the Netherlands Antilles with its offshore investment companies, and even the UK through its non-domicile benefits. Switzerland has dealt with treaty shopping unilaterally, the UK though limitation of relief to remittances, and the Netherlands Antilles by being excluded from the network of double tax treaties (except for its important treaty access route through its treaty with the Netherlands). The network of treaties negotiated by Cyprus commonly excluded offshore companies from benefiting, although such entities are now subject to a 'grandfathering' regime,[25] following the introduction of the new 10% tax regime in 2002 applicable for 1 January 2003.

25. I.e. allowing temporary preservation of legislation which exists at the time a law is amended or a tax treaty is concluded or modified.

United Kingdom tax treaties

Formerly, certain tax treaties could be utilised to shelter gains which would otherwise give rise to a charge under TCGA 1992, Section 86.[26] An offshore trust would become resident in a suitable treaty jurisdiction, such as Mauritius or New Zealand. Before the end of the year of assessment in which the gain is realised but after its realisation, a majority of trustees resident in the UK are appointed to the settlement. In this way, the trust could become UK resident and the trustees would therefore be subject to UK capital gains tax. If TCGA 1992, Section 77 applies to the trust, it is likely that the tax treaty would protect the gains.[27] Following the 2003 Protocols to the UK's tax treaties with New Zealand and Mauritius, respectively, these loopholes based on the nature of domestic legislation have been closed. In the case of the treaty with Mauritius, Article 13(5) of the 1981 tax treaty has now been replaced by the following:

> *The provisions of this Article shall not affect the right of a Contracting State to levy according to its law a tax chargeable in respect of gains from the alienation of any property on a person who is a resident of that State at any time during the fiscal year in which the property is alienated, or has been so resident at any time during the six fiscal years immediately preceding that year.*

The relevant article in the Protocol to the 1983 tax treaty with New Zealand contains a similar provision.[28]

4.4.3 1962 Swiss Federal Decree and 1999 Amendment

1962 Decree

Switzerland's tax treaty network is available to all Swiss-incorporated companies, regardless of concessions given at federal or cantonal level. This, therefore, permits treaty shopping by non-residents so that income may be received with low or no foreign withholding taxes deducted, even if Swiss taxation subsequently levied may be limited by concessions available to certain types of company. As long ago as 1962, the Swiss Federation realised that this would be unacceptable to its treaty partners, and comprehensive measures were therefore brought in by the decree of the Federal Council in 1962. The principal measures involve limiting

26. Compare §1.2.1. The UK HMRC is of the opinion that Section 86 simply calculates an amount of gain as arising to the settlor by reference to the gains of the trustees rather than deeming those gains to be the settlor's.
27. Section 77's mechanism allocates gains to the settlor in a different way from that in Section 86 and arguably, the treaty intercepts the gain before it can be attributed to the settlor.
28. It was announced in the 2005 Budget that treaty protection for temporary non-residents would be removed by Finance Act 2005, in a provision that overrides treaty protection for individuals ceasing to be resident or ordinarily resident after 16 March 2005.

the erosion of the tax base as well as requiring a minimum profit distribution, which would then be subject to the 35% Swiss withholding tax on dividends. First, Article 1 of the decree lays down the major principle for the introduction of anti-avoidance legislation, namely that reduction of tax withheld at source because of the provisions of a double tax treaty shall not benefit persons not entitled to such reduction. Thus, the formation of a Swiss subsidiary of a foreign company shall be an abuse if formed for the purpose of securing the benefits of reduced withholding taxes at source (but not other benefits) from the double tax treaty that exists between Switzerland and the third country. In the event of a perceived abuse, the Swiss tax authorities may:

- refuse application made for the reduction of withholding taxes; or
- recover any withholding taxes reduced by treaty provisions; or
- inform the contracting third-party state of the existence of such an abuse.

Cantonal and federal tax authorities shall keep each other informed of the existence of any suspected abuses.

Secondly, Article 2(2)(a) states that an abuse will occur where a substantial part of foreign income, for which double tax relief is claimed, is used to pay debt interest, fees, commissions, salaries, royalties and any other payments other than dividends to persons not entitled to the tax treaty reliefs if paid directly to them. The 'substantial part' is in practice 50%, so that at least 50% of the remainder is taxable income in Switzerland and subject to federal and possibly cantonal and municipal taxation. This is as opposed to the normal allowance in respect of the satisfaction of foreign interests out of income brought into charge from abroad, which is normally 80% of foreign income (received without the benefit of tax treaty provisions) that may be paid out of taxable income to third parties.

Thirdly, Article 2(2)(b) sets down further regulations where income from abroad, which has benefited from treaty provisions is received by a company owned by non-residents. The regulations are mainly aimed at preventing income from being accumulated by a Swiss company.[29] The regulations are also aimed at companies that are able to claim the participation deduction and are, therefore, not subject to any Swiss taxation on dividend income received. Accordingly, at least 25% of gross income received for which a tax treaty applies must be distributed to the ultimate non-resident beneficiaries entitled to the income, and the 35% Swiss withholding tax deducted from the distribution. This may or may not be refunded in part or in whole, depending whether or not a treaty exists between Switzerland and the country of residence of the recipient.

29. I.e. a company which enjoys holding company or domiciliary company status and pays the very low federal tax only on income retained.

It should be realised that the Decree is only applicable where foreign income has been subject to a withholding tax, which is reduced under a Swiss treaty. Swiss companies receiving income from, for example, the following countries are unaffected by the Federal Decree:

(a) countries which do not impose a withholding tax on that income; or

(b) countries where the treaty rate and the unilateral rate of withholding tax on that income are the same.

1999 Amendment

The 1999 Amendment to the 1962 Swiss Federal Decree emphasises the distinction between active and passive income. Thus passive income generated in Switzerland may not enjoy treaty protection in respect of withholding tax on royalties when more than 50% of treaty-protected income is subsequently forwarded to recipients outside Switzerland. It seems that income will indeed be split up as active or passive when determining whether treaty benefits apply. The Swiss tax authorities may put the burden of proof on the company in determining what is passive and what is active income. Key to overcoming this problem, however, is that value has to be added on a continuous basis by the company in order to enjoy this protection.[30]

The mechanics of tax treaty protection being disallowed are as follows. Suppose that royalties emanate from Spain. A certificate of Swiss tax residence may not be sufficient for the Spanish tax authorities. They will require a form to be completed by the Swiss company, which is then sent to the Federal Tax administration in Berne. It is at this stage that the Federal Decree may apply, since the burden of proof is on the company. The company will have to show in relation to the royalties (or other income) that it is adding value by, for example, specific exploitation activities.

4.4.4 Remittance provision in UK and other treaties

As outlined above,[31] the basic function of a double tax treaty is to avoid double taxation, rather than create an opportunity for income and capital gains to be exempt from tax. Thus, countries which provide certain concessions permitting this to happen may include in their treaties a limitation clause restricting the treaty benefits only to those persons who do not enjoy such concessions. UK treaties would generally include a limitation of relief provision restricting treaty

30. From 2005 all expenses have to be substantiated with relevant documentation to be allowable, effectively abolishing the 50/50 practice. In certain cases a transitional period applies until the end of 2008.

31. In §4.1.

benefits only to amounts remitted to the UK. This is because UK law relating to non-domiciled individuals only subjects remittances of non-UK-source income and capital gains to UK tax, so there should be no relieving provisions relevant if such income is not remitted.[32] This generally relates to the reductions in withholding taxes on dividends, interest and royalties, and to the absence of capital gains tax charges.

4.4.5 1994 Anti-treaty shopping law in Germany

The 1994 Anti-Abuse and Technical Amendment Act has extended the provisions applicable to the abuse of law doctrine in order to deny treaty benefits if shareholders would not be entitled to those benefits if such income were received direct by them. As with most anti-avoidance provisions, there is an exception where a foreign corporation has been set up for *bona fide* commercial purposes. The provisions deny treaty benefits to foreign companies where:

(a) they do not engage in a business activity of their own, and

(b) their interposition has no commercial or non-tax validity; and

(c) their shareholders would not be entitled to treaty benefits if the income were received direct.

However, since this is a threefold test, engaging in business activities would thwart treaty denial, and there may therefore be an argument that a conduit company is engaging in business activities. Subsequent to these provisions, several important issues have been clarified by the Bundesamt:

(a) holding companies do not qualify for treaty benefits unless they exercise some degree of management and control over their subsidiaries, which denotes the holding company having several employees and its own business premises;

(b) the provisions apply not only to withholding taxes but also to any other kind of treaty benefits or provisions under the EU Parent/Subsidiary Directive;

(c) the Bundesamt may look through a chain of tiered companies to the ultimate individual shareholder in order to determine whether he would be entitled to similar benefits if he received the income directly.

The Bundesamt will not entertain requests for advance rulings on structures.

32. Including, for example, Article 32 of the 2004 France/United Kingdom tax treaty (pending entry into force at the date of writing this book) and Article 27 of the 1977 Switzerland/Netherlands tax treaty.

[IV.] CASE STUDY 4

In this chapter, some of the functions and applications of tax treaties have been investigated. Clearly, although tax treaties are often used in international tax planning, countries are attempting to curb the use of their tax treaties to reduce tax burdens artificially by using treaties for purposes for which they were not intended.

When considering how the Filipes have been using tax treaties in their international tax planning endeavours, reference must be made to:

(a) the use of Lucca BV to avoid or reduce withholding tax in France, Italy and the UK (Diagram 4);
(b) the payment of invoices from Lucca Software SpA via the UK nominee company (Diagram 7);
(c) the use of Opus AG to collect royalties for Paolo (Diagram 8);
(d) pension issues for Giuliano (Diagram 9).

Diagram 4

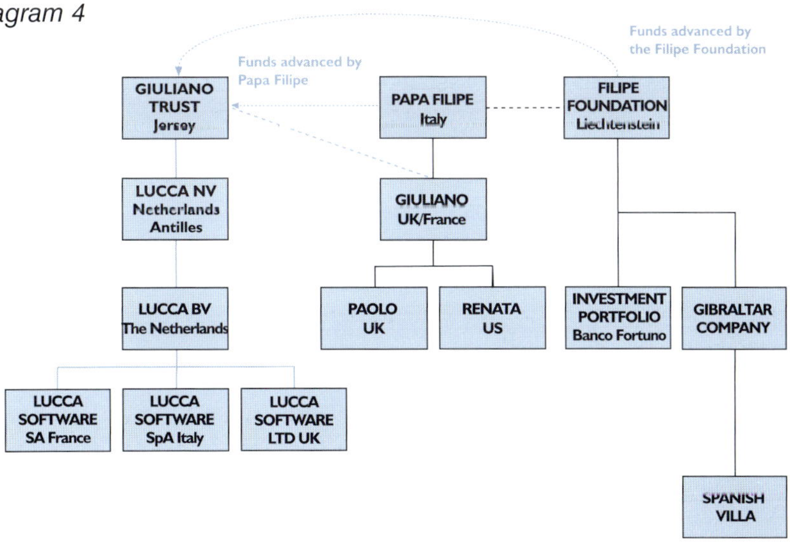

Diagram 7

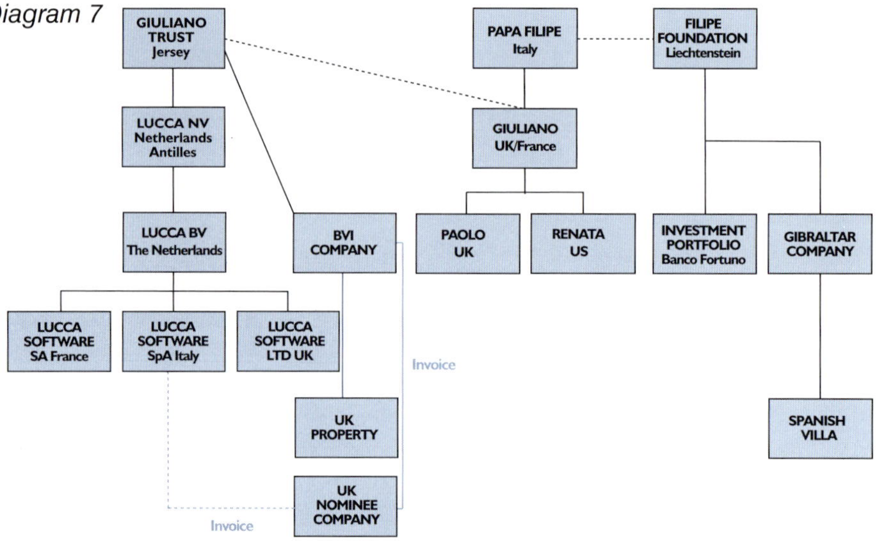

Diagram 8

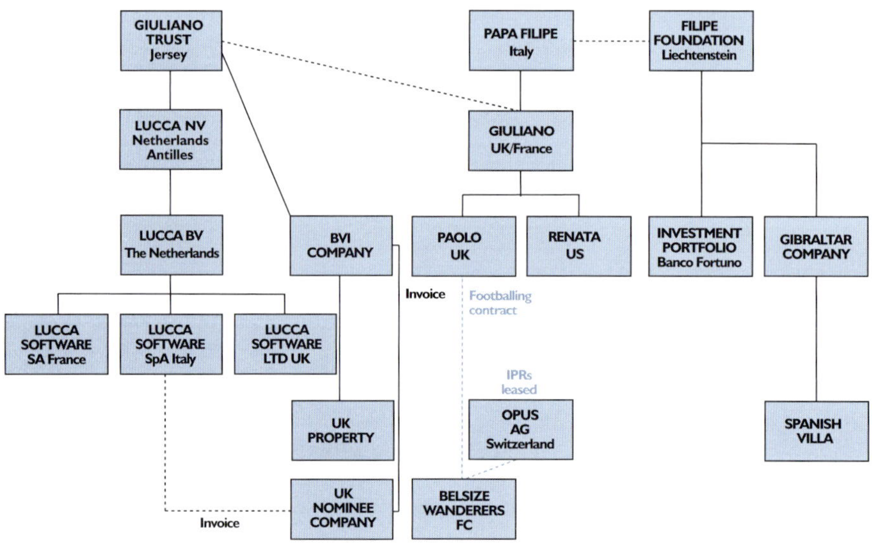

Diagram 9

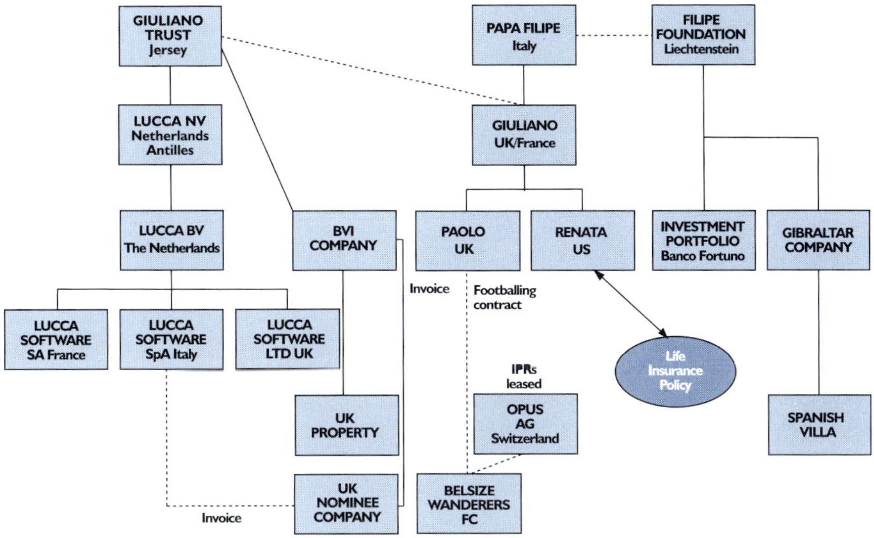

[IV.a] Use of Lucca BV for withholding tax exemption

Maurice Brightman originally advised Giuliano on the creation of a group holding structure, with Lucca BV, a Dutch company, holding the lower-tiered Lucca Software SpA. The Group later expanded into the UK and established Lucca Software Ltd UK, and then France, setting up Lucca Software SA.
At the time when the group structure was created, Maurice knew that by using Lucca BV as a holding company, withholding tax on dividends distributed to the Netherlands would be reduced in France, Italy and the UK, based on the tax treaties in place.

It was shown in the previous chapter that under the EU Parent/Subsidiary Directive, which came into force in 1990, dividend distributions from EU subsidiaries to their EU parents are generally exempt from withholding tax, so that the benefits of the Dutch treaty network are not as important as they were at the time of the creation of the group structure. However, Maurice advised Giuliano that if the latter wanted to expand the Lucca empire to non-EU countries, the Dutch treaty network would be a distinct advantage, including reducing withholding tax on dividends distributed to Lucca BV.

Nevertheless, Maurice had to point out some changes that have taken place since the initial recommendation of the NV/BV structure. First, the structure itself had become more expensive as a result of changes in Dutch tax legislation, initiated by the EU member states, so that the tax cost of distributing income through Lucca BV was now 8.3% as compared to (initially) total exemption.[33]

Secondly, Giuliano had to consider putting commercial substance in Lucca BV; otherwise distributions to the Dutch holding company may not benefit from the withholding tax exemptions originally envisaged.[34] This is particularly the case for distributions from any future German subsidiary of Lucca BV or distributions from a future US subsidiary, where a 'limitation on benefits' provision might prevent the application of lower withholding taxes as per the treaty.

Giuliano was therefore recommended to ensure that he employed a local managing director in the Netherlands who understood the Lucca business and who could take management decisions for the group in respect of its underlying subsidiaries, in order to secure that Lucca BV was managed and controlled within the Netherlands.

Giuliano and Maurice also discussed the option that as the business developed, Lucca BV could be listed to further ensure that a future US subsidiary of the company does not fall foul of the 'limitation on benefits' provision in Article 26 of the 2004 Protocol to the Netherlands/US tax treaty. Maurice informed Giuliano that Lucca BV would have to be listed and its stock regularly traded on a recognised stock exchange such as the Amsterdam Stock Exchange in order to meet this requirement.

[IV.b] Invoice payments from Italy via UK nominee company

The British Virgin Islands company has invoiced Lucca Software SpA via a UK nominee company in order to extract profits from the Italian subsidiary. This was one of Giuliano's ideas that he did not discuss with Maurice. Maurice spent a considerable amount of time banging his head against the wall of his office when he heard that Giuliano had not only thought of the structure, but also had gone ahead and implemented it.

Besides the concept of legal tax fraud, under double tax treaty provisions generally only residents of treaty countries are eligible for treaty benefits. Giuliano's structure interposed the UK nominee company between the Italian subsidiary and the BVI company in order to ensure that the benefits provided for by the Italy/UK tax treaty could be taken advantage of.

33. It seems that during 2006, 0% dividend withholding tax might be reintroduced for participations of 25% or more; however, at the time of writing this book, this was subject to confirmation.
34. See also [§III.d].

However, the UK Inland Revenue[35] had announced that it would generally not issue certificates of residency to nominee companies, such as the company in the Giuliano structure, the consequence of this being that the UK nominee company would be ignored in transactions between the BVI company and the Italian subsidiary. Since there is no tax treaty between the BVI and Italy, the result of ignoring the existence of the UK company is that no deductions will be allowed in Italy for payments made to the UK nominee company.

Based on Article 27 of the 1988 Italy/United Kingdom tax treaty, the Italian revenue authorities and the UK Inland Revenue are free to exchange information as is necessary for carrying out the provisions of the tax treaty, in particular to prevent fiscal evasion or fraud. The only limitations on the kind of information that may be exchanged between the countries' tax authorities is such information that is not obtainable under the respective legal systems of the two countries, for example disclosure of trade, business secrets, or information that would be contrary to public policy. Consequently, upon enquiry, the UK Inland Revenue would be able to disclose to the Italian tax authorities the amounts that were paid from the UK nominee company to the BVI company, ensuring that the Italian tax authorities disallows deductions from corporate tax of appropriate amounts in Italy. The Italian tax administration may itself ascertain the nominee nature of the UK company by reviewing the accounts of the company at Companies House. These publicly available documents would merely show a nominee fee receivable as opposed to the entire receipts for Lucca Software SpA as turnover. To do otherwise would risk the UK Inland Revenue denying the deduction for UK corporation tax of amounts paid to the BVI company.

Maurice suggested Giuliano reconsiders such 'tax planning', which was outmoded even in Mussolini's era.

[IV.c] Opus AG collecting royalties for Paolo

Belsize Wanderers transferred merchandising rights in respect of the No. 11 shirt to Opus AG in Switzerland. Royalties paid by licensees to this company are accumulated for Paolo in Switzerland. The royalties, paid from various countries in the world, are often subject to no or low withholding taxes based on the provisions in Swiss tax treaties.

Depending upon ownership of Opus AG and the tax ruling it had obtained, Paolo may not be able to benefit as much as he hoped from the

35. In Tax Bulletin 62.

accumulation of profits in Opus AG. The reason for this is the policy basis of the Swiss Federal Decree of 1962 – preventing individuals like Paolo, who is a resident of the UK, from using the Swiss treaty network by creating an entity in Switzerland to benefit from reduced withholding tax at source. Under Article 2(2)(a) of the decree, 50% of the foreign income must be subject to various levels of Swiss tax. Even if the income is not paid out to Paolo, as is the current plan, but is merely accumulated in Opus AG, at least 25% of the foreign income received that has benefited from treaty provisions will have to be distributed to Paolo. This amount will be subject to Swiss withholding tax at a rate of 35%. Furthermore, payments from the various licensees around the world to Opus AG in respect of Paolo's merchandising rights may be denied treaty protection if more than 50% of the royalties are paid to recipients outside Switzerland.

Based on the 1999 Amendment to the Swiss Federal Decree, however, the above denial of treaty protection does not apply if Opus AG meets the 'activity test'. A Swiss company, such as Opus AG, with an active business may be entitled to forward more than 50% of treaty-protected income to recipients outside of Switzerland, such as Paolo. However, Opus AG should actively enhance the value of the assets it is exploiting. Not only must Opus AG have offices and personnel in Switzerland, but its management team must also be involved from start to finish in the development of a Paolo's merchandising right enhancement: the instruction of specialist lawyers for the drafting of suitable contracts, negotiations with agents and companies, engagement of specialist intellectual property brand managers, and so on.

[IV.d] Pension issues for Giuliano

Although Giuliano had always liked to get the most out of life and had not had much opportunity to think about his age, his daughter Renata had been reminding him on a regular basis that he was 'not getting any younger' and that he should 'do something about taking care of himself when he gets really old'. (After such conversations, Giuliano often thought how much Renata reminded him of her mother, particularly in respect of the tenacity both women possessed.)

During Giuliano's recent visit to north London, he invited Maurice for pizza, particularly to raise the pensions issue after a glass (or, truth be told, two bottles) of Chianti. Giuliano told Maurice confidentially that his dream had always been to live Cyprus and that he hoped to move there after retirement.

Maurice replied that Giuliano had two options in respect of the pension fund he has been contributing to in the UK as a result of being directly employed by Lucca Software Ltd for his UK duties following his move to the UK from Lucca after his divorce. He could either leave it untouched in the UK once he moved to Cyprus, or 'emigrate' his pension scheme to Cyprus. Maurice said that it was a good thing that Giuliano had dreams about moving to Cyprus (and not Monaco, for example, with whom the UK has not concluded a tax treaty and would thus leave Giuliano's pension vulnerable to UK tax). The Cyprus/United Kingdom tax treaty provides under Article 19(1) for non-taxation of any pension derived from sources within the UK by an individual who is a resident of Cyprus and who is subject to tax in respect of the pension in Cyprus. Under Article 20 of the Cyprus Income Tax Law,[36] pension payments that are received by an individual resident in Cyprus for services rendered outside Cyprus will be subject to tax at the rate of 5%. Thus, should Maurice become resident in Cyprus he would not be subject to UK tax on his pension but only to Cypriot tax at the rate of 5%.

Alternatively, Maurice could 'emigrate' his pension scheme to Cyprus, but the UK Pensions Schemes Office would only allow this if Giuliano is to take up real residence in Cyprus for several years. He must also take up real employment in Cyprus for a Cyprus-resident company and ensure that Cypriot trustees take over the administration of the pension scheme after its 'migration'. Under these circumstances, the Cypriot tax rate on the pension would still be 5%.

Maurice and Giuliano agreed that it seemed simpler to leave the pension scheme in the UK and benefit from the tax treaty provisions once Giuliano reaches retirement age.

[IV.e] Conclusion

Double tax treaty provisions are very important to the international tax consultant. First, there is clarification as to which state has the taxing right on a certain portion of income, which prevents double juridical taxation. However, the tax planner who is also hoping to use tax treaties to reduce his client's tax burden by, for example, 'shopping' for the most favourable treaty should be aware that a significant role of tax treaties is also to prevent fiscal avoidance – thus, domestic and treaty anti-avoidance legislation should be investigated during the international tax planning discussions.

36. 118(I)/2002.

Chapter 5

Can Domestic Taxation Be Mitigated by the Use of Offshore Structures?

In Chapter 3, the issue of whether income and capital has a local source was considered and in Chapter 4 a study was made as to whether the relevant taxes are reduced or eliminated by virtue of an appropriate double tax treaty. It is now necessary to consider whether the income and capital is taxed in the country where the owner is resident, even if the income and capital are not remitted to the country but remain offshore.[1]

The first requirement in considering this third primary consideration is to understand the definitions of what constitutes residence in a particular country, and then consider whether foreign income and capital can be attributed to the individual or corporate beneficial owner in the absence of an actual remittance.

1. It might be useful for the reader to recall the fundamental questions asked at the beginning of Chapter 3, and particularly 'Will one have to pay domestic tax because of one's residence, even if one does not remit the income or capital?', which is the main question relevant to this chapter.

5.1 RESIDENCE, DOMICILE AND CITIZENSHIP

The concepts of residence in respect of companies and, in addition to this, domicile and citizenship in respect of individuals are important to consider within the context of determining the basis on which any taxation might take place.

5.1.1 Individuals

Residence

Residence, perhaps unlike the UK concept of domicile, which is discussed below, is a generally recognised concept to tax planners wherever they may be. It is used in many countries to define the liability of the person to tax in that country. With regard to individuals, a number of tests are employed in order to determine whether a person is a resident of a country, but these can generally be broken down into one or a combination of the following:

(a) a mechanical test under which a person is resident if they spend a set amount of time in that country (183 days in, for example, Spain or the UK);

(b) the home (*foyer*) or principal abode (*lieu du séjour principal*) used in France or Spain;

(c) a centre of economic interests test such as that used in France or Spain;

(d) a professional activities test such as that used in France or Spain;

(e) a cumulative presence test, such as that used in Norway, Ireland and the US, and to a lesser extent in the UK (the '90-day rule').

These tests raise a number of issues for the international tax adviser. The first is that, with the possible exception of tests (a) and (e), they are obviously open to interpretation, and countries will have their own definition of 'centre of economic interests'.

Under the Italian Civil Code, for example, an individual is resident in the place where he has his habitual abode. Having a habitual abode in Italy means that the person considers Italy as his home country. This is similar to the concept of domicile in the UK, and if an individual's presence in other countries is merely incidental and of a temporary (although not necessarily short) nature, this may not disrupt their Italian residence. Hence, if factual circumstances show that such individual considers Italy as his home country (for the greater part of the taxable period), he might be regarded as a resident even if he is not physically present in Italy. Typically, such factual circumstances are family ties and the availability of accommodation that is not of a temporary nature.[2]

Even under the mechanical test, there is room for discord, with a 'day' being calculated as being from midnight to midnight in the UK, but not in the US, where any part of a day spent in the US would be counted. The second ground for disagreement is that any one country may apply more than one test and an individual may be resident under any one. The third issue leads on from the first two, and is simply that with a number of different definitions and tests applied by each country, there is clearly the potential for overlap. It is at that point that one must revert to a double tax treaty (if one is in place) as reviewed in detail in Chapter 4.

The mechanical presence test of 183 days per fiscal year is generally applied in most countries, but increasingly, the cumulative presence test is taken as an alternative measure of residence. Thus, the UK has its '360 days over four years' test of ordinary residence; Ireland has a '240-day test over two years' and with effect from 1 January 2004, Norway has its '270 day over three years cumulative presence' test. The US is often more complex and has a cumulative presence formula where one takes the entire number of days in a particular calendar year ('the relevant year'), one-third of the days of the preceding year and one-sixth of the days of the second preceding year, and if this aggregates more than 183 days in the relevant year, the cumulative presence test is met.

Domicile

Generally, domicile is a concept of international law which determines an individual's civil status for jurisdictional purposes, such as marriage, divorce or property ownership. It is often described as nationality or citizenship; however, under UK law, it is really the country that is regarded as one's natural home and for most people is their country of birth.

For UK purposes, an individual normally follows the domicile of his or her father but may also take a domicile of choice if residing in another country and

2. Luciano Pavarotti was acquitted on a charge of tax evasion in a decision (Commissione Tributaria Regionale di Bologna, Sez.XIX, n.16) dated 27 March 2000. The Italian Finance Ministry claimed that the tenor's centre of vital interests was in Italy but Pavarotti's lawyers argued that virtually all of his professional activity took place outside Italy and that Modena and Italy in general were merely a holiday destination. Pavarotti's trial ended with him being acquitted on the basis that a declaration made in bad faith is not a crime. However, had the Finance Ministry been able to prove that Pavarotti regarded Italy as his home country (e.g. through having close economic and personal ties with the country), the outcome might have been different for the singer. The case is a salient reminder to anyone looking to establish non-residence that to do so is often fraught with potential pitfalls, especially if it is tax-motivated.

intending to live there permanently. While it is possible to be resident in more than one country and in some cases to have more than one nationality, an individual can have one UK domicile only.

There are essentially four types of domicile, which are:

(a) domicile of origin – an individual will be born with a domicile of origin which is usually that of his/her father;

(b) domicile of choice – an individual may replace his/her domicile of origin with a domicile of choice on attaining 16 years of age. In order to lose a UK domicile of origin, an individual must sever all ties with the UK;

(c) domicile of dependency – women who married prior to 1 January 1974 retain the domicile of their husband but after that date, this is determined by the same factors as for any other individual who is able to have an independent domicile;

(d) deemed domicile – the question of deemed domicile is relevant where an individual, other than somebody who has been born here, has been resident in the UK for a long time.

A UK domiciled person remains UK domiciled for inheritance tax purposes for three calendar years after he/she ceases to be UK domiciled under general law. Note also that a person will be treated as if he/she was in fact UK domiciled if the individual has been resident for tax purposes in the UK in not less than 17 of the 20 years of assessment ending with the year of assessment in which the relevant time falls.

Deemed domicile is relevant only in the context of inheritance tax (the estate of a deemed domiciled individual is subject to UK tax), while domicile of an individual is relevant particularly to determine whether the remittance basis[3] of taxation applies – usually only non-domiciled individuals resident in the UK can enjoy this advantage.

Citizenship

US citizens, even if non-resident, and resident alien individuals are taxable on their worldwide income. The only way for a US citizen to avoid the necessity of filing US tax returns during a period of non-residency is to relinquish his US

3. Where the remittance basis applies, UK resident but non-domiciled individuals are only liable to UK tax on the amount of their overseas income that is remitted to the UK. Income is remitted if it is paid or transmitted or brought to the UK in any way. In determining the tax liability, all income remitted to the UK will be included.

citizenship, a right which most US citizens consider sacrosanct. Moreover, a US citizen who gives up his citizenship for the principal purpose of avoiding US tax would continue for a period of ten years to be taxed in the same manner as previously. The US government has now gone beyond the freedoms established by the US Constitution by amending the US Immigration and Nationality Act on 1 October 1996 to allow any individual to be barred from entry to the US if he has previously renounced citizenship for tax avoidance reasons. Proposals at the US Senate may have even more onerous tax consequences for US citizens wishing to relinquish citizenship, such as treating loss of US citizenship as a taxable event in itself with retroactive effect, but such provisions are yet to be finalised.

5.1.2 Companies

One of the major factors[4] used to determine the residence of companies is the place where a company is managed and controlled, aspects of which are discussed below.

Management and control[5]

The classic UK case of *De Beers*[6] considers 'where the real business of the company is carried on, where the central management and control actually abides'. In this case, a South African company operating in South Africa, but whose affairs were controlled from the UK, was held to be resident in the UK, because that was where it 'keeps house and does business' (even though the 'nuts and bolts' of the business was, in fact, in South Africa). It was held that since the principal office was in the UK, and the majority of directors met in the UK, the profits were therefore realised in the UK.

While the basic concept has been developed over the years, the principle remains the same. The position in other selected countries is discussed below.

Australia

Section 6(1) of the Income Tax Assessment Act 1936 defines 'resident in Australia' in terms of a company, as a company which is incorporated in Australia or which, if not incorporated in Australia, carries on business in Australia and has either its central management and control in Australia or its voting power controlled by shareholders who are residents of Australia.

4. The other main factor is the place where a company is incorporated. Some countries take other factors as determining, including where the principal activities of the company take place or the nationality or tax residence of controlling shareholders or directors. Aspects of relevant factors are discussed in the individual country sections below.
5. For determining residence of trusts by using the management and control test, refer to §2.5.1.
6. *De Beers Consolidated Gold Mines v. Howe* [1906] AC 455.

By the first limb of the test, a company is indisputably a resident of Australia if it is incorporated in Australia. Present case law asserts, in terms of the second limb of the test, that a company whose central management and control is in Australia necessarily results in that company carrying on business in Australia. The concept of central management and control, in the case of a company incorporated outside Australia, is therefore of critical importance and is a matter of extensive case law, much of it under the law of England and Wales. It should be observed that while, in most cases, a company will reside where its board of directors habitually meets for the purpose of conducting the business of the company, this is not universally true. The real test of central management and control is found in the determination of where the actual business of the company is carried on; not in the sense of where it trades, but in the sense of from where its operations are controlled and directed. This determination can only be made after an examination of the course of the company's business and trading operations.

Thus, in the case of *Koitaki Para Rubber Estates*,[7] criteria considered as secondary tests included: the place where dividends are declared; the place where general meetings are held; the fact that the company operates a bank account in the country; and the place where the company's books and corporate seal are kept.

Canada

Companies are considered to be resident in Canada in circumstances where they are either incorporated in Canada or are deemed to be resident in Canada by virtue of factors such as the location of business activities and location of central management. Canadian courts follow the rulings of UK courts that a corporation is resident according to the country where its real business is carried on, and that its real business is carried on where its 'central management and control' is actually located.

In most cases, the central management and control will be located where the board of directors of the company meets and carries out its responsibilities. It is important to note, however, that *de facto* control is the determining factor (in this respect legal control, based on the percentage of voting shares, is not important). In order to establish where central management and control are exercised, factors such as where the effective decision-making relating to the activities of the corporation takes place are considered. The courts have also considered factors such as the place of incorporation, the country of operation, the residence of shareholders, the place where books are kept and bank accounts opened and the place where shareholders meet.

7. *Koitaki Para Rubber Estates v. FCT* [1941] 64 CIR 15.

Cyprus

A company is regarded as resident in Cyprus if it is managed and controlled in Cyprus. The test of management and control has not been defined, but the following factors are expected to be important in determining whether or not the management and control of a company are exercised in Cyprus:

- Does the board of directors have a majority of Cypriot residents?
- Are all the strategic decisions affecting the company made, and can they be shown to have been made and implemented, by the board of directors and in Cyprus?
- Does the company maintain its headquarters in Cyprus?
- Does the company operate an account with a bank in Cyprus?

Registration or incorporation in Cyprus alone will not be enough to render a company liable to tax in Cyprus.

France

Companies are resident where the registered seat (*siège social*) is located, or again where central control and management lies. Whether resident or not, however, they are taxed according to the principle of territoriality, so that although their total income is taxed in France, income earned abroad through subsidiaries and branches is in principle exempt from French taxation. This may only be changed: (a) at the option of a company that elects to be taxed on its worldwide income, if the company elects to create provisions reflecting foreign losses, or (b) if the French controlled foreign company legislation applies.

Germany

Residence is determined either according to where the seat of the corporation is, or where the place of management is located. In view of the strict tax legislation in Germany regarding tax avoidance, great care must be taken that income which seems to fall outside the German tax net is not in fact considered to arise in Germany because it is connected to a German source, or because the management of the non-resident entity receiving the income is deemed to exist in Germany. The German authorities regard the place of central management and control of a company as being that place where basic management decisions are carried out and translated into acts of real management. It therefore follows that a company whose central place of management and control is located in Germany will be governed by German tax law.

Israel

The Israeli Circular 4/2002, *Guidelines for Determining Control and Management,* makes clear that the substantive issues of who is really responsible for the conduct of the entity are key. The most significant issues are where the most important decisions are made, business strategies are set and the decisions that allow the company to function are taken. Important aspects of the decision-making process that should be examined include: the whereabouts of the source prompting the need for a decision, the place where the alternatives were prepared and discussed and where the final decision was agreed. The location of certain decisions is particularly important, including entering into certain dealings which impact heavily on a company's future, certain financing decisions, and those concerning large investments. It is clear that the Israeli position bears a close resemblance to the concept of management and control in the UK, but both can be contrasted with that of the US.

Singapore

A Singapore company is taxed on a territorial basis. The tax residency of a corporation is determined not so much by its place of incorporation, but defined in the Singapore Income Tax Act as 'a company or body of persons, the control and management of whose business is exercised in Singapore'. In this context, control and management is taken to be the place where the directors meet and exercise *de facto* control.

The Netherlands

A legal entity incorporated under Dutch law is in principle subject to tax in the Netherlands.[8] Under most tax treaties, a company may be resident in the place of its effective management and control. As such, a foreign legal entity with effective management and control in the Netherlands will be subject to tax in the Netherlands.[9] On the other hand, a legal entity incorporated under Dutch law with effective management and control in another country, with which the Netherlands has concluded a tax treaty with a tie-breaker clause, will be subject to tax in that other jurisdiction. In that case the Dutch incorporation principle is subordinate to the tax treaty.

Case law highlights that the most important factor is the place of effective management. This is considered to be the place where the managing directors pass management resolutions, which is usually where they meet and carry out their management duties. It has, however, been recognised that there are instances where management cannot be considered to be in the hands of the managing directors, such as where their functions are restricted to management of day-to-day matters, with more important aspects lying within the domain of the shareholders' meeting which must then be approved by the board of directors. Therefore, management is deemed *not* to be carried out by the managing directors in the following cases:

8. Corporate Income Tax Act 1969 (Wet op de vennootschapsbelasting 1969), Article 2.
9. General Tax Act (Algemene Wet inzake Rijksbelastingen), Article 4.

(a) where the type of business in which a company is engaged requires specialist knowledge (which they do not have); or

(b) where one individual acts as managing director of numerous companies and cannot therefore be considered to have the specialist knowledge required for all of them.

The latter case must clearly sound a warning note to trust companies, who generally will not have the specific skills or knowledge required to manage each Dutch company under their 'management'.[10]

United Kingdom

Similar to the position in the US, companies resident in the UK are liable to corporation tax on their worldwide income, while non-resident companies carrying on a branch or agency (now replaced by the term 'permanent establishment') in the UK or any other business activity are taxed only on UK source income (subject to double tax treaty provisions). From 15 March 1988, companies incorporated in the UK are treated *per se* as resident in the UK for tax purposes irrespective of where their central management and control is situated, unless the provisions in an applicable tax treaty changes this general rule.[11] However, the Inland Revenue has explained[12] that it will not issue a certificate of residence for tax treaty purposes to companies who act as agent for another person rather than as principal ('nominee companies') or where the proper person to claim treaty relief is not the nominee company, but the beneficial owner of the income.

United States

US corporations, irrespective of where they are managed and controlled, are taxable on their worldwide income, so that income from foreign branches, foreign real estate and foreign investment income is fully subject to US tax, with unilateral and bilateral credits allowed for foreign taxes incurred on that income.

However, in contrast to the management and control principle examined above, the US has the concept of taxable income 'effectively connected' with a US source, and if a foreign corporation has effectively connected income, then the foreign corporation will be subject to US tax on such income.[13] Moreover, if 25% or more of a foreign corporation's gross income is effectively connected income,

10. Reference should be made to §6.3.4 for Ministry of Finance considerations of what constitutes 'substance' for a Dutch conduit or holding company.
11. The general approach has been outlined in §5.1.2 under Management and Control.
12. See Tax Bulletin 62.
13. IRC, Section 864(c)(4)(B).

then any dividends paid by the foreign corporation to a non-US resident will be subject to US withholding tax unless an applicable tax treaty provides otherwise. The US is exceptional in imposing this second dividend tax on foreign corporations.

Ensuring non-residence

If an overseas incorporated company is to remain non-tax resident in a particular country (country A), but resident overseas (in country B) where it is managed and controlled, it is necessary to ensure that:

(a) no country A resident director takes decisions or gives instructions affecting the business of the company in country A, nor even really considers the business of the company while in country A;

(b) there is a majority of non-country A resident directors, some of whom have expertise in the commercial business of the company;

(c) regular board meetings take place outside country A and preferably in the same location where the administration office of the company is situated (country B);

(d) agendas and minutes of board meetings are accurately recorded and clearly reflect the decisions effected at the meetings;

(e) the statutes of the company reflect wherever possible that the company operates in the desired manner;

(f) the administration of the company, separate from policy decisions affecting the company, is conducted as far as possible in country B, being the country of desired residence, including *inter alia* the maintenance of an office, employment of local individuals, operation of a local bank account, keeping statutory books and conducting accounting operations there.

It is therefore rather short-sighted to give advice which involves the incorporation of a foreign company in order to save tax where that foreign company is obviously only incorporated for tax avoidance reasons and has no substance in actual effective management. If the foreign company is incorporated in a country which has a double tax treaty with the domestic country, then the foreign company may be taxed separately but, even so, the absence of effective management may negate successful tax planning.

Place of effective management under OECD Model Treaty

It may be that two countries consider a particular company to be tax resident, perhaps one on the grounds of its place of incorporation and the other on the grounds of where its management and control are located. In such circumstances, a relevant double tax treaty would be helpful in clarifying which country has the applicable taxing rights. The Commentary to Article 4 of the OECD Model Treaty considers the overriding intention to be 'the place of effective management', which is considered to be the place where:

> *... key management and commercial decisions that are necessary for the conduct of the entity's business are in substance made. The place of effective management will ordinarily be the place in which the most senior person or group of persons (for example a board of directors) makes its decisions, the place where the actions to be taken by the entity as a whole determined; however, no definitive rule can be given and all relevant factors and circumstances must be examined to determine the place of effective management. An entity may have more than one place of management, but it can only have one place of effective management.*

It should be noted that the OECD released a discussion draft on 27 May 2003 concerning the 'place of effective management' concept. The draft has developed two proposals: the first would refine the current concept of place of effective management by expanding the Commentary explanations as to how the concept should be interpreted, whilst the second, known as the 'hierarchy of tests', would provide for different tests applying in succession. In addition, much of the above Commentary would be struck out and replaced with wording indicating that the place of effective management will usually be the place where the most senior person or group of persons makes its decisions. Where key decisions are made in one place but formally finalised in another, the place of effective management of a company would be where the key decisions are made. Also, the place where a person or entity with a controlling interest makes key decisions in respect of the company may be deemed to be the place of effective management. Where a board of directors routinely approves the strategic decisions made by the executive officers, the place where the latter make their decisions is important in determining the place of effective management of the entity.

The importance of determining residence is that the taxing rights of any particular country are usually defined by reference to whether an entity is resident or non-resident. Depending upon the taxing policy of the country in question, residents will often be subject to tax on their worldwide income while non-residents may find that the taxation rights of the jurisdiction concerned are restricted to income, gains or profits derived within the relevant jurisdiction.

As already seen, there is no point in advising a client to form a foreign subsidiary company for tax avoidance reasons if the parent company will be taxed in any event on the income of the foreign subsidiary. Management and control is only one consideration and, in fact, it may be irrelevant in the light of a particular country's unilateral tax legislation in determining whether or not domestic tax is avoided.

5.2 WORLDWIDE v. TERRITORIAL PRINCIPLES OF TAXATION

5.2.1 Worldwide

Some countries operate a worldwide system of taxation, i.e. their residents are taxed by that country based on the mere fact that the individual or company resides within that country's borders irrespective of the source of the income or gains. Some countries also tax their citizens on a worldwide basis regardless of an individual's tax residence. The United States and South Korea, for example, tax their citizens on a worldwide basis, irrespective of their place of residence, whereas Israel and South Africa tax their residents only (individual or corporate), on a worldwide basis.

5.2.2 Territorial

Some countries practise a system of full territoriality, which means that the residents are taxed only on the taxable items sourced within the borders of that country, as opposed to taxation on the basis of partial territoriality, described below. Countries that tax individuals resident within their borders on the basis of a fully territorial system include Hong Kong, Singapore and Thailand. These countries may also tax foreign-source income remitted to residents.

Some countries may practise partial territoriality in respect of individuals resident within their borders – this revolves around the concept of ordinary residence of an individual within that country, which means he may not be taxed on foreign-source income unless he is resident within that country on a regular or reasonably permanent basis. Countries that tax their residents on this basis include Japan and the UK. Certain countries tax their residents or individuals who are ordinarily resident within that country's borders, but who are not domiciled there, on a remittance basis. Examples of such countries include Ireland and the UK.

Some countries tax corporations resident within their borders on a full territorial basis, i.e. tax is imposed only on items of income or gain sourced within their borders. Countries that operate this system include Hong Kong and Singapore.

5.3 CFC LEGISLATION AND APPORTIONMENT OF FOREIGN PASSIVE INCOME

5.3.1 General background

Where a country operates the worldwide system of taxation, foreign income may be subject to domestic taxation, and the formation of a foreign base company to divert income from the domestic tax net will have to be legislated against. However, many countries exempt certain types of foreign income under certain conditions, for example foreign branch income and dividends from foreign subsidiaries, thus operating the territorial system of taxation, which has been explained above. In this event, there is no need to form a foreign base company since the income, which would be diverted to it, would be tax exempt in the domestic country. There may also be a combination of systems whereby active income is taxed on a territorial basis whereas passive income is taxed on a worldwide basis, as described in the anti-avoidance legislation below.

The exact terms and conditions of controlled foreign company (CFC) legislation varies with each country seeking to apply it, but in general terms it is designed to repatriate the income of a company deemed to fit the criteria of a CFC and include it in the income of resident shareholders, regardless of whether it is actually distributed to them or not. For many countries the basis of the legislation is to prevent income accumulation in tax havens where the nature of the underlying transactions has no genuine business purpose.

It is interesting to note that many of the CFC regimes are based upon the famous subpart F provisions contained within the US Internal Revenue Code (IRC), described below. Legislation often differs in the percentage requirement owned by domestic residents before a foreign company will be considered a CFC. Many regimes include provisions requiring the tax paid by the overseas company in its country of residence to be of a certain proportion of domestic tax. The CFC legislation in the UK is particular among its equivalents in Europe in applying to companies only (France is another notable exception), although there is an equivalent section applicable to individuals.[14] In common with France, Finland and Portugal, the UK legislation looks at the CFC on a territorial basis and can impose domestic tax on all profits earned by that CFC. This should be contrasted with the approach in the US, Canada, Germany and Spain, which would generally impose the legislation only where the foreign profits comprise passive income. The UK legislation is unique, though, among its European counterparts in that it does not attack capital gains earned by a CFC which is owned by a UK company, this being caught under separate provisions of UK tax law,[15] which may be superseded by the provisions of relevant double tax treaties.

Countries operating CFC legislation usually publish a list of countries to which it will not apply,[16] thus targeting the measure at those jurisdictions considered to be tax havens or those operating a particularly low level of taxation. Of course, CFC legislation is an anti-avoidance measure and in circumstances

14. ICTA 1988, Section 739.
15. TCGA, Section 13.
16. Most developed countries now have a form of black or white list arrangement. The purpose of such lists is to apply, or to disapply, certain aspects of that country's anti-avoidance provisions. The effect is to target those jurisdictions which are considered to be undesirable, usually on the basis that little or no tax is payable there. There are generally three forms of list:
    (a) Black lists: Black lists, such as those issued by the tax administrations of France, Denmark, Australia, Germany and Spain, are used to specifically apply certain strands of anti-avoidance legislation to listed countries.

Continued on facing page...

where there is a genuine economic activity, as opposed to one of a financial or passive nature, it is certainly possible that the rules will not apply.

It is not essential to provide a comprehensive list of the differing anti-avoidance legislation in various developed countries: examples of such types of legislation suffice to illustrate that the international tax adviser has to keep this issue in mind at all stages of tax planning.

5.3.2 France

The French CFC provisions are contained within Article 209B of the French Tax Code. The provisions do not apply if the main activity of the foreign company located in a tax-privileged regime is an industrial or commercial activity, and if it predominantly trades on the local market which may be a regional market covering several countries in the region. A French parent company may claim that the profits generated within the low-tax regime were not created for the purpose of avoiding French taxation. However, even if this is the case, if the result is that the foreign company has achieved tax savings, even if this is not the principal intention, then the French tax administration may invoke the section. The local market test only creates a so-called safe harbour if the local manufacturing, sales or service activities or local purchase of goods or raw materials accounts for more than 50% of the foreign corporation's income. Moreover, these activities should have substance as the instructions of the French tax authorities emphasise that the question is not merely one of intent.

Contrary to the practice in many countries, French companies do not necessarily have to own more than 50% of the shares in a subsidiary company located in a low tax jurisdiction to be subject to Article 209B – only 10% of the financial or voting rights is required. Therefore, the description 'controlled foreign corporation' is not particularly apt for French commercial law purposes. If the participation is below the threshold, for example, where ten French companies own 9.9% each in the same foreign entity, the CFC rules do not apply. If this artificial division of shares is created to thwart the provision of Article 209B, however, it is likely that the French authorities would consider invoking the abuse of rights legislation.

(b) White lists: The white list, by contrast, is generally used to identify countries to whom certain legislation, for example that referring to controlled foreign companies, does not apply, thereby allowing companies to operate subsidiaries in white-listed countries without the threat of domestic attribution of foreign profits even if they are undistributed.

(c) Grey lists: Grey lists generally exempt listed countries from anti-avoidance provisions in circumstances where a company meets certain conditions. For example, in New Zealand, income will be attributed from CFCs resident in grey-listed countries in circumstances where the CFC income is exempt from tax resulting from carrying on a business outside its country of residence, or where certain tax privileges have been granted.

5.3.3 United Kingdom

The UK CFC legislation[17] is aimed solely at preventing the accumulation of corporate funds outside the UK tax net. Its provisions touch upon any UK resident person, which in practice only affects companies with an interest in an overseas company and apply if:

(a) the company is resident outside the UK; and

(b) the overseas company is controlled[18] by UK residents; and

(c) the overseas company is subject to a lower level of taxation in the territory in which it is resident.

The provisions[19] state that the Inland Revenue will have no power to make a direction or raise an assessment where:

(a) the tax paid by the overseas company in its country of residence is at least 75% of the amount that would have been payable in the UK had it been resident in the UK; or

(b) the overseas company is engaged in activities which fulfil specified conditions for exemption (the 'exempt activities' test); or

(c) the overseas company remits by way of dividend a substantial proportion of its commercial profits to the UK (the 'acceptable distribution' test); or

(d) a main purpose of the transactions carried out by the overseas company is not to achieve a significant reduction of UK tax and it is not an underlying reason for the company's existence to achieve a diversion of profits from the UK (the 'motive' test); or

(e) at least 35% of the shares of a CFC are beneficially held by the public and during the accounting period were quoted on and were the subject of

17. ICTA 1988, Sections 747–756 and Schedules 24–26.
18. 'Control' is broadly defined and exists not only in circumstances where a company resident in the UK holds enough shares, voting power or powers granted by other documents (for example by the Articles of Association) to secure that the affairs of the overseas company are conducted in accordance with its wishes (ICTA 1988, Section 755D(1)) but also in circumstances where a UK resident company holds at least 40% of the shares in a overseas company and between 40% and 55% is owned by a second person resident outside the UK (ICTA 1988, Sections 747(IA) and 755D(3), (4)). Thus a UK resident company holding just 40% of the shares in an overseas company can fall foul of the definition of control for the purposes of the UK's CFC legislation.
19. ICTA 1988, Section 748.

dealings on a recognised stock exchange in the CFC's country of residence, and the 'principal members' of the company do not hold more than 85% of the voting power (the 'public quotation' test); or

(f) the chargeable profits of the CFC do not exceed £50,000 per annum (the *de minimis*) test.

In any case not falling within the above six exclusions, the Inland Revenue may raise an assessment on the UK company equal to the UK tax that would have been payable on the income of the overseas company if it had itself been UK resident. In computing the profits of the overseas company for the purposes of such an assessment, the full range of capital allowances, stock relief and double taxation relief are ordinarily available; however, the profits of the CFC will be subject to tax at the full rate regardless of the profits of the company to which they are attributed.

The incorporation by UK companies of subsidiaries resident in low-tax jurisdictions has for many years fallen within the scope of UK CFC laws. However, the use of international business companies[20] that are able to elect a rate of corporation tax, thus making it possible to fall outside the UK CFC rules by having a tax rate of 75% or more of the rate applicable in the UK, forced the Inland Revenue to introduce changes to the anti-avoidance rules. These rules applied to CFC accounting periods beginning on or after the 6 October 1999, under which companies such as Isle of Man or Jersey international business companies which can elect to pay a designer rate of tax, now fall within the definition of a CFC, irrespective of the level of tax actually paid.

In common with many other developed countries, the Inland Revenue has published a provisional list of countries which are not regarded as low-tax areas.

The entire matter of the compatibility of CFC legislation with the provisions of the Treaty of Rome is currently being considered in the UK, France and other EU countries with CFC legislation. For example, should CFC legislation apply to EU parents with subsidiaries in Cyprus or Ireland where the rates may be 10% or 12.5% respectively, or is this discriminatory under EU rules? Indeed, a case concerning a UK company with Irish subsidiaries is working its way through the ECJ at the time of writing and it would seem that unless there is a clear justification for CFC legislation, it is likely to be considered contrary to the founding principles of the EU, such as freedom of establishment.

5.3.4 United States

One provision which succeeds in preventing income accumulation abroad for the benefit of US individuals is Section 551 of the IRC, which gives the IRS

20. So-called 'designer-rate CFCs'.

power to tax US shareholders of a foreign personal holding company (which is 50% or more owned by five or less US citizens), on their apportioned share of the total net income of such company.

However, probably the best-known tax provision which subjects the income of a foreign subsidiary to domestic taxation is the subpart F legislation in the US. Section 951 *et seq* of the IRC includes the income of a foreign company which is a CFC with the income of US resident shareholders even if the income is not distributed to them. A CFC is one which is 50% owned by US residents who each own more than 10% of the voting rights or the share capital and whose income is 25% or more passive income, i.e. income such as dividends, interest, royalties and rents. This also includes income of captive insurance companies insuring US risks. The US shareholders may be corporate or personal, and they are taxed on their apportioned share of the undistributed foreign income earned by the CFC, thus preventing a deferment of US tax by income accumulation abroad.

Thus, if a US company is receiving dividend income from foreign subsidiaries and decides to create a foreign holding company in a country which levies little or no tax on dividend income, the subpart F legislation will enable the IRS to tax such dividend income in the hands of the controlling US shareholders, even if the dividend income is accumulated by the foreign base holding company and not remitted to the US parent.

Another provision is Section 1248 of the IRC which subjects earnings of CFCs which are not caught by subpart F provisions to US income tax when the CFC is sold by the parent, with the provision that only the balance of sale proceeds over accumulated earnings is treated as a capital gain. Thus, if income is accumulated abroad without being previously subject to US income tax, then, when the CFC is sold, that accumulated income will be subject to US income tax and not treated as a capital gain. There is in fact an escape under this section if shareholders hold less than 10% of the CFC or if a US company has 50% of a CFC and a foreign corporation holds the other 50%, so that US shareholders do not have a majority interest. If the foreign corporation holding the other 50% is in any way related to the US shareholders, then Section 1248 can be invoked.

5.3.5 Canada

The 'foreign accrual property income' (FAPI) concept[21] is Canada's equivalent to the US subpart F rules. Where a non-resident corporation earns income from property or income from passive business, there is attribution and immediate taxation in the hands of a Canadian shareholder, whether or not the income is distributed, where such non-resident corporation is considered a controlled foreign affiliate.

21. Income Tax Act, Sections 91–95.

The above rules apply where a Canadian shareholder, at the end of any taxable year, owns directly or indirectly not less than 1% and together with persons related to the shareholder owns directly or indirectly 10% or more of the shares of any class of the corporation,[22] and such shareholder alone or together with no more than four other Canadian residents or any number of related persons controls the affiliate. In such circumstances the FAPI is taxed in the hands of the shareholder proportionate to his participating percentage. Effective credit is granted for underlying corporate taxes and certain inter-affiliate withholding taxes, and there are procedures to avoid double taxation upon actual distribution of such FAPI. Capital gains may also be included in attributable FAPI income in respect of certain passive assets held by the foreign affiliate.

The FAPI rules also extend to certain non-resident trusts that have been set up by Canadian residents and which have Canadian beneficiaries. However, there is a *de minimis* rule of C$5,000 before FAPI income is attributed to the Canadian shareholders.

5.4 ANTI-AVOIDANCE PROVISIONS IN RESPECT OF TRUSTS

CFC provisions are particularly aimed at preventing unacceptable tax deferral in respect of foreign source income beneficially owned by residents of the particular country through direct or indirectly owned foreign companies. Countries may adopt various other anti-avoidance measures to prevent tax revenues from escaping their reach. Some of the most important guises in which anti-avoidance measures appear include exchange of information,[23] anti-treaty shopping provisions,[24] transfer pricing rules and thin capitalisation rules.[25] In respect of trusts, although these are useful tax planning tools as pointed out in Chapter 2, this fact alone has inevitably led to legislation of anti-avoidance measures regulating the use of trusts.

5.4.1 United Kingdom

In the simplest example, the transfer of assets from an individual to a company owned by a trust will vest income in a legal entity entirely separate from the individual.[26] Consideration must be given therefore not only to the fact that the higher personal rates of tax may be avoided by the use of a company, which may pay a lower rate of tax, but also to the fact that the after-tax profits of the company are not the property of the individual. If the taxpayer for whom the structure has been set up does not require the income of the trust then,

22. Giving rise to foreign affiliate status.
23. Discussed in Chapter 1.
24. Discussed in Chapter 4.
25. Both topics are discussed in Chapter 8.
26. Compare Chapter 2.

depending upon how the trust has been formed, substantial tax savings may result. However, once the taxpayer needs and actually uses the income of the trust in some way, he becomes subject to tax in his own country and the tax initially 'saved' by the structure will eventually be payable.

ICTA 1988, Sections 739 and 740

In order to be able to benefit from the tax savings, the trust deed may allow the taxpayer who has created the trust to be a beneficiary. Thus, the individual may have 'power to enjoy' the income of the trust. This phrase 'power to enjoy' is used within Section 739; when a UK resident has power to enjoy the income of the above trust, whether or not he personally does enjoy such income, he will be liable to the UK tax originally saved through the creation of the trust.

Thus, in circumstances where an individual ordinarily resident in the UK has made a transfer of assets (and can benefit therefrom), further to which income is payable to a non-resident person (trust or company), he will fall within the wording of Section 739 in circumstances where he is the transferor or settlor, or Section 740 in circumstances where he is only a beneficiary. The only reason allowed in the Act for which Sections 739 and 740 will not be invoked is if tax avoidance was not the purpose behind the transfer and the transfers were *bona fide* transactions.

As with CFC provisions, Section 739 attributes such income to the taxpayer on an arising basis, as opposed to Section 740 under which a tax charge is only incurred when income is remitted to the taxpayer.

Again, as for CFC provisions, it is arguable whether Section 739 can be invoked where the income is earned by a company resident in another EU jurisdiction. The argument by HMRC is that it is not the foreign EU resident company that is taxed in the UK on its profits, but the UK individual that is taxed 'by reference to' such profits. It remains to be seen how such a fine distinction is viewed by the European Court of Justice.

TCGA 1992, Section 13

The anti-avoidance legislation of many countries relates not only to taxation of income but also to taxation of capital gains derived through the use of foreign entities. In the UK, Section 13 taxes individuals resident in the UK who own shares in a non-resident company which would be a close company (five or fewer participators or any number of directors who are participators) if it were resident in the UK and which makes a chargeable gain; this chargeable gain is then attributed to the UK resident in proportion to his respective shareholding, provided that it is more than 10%. It may be noted that in circumstances where part of the gain is attributed to a connected person, the combined share must not exceed 10%.

It may also be noted that unlike Section 739, HMRC accept[27] that double tax treaties override Section 13. The capital gains tax article (Article 13 of the OECD Model Treaty) gives taxing rights in connection with capital gains made by a foreign company resident in the tax treaty jurisdiction solely to that country, and this appears to thwart the 'fine distinction' discussed above.

TCGA 1992, Section 86

A similar section, Section 86, applies to capital gains accruing to a non-resident trust as opposed to a company, and attributes the gain to the resident and domiciled settlor if they have an interest in the trust (which is widely defined). Additionally, where the settlor or one of the settlors was domiciled and either resident or ordinarily resident in the UK, any UK domiciled beneficiary under the settlement who is resident or ordinarily resident in the UK during that year shall have part of the capital gain attributed to him in proportion to his interest in the settlement.[28]

5.4.2 United States

Where income and capital gains are earned by an offshore trust which has been established by a US citizen or resident individual, such a trust will be considered a grantor trust[29] and will effectively be transparent for US tax purposes. Therefore, the relevant income and capital gains will be subject to tax on the US grantor as if it had been earned by him, and the capital will form part of his estate. Recent changes to US tax law in connection with offshore trusts have now created a similar tax liability for a US citizen and resident beneficiary, even if the individual is not considered to be the grantor of an offshore trust. Thus, where there is a US citizen or resident beneficiary, the income and gains of an offshore trust are attributed to the beneficiary in the proportions in which they are entitled to benefit from the trust.[30] With the exception of so-called 'Rabbi trusts'[31] which allow an element of current tax deferral, offshore trusts are of little tax planning benefit for US citizens or resident beneficiaries, and are now principally used for asset protection purposes.

5.4.3 Canada

Deviating from the relatively harsh treatment outlined in respect of the examples of the UK and the US above, Canada allows 'immigrant trusts' when the income may be kept offshore without penalty.

27. IR Capital Gains Manual, paragraph 57380.
28. CGA 1992, Section 87.
29. See also Chapter 2.
30. In accordance with Section 6048 of the IRC and by filing Forms 3520-A and 3520.
31. See also §3.4.1.

As a general rule, a foreigner becomes Canadian for tax purposes if he stays in Canada for more than 183 days in any tax year. Canadian residents are subject to Canadian tax on their worldwide income.

However, by establishing a properly planned offshore immigrant trust prior to taking up Canadian residency, investment income earned during the first five years of Canadian residency may be exempt from Canadian taxation. Furthermore, if the individual's transfer to Canada will last less than five years, this exemption becomes permanent.

A non-resident trust created and settled with property outside Canada is not resident in Canada for the purposes of Canadian tax law if:

- all of its property is acquired from a non-resident settlor;
- it does not receive any financial assistance from any person resident in Canada at any time;
- its non-resident trustees constitute a majority of the trustees; and
- the non-resident trustees actively exercise their responsibilities as trustees.

If the above conditions are satisfied, the trust is not deemed to be resident in Canada. Such a trust is not subject to Canadian tax on any of its income and gains that the trustees resolve to accumulate offshore in each year. Any amounts paid to or for the benefit of a Canadian resident beneficiary (including taxable capital gains realised or deemed to be realised in any year) are taxable in the hands of the beneficiary. Distributions of capital are not subject to Canadian tax.

The general steps in establishing an immigrant trust entail the following:

- the trust would be settled in an offshore jurisdiction by way of a gift from non-residents of Canada;
- non-resident trustees would be appointed;
- the trust would be irrevocable and discretionary;
- all investment decisions in respect of the trust and meetings of trustees would occur outside Canada;
- the trust deed would provide that the annual income of the trust should be accumulated and that the trustees would have the discretionary power to make capital distributions to the beneficiaries.

5.5 ACCESSING OFFSHORE FUNDS

The problems caused by having money in a foreign entity, which cannot be used when and where it is required, should not be underrated. Very often tax consultants may advise clients to extract profits from a high-tax country in the form of interest, royalties, fees and the other types of expenditure, whereas the taxpayer really needs the money to be retained by the payor company. For example, an international group with a properly constituted trading company in Liechtenstein and one in Germany, may well attempt to extract profits from the German company to the Liechtenstein company in order to reduce the overall tax burden of the group; however, if the German company requires the profits for reinvestment, then the current year's tax may be saved at the expense of future profits, clearly a totally false saving.

5.5.1 Companies – cash flow problems

In the above example, the Liechtenstein company may lend the German company the amount of profits extracted. There are, however, several problems which may arise: the German tax authorities may immediately suspect that the Liechtenstein company is related to the German company, for it is unusual for a non-related company to receive fees or other income and then philanthropically hand it back to the payor, albeit by way of loan. The deductibility of the fees or other type of expense paid by the German company will then be questioned by the tax authorities, and the end result may be that the group is unable to deduct the expense against German taxable income, thereby ruining a scheme for profit extraction. A hidden distribution of profits may then be construed by the tax authorities, and German withholding tax payable on the constructive dividend.

Additionally, the Liechtenstein company must, to ensure that the loan appears to be a commercial transaction, charge a realistic rate of interest on the loan. Although Germany does not levy withholding tax on interest payable on unsecured loans, many countries do impose a withholding tax, which may be 25% of the interest payable, and, since Liechtenstein and most other low-tax or no-tax countries do not have tax treaties with the higher tax countries to reduce the level of withholding taxes, this tax may well be an additional tax burden on the group. Furthermore, the interest, when paid, may not be deductible against the taxable profits of the payor company unless the entire transaction is proved to be a commercial one entered into between non-related parties. In other words, by not planning ahead and considering which company in which country requires the cash extracted for tax mitigation purposes, an additional and unnecessary tax burden will be created because of the dictates of cash flow.

5.5.2 Trusts

Stockpiled gains

United Kingdom

The 1991 Finance Act introduced a number of measures to make the use of offshore trusts less attractive for UK domiciled and resident individuals. The measures were introduced to discourage the retention of capital gains realised by offshore trustees rather than the distribution of those gains to beneficiaries.

The penalty is calculated by reference to the number of UK tax years for which the gain has been accumulated. The penalty is calculated at 10% per annum of the tax payable by the beneficiary on the distribution, but limited to a maximum of six years' penalty. Thus the maximum penalty is 10% of 40% (maximum income tax rate at present) for six years, or 24%. This is in addition to the 40% tax payable when the capital gain is distributed, making a total tax charge of 64%, the highest payable under the UK tax code.

The rules do not affect the position of those trusts created prior to 19 March 1991 ('golden trusts'). However, no further settled sums should be added to these trusts, nor should any benefits (e.g. interest-free loans from the settlor) be provided, nor should any new and unexpected beneficiary be appointed. If changes of this sort occur, then the trust could lose its status, and become subject to the new rules.

Undistributed net income

United States

In the case of a non-US, non-grantor trust, income (including realised capital gains) that is not paid out of the trust each year will become undistributed net income (UNI). If in a future year the beneficiary receives distributions that do not exceed the annual income amount of the trust, he will pay income tax only. However, if he receives in any year distributions that exceed the current year's income, the excess will carry UNI from the first year when such UNI was originally earned by the trust, with the following consequences:

(a) capital gains treatment is lost;

(b) there is an interest charge (about 8%) on the tax payable, going back to the year the income was originally earned;

(c) the 'throwback' rules apply, i.e. the beneficiary will be taxed based on his income tax bracket in the year the income was earned, not in the year it is paid out.

5.6 TAX AMNESTIES

Recognising that citizens may have inadvisedly accumulated wealth offshore which had not been declared as taxable under relevant anti-avoidance provisions, but that proper declaration would now put them between a rock and a hard place, an increasing number of countries have introduced tax amnesties for such individuals. This is not through benevolence, but recognising that tax revenue may increase as a result of permitting past errors to go unpunished.

The first amnesty of any substance was the Italian one, shortly followed by the

German and subsequently the US amnesties. Some of these tax amnesties are discussed below.

5.6.1 Belgium

One of the most recent countries to utilise a tax amnesty is Belgium, which has clearly seen the benefits derived from earlier tax amnesties, specifically those in Germany and Italy. Clearly, the success of any of these amnesties depends on the tax liabilities incurred on declaration of foreign capital and income; however, the most successful of all amnesties, the Italian one, may have owed its positive results to the confidentiality afforded to taxpayers so that they would not become future targets for local Revenue investigations.

5.6.2 Italy

Under the Italian tax amnesty (*condono fiscale*), Italians were allowed to either repatriate their undeclared offshore assets (held on 1 August 2001) or own up to their existence (applicable to assets held on 27 September 2001). The terms of the amnesty required that Italian residents pay either 2.5% of the value of the assets or used 12% of the value of the assets to purchase Italian Treasury bonds. The deadline for the amnesty, which started on 1 November 2001, was later extended from 28 February to 15 May 2002 (and in certain circumstances June 2002) and widened to provide that individuals who held funds derived from certain criminal activities would be covered if these had lapsed or been decriminalised.

5.6.3 South Africa

The South African tax amnesty got under way on 1 June 2003 and ended early in 2004. Under the terms of the amnesty, individuals or entities repatriating funds paid a 5% charge, while those declaring funds, that they intended to keep offshore, were required to pay a 10% charge.

5.6.4 United Kingdom

The UK appears unlikely to announce a tax amnesty, but if one is introduced after all, it will probably take on a form similar to that of the tax amnesty in the US.

5.6.5 United States

The US tax amnesty closed its doors to new entrants on 15 April 2003, with reports indicating that over 1,200 taxpayers had provided information about offshore bank accounts and credit cards, as well as those promoting such schemes, with the IRS expecting to generate over $100 million as well as identifying a number of individuals or entities promoting such schemes. Unlike the Italian amnesty, US citizens would not enjoy a tax holiday, but be liable to back taxes together with interest and also a flat 20% charge. US individuals who have used offshore schemes to mitigate tax were given three months to report and pay up or face fines and criminal charges.

5.7 EXIT TAX

5.7.1 Exit tax on individuals

Individuals resident in high-tax countries may view with dismay the above plethora of tax laws preventing accumulation of tax-free income and gains. Even with the availability of tax amnesties, they may decide that enough is enough. However, they may find additional obstacles in their way when considering leaving their country of residence.

An exit tax may be based on the emigration by individuals from that country to another, primarily on the deemed sale of assets immediately prior to departure. Exit taxes are certainly a weapon in the arsenal of those jurisdictions that have such provisions. However, following the ruling of the European Court of Justice in respect of France and discussed below, how much longer these will be sustained legally in the EU remains to be seen. The decision raised concerns in many countries, as it seems that it will not be limited to individuals but will also apply to companies, which many believe will initiate the departure of companies from jurisdictions such as the UK. Such companies are currently locked in by the imposition of exit taxes which would be levied should they wish to leave.

Denmark

Individuals emigrating from Denmark are subject to an exit tax on the deemed sale of assets immediately prior to departure. New provisions mean that all assets will be subject to departure tax, rather than just those held for three years of more. Individuals will be subject to the tax in circumstances where they have been subject to tax in Denmark for at least five of the ten years prior to emigration.

France

In France the exit tax, effective as from 1 January 1999, applies to individuals who transfer their domicile abroad and is calculated on the capital gains recorded at the exit point on substantial participations (i.e. shares representing more than 25% of the right to dividends distribution). The exit tax applies to individual taxpayers who have been resident in France for at least six years during the ten preceding years. In this case they are deemed to have realised the latent capital gains on their substantial participations in French and foreign companies at the time of emigration.

However, the European Court of Justice stated recently that the French exit tax on hidden capital gains, as provided by Article 167 *bis* of the French Tax Code, contravenes the principle of free establishment.[32] As a consequence, this regime should no longer apply to French residents leaving their country for another member state of the EU (and possibly to other countries such as Switzerland, an issue which remains pending).

Ireland

New anti-avoidance legislation, introduced by the 2003 budget, may also be considered a form of exit tax. The legislation is aimed at catching individuals leaving Ireland to escape from capital gains tax on the sale of shares in a company in which the individual owns 5% or more of the shares, or where the individual's holding is worth more than €500,000. Under existing rules, individuals ceasing residence in Ireland remain liable to capital gains tax on the sale of assets such as those in question for three years. The rules affect individuals who have been non-resident in Ireland for a period of at least three years, but less than five years. Under the rules the taxpayer is deemed to have disposed of the shares and reacquired them prior to their departure.

Israel

Israel has introduced an exit tax, beginning in 2003. The provisions deem there to be a sale of capital assets by individuals ceasing to be resident in Israel immediately prior to departure. However, the provisions, similar to those in force in Denmark, provide that tax payable is deferred until the actual disposal of the assets in question. Tax is only due on the portion of the gain attributed to the period prior to the deemed disposal/departure from Israel and is levied at the rate of 25%.

United States

As mentioned earlier,[33] a US citizen who gives up his citizenship for the principal purpose of avoiding US tax would continue for a period of ten years to be taxed in the same manner as previously. The rules also apply to long-term resident aliens. Individuals will be regarded as having such a motive in circumstances where their income over the past five years has averaged more than $124,000, or their net worth is equal to or greater than $2 million.

32. ECJ, 11 March 2004, C-9/02, *Hugues de Lasteyrie du Saillant.*
33. In §5.1.1.

5.7.2 Exit tax on companies

United Kingdom

The UK effectively imposes exit taxes on companies but not individuals.[34] In respect of individuals leaving the UK, any gains made from the disposal of assets during a period of non-residence and non-ordinarily residence will be subject to capital gains tax in the UK if that individual subsequently returns to the UK within a period of five years from departure.[35]

United States

'Corporate inversions' have been topical in the US for a number of years. In its simplest form an 'inversion' is the process by which a new company established in another country acquires an existing US company through asset or share purchase. In essence, the legal location of the parent company changes from the US to another country. The restructuring allows the company to take advantage of certain laws in that country. Typical advantages that draw US companies to incorporate elsewhere include lower tax rates, more accommodating corporate governance rules and more flexible banking laws. Bermuda is one of the most popular destinations for corporate inversions for several reasons. The primary factor is that Bermuda does not have a corporate income, profit or dividend tax and does not tax capital gains.

A short-term result of a corporate inversion is an increase in federal tax collections from the capital gains realised in the hands of the selling shareholders upon completion of the initial transaction. This factor and a requirement on companies to inform the Internal Revenue Service and the companies' shareholders when they move headquarters offshore or are acquired by foreign companies, combine to form what is essentially an exit tax.

34. Note, however, an exit tax on trusts migrating from the UK under Section 80 TCGA 1992, where trustees are deemed to have disposed of and immediately reacquired all the settled property at its market value. The gains resulting from the deemed disposal accrue to the UK trustees.
35. Section 10A TCGA 1992.

[V.] CASE STUDY 5

It is clear that, under certain circumstances, the fact that income remains offshore is not always relevant to the question of whether such income will be taxed domestically. When some of these principles are applied to the activities of the Filipes, it would be useful to refer to:

(a) Papa Filipe's income in Liechtenstein from the Filipe Foundation (Diagram 2);
(b) Giuliano's tax liability in respect of Giuliano Trust income and gains (Diagram 4);
(c) determining whether Giuliano is a tax resident of France or the UK (Diagram 7);
(d) Lucca BV as a Dutch holding company of the Lucca Software subsidiaries (Diagram 4);
(e) Paolo's cash flow situation resulting from Opus AG collecting royalties (Diagram 8);
(f) Determining Renata's tax residence (Diagram 9).

Diagram 2

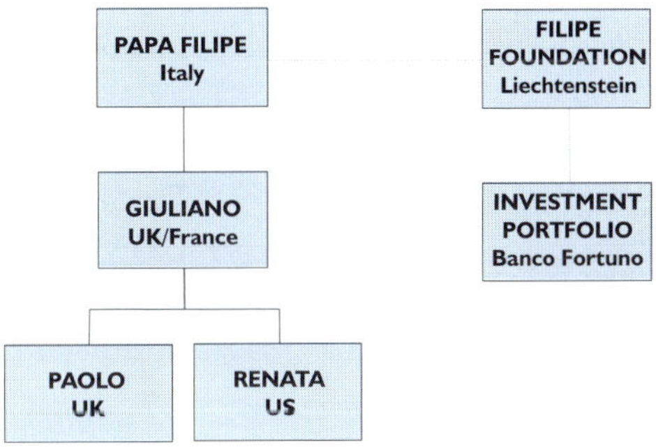

Diagram 4

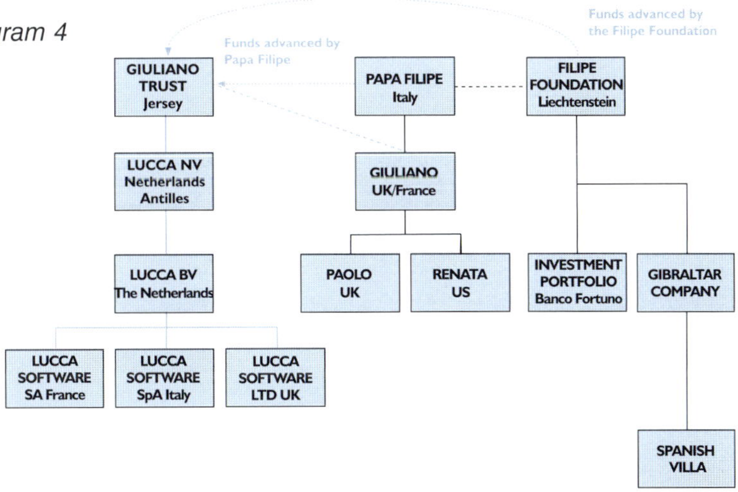

Diagram 7

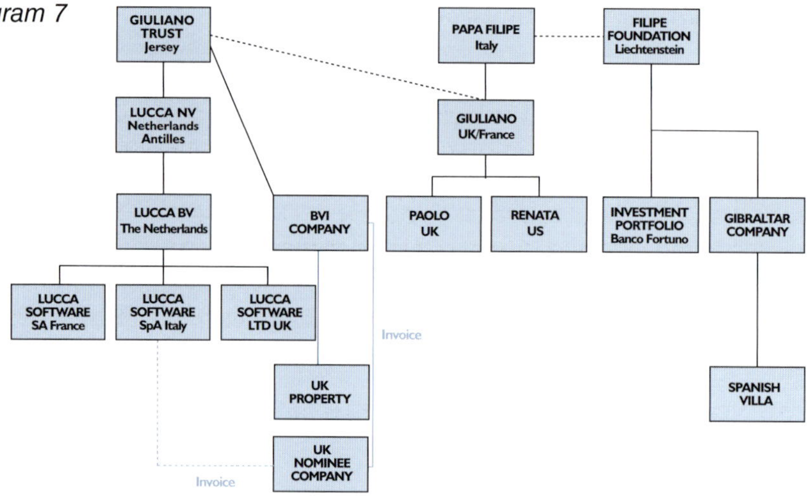

Diagram 8

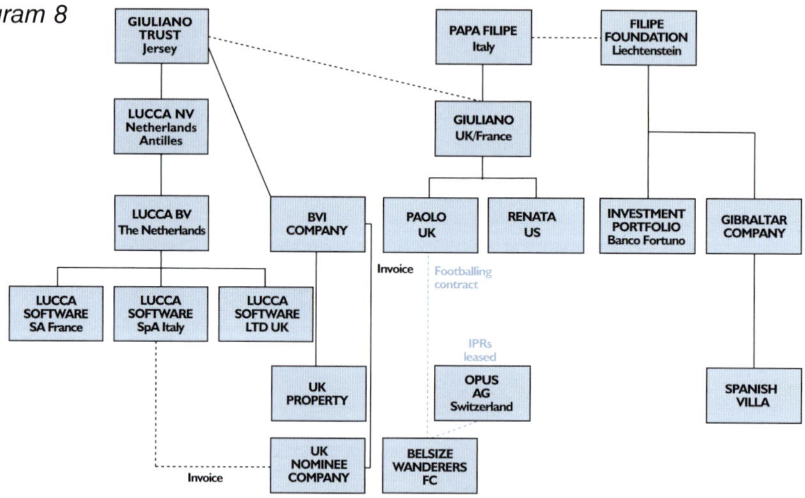

Diagram 9

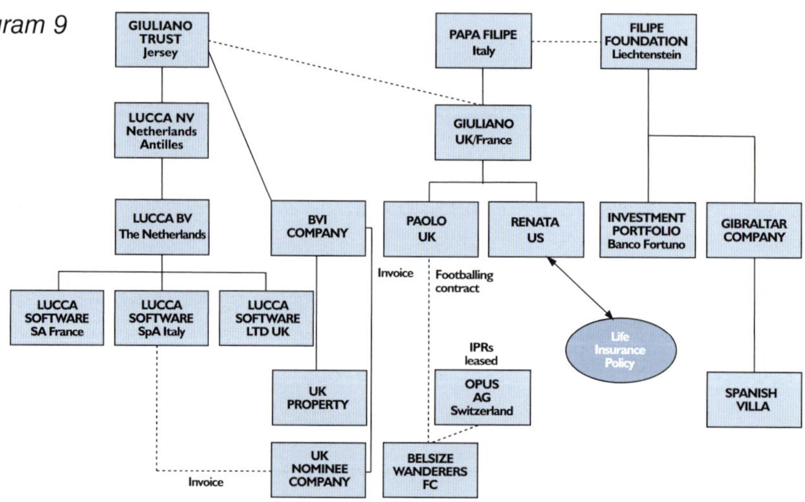

[V.a] Papa Filipe's income from Filipe Foundation

Although Maurice Brightman, the family's tax planning adviser, was not familiar with the exact details of CFC-like legislation in Italy, he cautioned Papa that even if the income in Liechtenstein were not included in his annual Italian income tax return, the Italian tax authorities might insist on current inclusion based on their version of the CFC rules. He based his opinion on the facts that Papa essentially controls the foundation and is planning to keep most of the income offshore (i.e. in Liechtenstein, a low-tax jurisdiction) to avoid Italian tax, and the fact that income that Papa receives from Switzerland into the foundation is essentially passive income, namely dividends. Maurice might have been interested in the Italian tax amnesty and would have brought this to Papa's attention, particularly since the provisions of the amnesty would have given confidentiality without full disclosure of Papa's identity.

[V.b] Giuliano's and Renata's tax residence

Whether a person is a resident of a country is important in determining whether he or she is liable to tax in the country. It has been seen that countries apply different tests to determine whether an individual is resident or not.

[i.] Giuliano

Giuliano spends much of his time in France while looking after Lucca Software SA and in fact had partially moved to Paris, renting a flat overlooking the Rive Droite for a three-year rolling period. He also maintained the property in London owned by the BVI company in order to ensure (or so he had hoped) that he remained a tax resident of the UK.

The French tax authorities would obviously be keen to prove that Giuliano is actually a tax resident of France. The French tax authorities may use the following arguments to prove their position, based on some of the tests that are used in this country to determine residence:

(a) Giuliano has moved to France, since he is renting a flat in Paris and spends much of his time there. The French tax authorities will therefore no doubt argue that the flat in Paris has essentially become his *principal abode* (*lieu du séjour principal*) and under the test of the same name, Giuliano has become a tax resident of France;

(b) the French might also try to argue that Giuliano's professional activities take place mostly in France – he is partially being paid by the French subsidiary and also spends most of his time in France;

(c) the French will possibly also try to argue that under the *economic interests* test Giuliano has become a tax resident of France. Maurice explained to

Giuliano that since he is spending much of his time in France and the greatest portion of his salary is derived from the work that he is doing for Lucca Software SA, Giuliano could easily be caught under this test as being a tax resident of France.

Giuliano was not at all pleased when he learned that he might be found to be a resident of France – individuals who are 'fiscal residents' of France are taxed on their worldwide income. This means that the French tax authorities would be interested in taxing not only the employment income earned from his work done for the Lucca subsidiaries, but also any income and gains he realises through the Giuliano Trust.

However, the UK Inland Revenue might want to argue that Giuliano is actually a tax resident of the UK, an argument based particularly on the number of days spent in the country. Since he has been in the UK for, on average, three months or more in the past four years and his visits to the UK have become part of his normal lifestyle, he will become a tax resident of the UK at the start of the fifth year.

In this case, Maurice had to advise Giuliano which country has the dominant taxing rights according to the provisions of the French/United Kingdom double tax treaty.[36] He pointed out that this only clarifies the position as regards items of income and capital covered within the double tax treaty, and therefore does not cover capital assets for inheritance tax purposes (where France and the UK in fact have a separate inheritance double tax treaty which has substantially similar provisions regarding residence as the income tax treaty). The 'tie-breaker' clause of the double tax treaty has subsidiary tests, which, in order of their importance, start with where Giuliano has a permanent home available for his use. The flat rented in Paris is a permanent home, despite a three-year rental period only, and the house in the UK is also a permanent home, despite the fact that it is not owned by Giuliano personally but by the BVI company.

The next test is where Giuliano has his centre of vital interests. This is not clearly France as opposed to the UK, because he also has substantial economic activities in the UK and his son Paolo is resident in the UK.

The third test is the test that Maurice described as most appropriate for the circumstances, which is Giuliano's habitual abode. This refers to the country where Giuliano spends most of his time, and Maurice advised Giuliano that he should spend more time in the UK than in France in order to be able to demonstrate a dominance of UK tax residence (which is more favourable in the case of Giuliano) than French tax residence.

36. See the 'tie-breaker' clause of Article 4 OECD Model Treaty under §4.3.1.

If habitual abode cannot be determined, the next test is where Giuliano is a national, but as an Italian he is neither national of the UK nor of France, and therefore it would remain with the competent authorities of France and the UK to determine his residence status (for the purposes of the treaty), if no other determination can take place. Maurice winced at this possibility, since a determination by such august authorities could take many years and ultimately not benefit Giuliano. Maurice therefore suggested that Giuliano terminate his rental agreement on the Rive Droite flat in Paris and, if he wants to stay there and can convince his landlord to play ball, he enters into a short-term annual tenancy. In this way, the Paris flat cannot be construed as permanent accommodation. He then has to consider restructuring his ownership of the house in London by acquiring it from the BVI company, something Maurice considers desirable in any event to avoid the UK 'benefit in kind'[37] legislation. Thus Giuliano would pass the first test of the 'tie-breaker' clause, namely that he has a permanent home in the UK and not in France, denying the French authorities taxing rights over his income and capital.

[ii.] Renata

The world-famous model Renata spends much of her time globetrotting. However, she manages to stay put in the US for three months a year and stays with her mother in Italy for the same amount of time. The question now arises of where Renata would be resident for tax purposes.

The Italian tax authorities might argue that since Renata has her habitual abode in Italy, this is the country of her residence. They may base their argument on the following: Renata's mother still lives in Italy on a continuous basis, her mother's house being Renata's usual abode in between her trips. This, according to the Italian tax authorities, shows that Renata regards Italy as her home country, which, among all the other benefits connected with being Italian, permits her the privilege of paying income tax in that country.

Maurice, who has a particular fondness for the intricacies of US tax law and knows it well, cautioned Renata that the US applies a cumulative presence test to determine the tax residence of visitors to the country. He advised her that it would be a good idea to keep track of the duration of her visits to the US by retaining documents such as hotel reservations and flight tickets to disprove any assertion by the IRS that she spent the number of days in the US required to meet the cumulative presence test. Thus once she spends 31 days in any tax year in the US, provided that the number of days in that calendar year, plus one-third of the days of the preceding year, and one-sixth of the days in the pre-preceding year, did not amount to more than 183 days in total, she would not be considered a US tax resident. Maurice explained that according to entries in

37. See §3.3.1

her passport, she had spent 84 days in the US 3 years ago, 120 days 2 years ago and 126 days 1 year ago. According to Maurice's calculations, this meant that her cumulative presence last year was 14 + 40 + 126 = 180 days. So she had just escaped being considered US tax resident last year. But this year, she is already carrying forward 20 + 42 days, so she only has 120 more days in the US this year before being considered US resident. If Renata intends to avoid Italian tax on the basis that she is not really present in Italy to the degree of frequency required for Italian tax residence purposes, she cannot rely on the 'tie-breaker' clause of the Italian/US double tax treaty. Accordingly, Maurice's advice is to ensure she is in the US for less than 120 days this year.

[V.c] Lucca BV and Lucca Software subsidiaries[38]

Lucca BV was incorporated in the Netherlands to hold the three Lucca Software subsidiaries in France, Italy and the UK, respectively. In the Netherlands the place of incorporation is generally decisive to determine residence, thus Lucca BV would be a Dutch tax resident company.

Maurice reminded Giuliano that even though Dutch holding companies are indeed tried and tested, the legal circumstances surrounding these entities have been changing to some extent. Under some amount of pressure from its EU partners, the Netherlands has increased the cost of dividend distributions through to Netherlands Antilles parent companies from a zero rate to an effective 8.3%.[39] Also, EU countries are increasingly aware of Dutch entities in international tax structures. Thus, the German tax authorities, for example, are generally sceptical about the commercial substance of Dutch recipients of interest, royalties[40] or dividends, and disallow withholding tax exemptions unless the company can prove it has sufficient substance (e.g. an office independent from any trust company managing its affairs, directors who have an understanding of the company's business and employees who administer the affairs of the Dutch company). The Dutch Ministry of Finance has also set out requirements to reflect substance in Dutch companies.[41] Consequently, Giuliano's suggestion of becoming a director of the Dutch company Lucca BV and of visiting Amsterdam on regular occasions to attend board meetings is welcomed by Maurice, who nevertheless remained suspicious of his non-fiscal motives for doing so!

---

38. This aspect has already been referred to briefly in [§III.d].
39. Based on a proposed amendment of the Dutch Antilles' profits tax regulations, a 0% dividend withholding tax on participation distributions from the Netherlands to the Netherlands Antilles may be reintroduced as from 1 January 2006.
40. Although the EU Interest and Royalty Directive exempts in principle from withholding tax payments of interest and royalties between associated companies in different member states, Article 5 of the Directive leaves member states the discretion to disallow application of the Directive in cases of tax avoidance or abuse.
41. Compare §6.3.4.

[V.d] Paolo's cash in Opus AG

Instead of Paolo paying UK tax on the royalties for merchandising rights related to the No. 11 shirt, Opus AG licensed Paolo's image rights and accumulated the royalties. The plan was that the company would pay a substantial premium into an offshore pension plan to provide for Paolo's retirement from football.

Provided that Paolo has no ownership rights over Opus AG, and there is commercial justification for the contracts entered into by Opus, the plan has a lot of merit, particularly bearing in mind the limited career of professional footballers. However, should Paolo wish to enjoy the benefit of the royalty income by way of salary from Opus AG, he will have to consider whether UK tax will be levied. On the basis that the salary is for non-UK services (promoting the No. 11 shirt back in Italy, for example) and it is not remitted to the UK, then as a non-domiciled individual, Paolo is one of the fortunate few who can avoid UK tax on such income. However, if Paolo needs the cash in the UK, for example, and the amount is remitted (or constructively remitted by way of credit card expenditure) to the UK, UK tax will be chargeable.

For a spendthrift like Paolo this could create a serious dilemma – there is, after all, a limited amount he can do with the £50,000 a week he is being paid by Belsize Wanderers FC – and a Ferrari 355 Spider doesn't come cheap these days.

[V.e] Conclusion

The question asked at the beginning of this chapter was whether domestic taxation could be mitigated through use of offshore structures. The answer to this question is undoubtedly 'yes'. However, the use of offshore structures now relies upon the doctrine of substance over form to a greater extent than ever before. So too is the importance of double tax treaties and their use (rather than abuse) if effective planning is to be undertaken. While tax systems have become more complex and sophisticated, it is certainly the case that domestic exemptions such as taper relief and business property relief for capital gains and inheritance tax respectively in the UK, for example, may provide excellent 'Revenue-approved' tax mitigation possibilities without the associated cost, risk or uncertainty that some offshore planning carries.

Chapter 6
Is the Structure Artificial?

It is not only specific foreign entities that may be disregarded in tax planning structures, but also the entire structure itself, on the basis that it has no commercial merit. Thus the transactions underlying the structure may be carefully investigated, and if there is an element of artificiality to the transactions, this may be regarded as a legal fraud on the tax administration. However, the mere fact that low-tax jurisdictions are involved in international tax structures does not prove the artificiality of the arrangements and, as has already been mentioned, taxpayers certainly have the right to minimise their tax liabilities in accordance with legally accepted doctrines. Nevertheless, unless there is significant commerciality in the arrangements, their effect may be negated by general anti-avoidance regulations. Within this context, this chapter focuses on sham transactions and tax schemes, substance over form and similar concepts.

6.1 SHAM TRANSACTIONS

6.1.1 Sham – meaning of the term

A 'sham' was described in *Snook v. London and West Riding Investments Ltd*[1] as:

> *... acts done or documents executed by the parties to the 'sham' which are intended by them to give to third parties or to the court the appearance of*

1. [1967] 1 All ER 518.

creating between the parties legal rights or obligations different from the actual legal rights and obligations (if any) which the parties intend to create.

Lord Templeman referred to the sham in *CIR v. Challenge Corporate Ltd*[2] as 'a transaction constructed to create a false impression in the eyes of the tax authority'.

6.1.2 Features and examples of a sham

The word 'sham' is widely used outside tax matters but it is particularly common in the tax planning profession and could be defined as a transaction that is purported to have taken place but which is not intended to have effect by the parties concerned.[3]

A familiar example of sham transactions is what is known as invoicing operations,[4] which used to be very common but which have become less so as anti-avoidance legislation in each country has strengthened. Invoicing operations exist where a specially formed company located in a low-tax regime earns an artificial profit as a result of pricing arrangements between related parties. Thus, a French company selling goods to a German company for €10 per unit at a profit of €5 per unit may attempt to circumvent French tax by forming a Swiss domiciliary company, for example, to buy the goods from the French company at €6 per unit, and earn the additional €4 per unit profit itself which will then be subject to a reduced rate of tax.

Another example of a sham may arise where there is a tax advantage if an asset is transferred from one person to another person. Specific provisions aside, it may be that there is an advantage for the transferee, as against the transferor, holding the asset. In such a case, the two people may agree to go through whatever legal formalities are required to effect a transfer, but otherwise to act as if the asset continued to be held by the original owner. However, the relevant tax authority may assert that the transfer was a sham, in that the parties to the transfer in reality intended the ownership of the asset to remain with the transferor, despite the outward appearance of the asset having been transferred to the transferee.

An element of deceit must be present before a sham transaction can be ascertained. If, however, the legal rights and obligations that are purported to have been created have, in fact, been created (and documentation will clearly be useful to show this), it will be difficult for the relevant tax authority to prove a sham.

2. (1986) 8 NZTC 5,219.
3. *Newstead v. Frost* (1980) 53 TC 525.
4. This has already been explored in various instances in previous chapters in respect of the UK nominee company rendering invoices to Lucca Software SpA on behalf of the BVI company in order to extract profits out of Italy.

6.1.3 Cases involving sham transactions

Sham transactions and structures are fragile and, although they may succeed, this success is often based upon the fact that they escape detection as opposed to standing up to investigation on their own merits. Before discussing the methods by which various countries attack tax avoidance schemes which rest on the formation of entities which have no real individual identity, or transactions which have no commercial foundation, it is useful to give some examples of sham structures and transactions which have been brought before courts of various countries. The following well-known cases illustrate the extent to which some tax avoidance schemes rely on completely artificial structures.

The Netherlands

In a Supreme Court case published in BNB 1974/2, a company was formed in the Netherlands purely for tax avoidance reasons. The case involved a Dutch holding company specifically formed by private investors in order to obtain exemption from tax on dividend income received from foreign subsidiaries. Prior to the formation of that company, the private investors were fully taxed on foreign dividend income but, in view of the Dutch qualifying participation privilege, which under certain conditions at that time allowed foreign dividend income receivable by a Dutch company to be tax exempt in the Netherlands, they decided to form a Dutch company for tax avoidance purposes. The Supreme Court decided that the exemption should not be given because the Dutch company did not carry on any business. At the time, this decision caused a temporary panic among tax consultants who had been using Dutch holding companies to reduce the overall tax burden of their international clients, but the Minister of Finance issued a resolution[5] stating that a Dutch holding company, performing an essential function within a group, such as management or provision of financial services, would still be able to obtain exemption in respect of income from a qualifying participation.

The issue of denying tax benefits was not a topic of discussion in later cases as the resolution provided clear benchmarks. There have been discussions, however, about the characterisation of debts. In a long list of decisions an approach was developed regarding hybrid loans and profit-sharing loans (participation loans). Supreme Court decisions in this respect have found their way into codification, now Article 10 of the Corporate Income Tax Act 1969. As far as uncollectable receivables and the principle of substance over form[6] are concerned, the Supreme Court decision of 27 January 1988[7] is still valid when characterising debts.

5. *BNB* 1975/11.
6. See also §6.3.4.
7. *BNB* 1988/217.

United Kingdom

The decision in the case of *Ramsay*,[8] followed by a number of other cases[9] in which the provisions have been refined, has had a profound effect on the treatment of 'artificial transactions'. The effect of *Ramsay* was that tax avoidance schemes should be disregarded as artificial and fiscally ineffective if the following four major principles apply:

(a) the scheme has no commercial justification insofar as there is no prospect of the taxpayer making a profit;

(b) the transactions are self-cancelling, designed to make neither gain nor loss, and the taxpayer would not enter into the transactions if a loss could be incurred;

(c) the transactions are steps in a series which returns the taxpayer to the same position from where he started, other than tax benefits sought;[10] and

(d) the money required for the transactions is advanced solely for the purposes of the scheme and is returned on completion of the scheme.

To summarise, *Ramsay* outlined that, in circumstances where a series of transactions were entered into to avoid tax, the courts are allowed to look at the overall result of the individual transactions, and not only at each transaction in isolation, to determine whether a sham transaction was entered into.

A subsequent case, the *Burmah Oil* case[11] went even further than *Ramsay,* stating that it is not necessary for the funds in (d) above to be advanced for the purposes of the scheme, and confirmed that the precedent established by the *Ramsay* case would hold even for genuine commercial transactions if their motive was to achieve a tax benefit, and no real loss was incurred.

The next case to appear before the House of Lords was *Furniss v. Dawson*,[12] where the Lords ruled that schemes which included a tax avoidance motive can be ignored by the courts even if in fact they are commercially justifiable. In the *Furniss* case, the scheme adopted resulted in enduring legal consequences as opposed to a circular transaction bringing a taxpayer back to his initial stance, and no artificial loss was created, contrary to the facts in the *Ramsay* case.

---

8. *W.T. Ramsay Ltd v. IRC* [1981] STC 174.
9. E.g. *Inland Revenue Commissioners v. Scottish Provident Institution* [2004] UKHL 52; [2005] STC 52, confirming the *Ramsay* principle.
10. Most recently addressed in *Barclays Mercantile Business Finance Ltd v. Mawson (HM Inspector of Taxes)* [2004] UKHL 51; [2005] STC 1.
11. *IRC v. Burmah Oil Ltd* [1982] STC 30.
12. [1984] STC 153.

United States

In *Ingemar Johansson v. USA*,[13] Johansson, had formed a Swiss corporation, Scanart SA, to hire him out and receive fee income from his boxing. When Johansson went to the United States to fight Floyd Patterson, Scanart SA, supposedly an entity independent from Johansson, signed the contract. According to the double tax treaty between the US and Switzerland, Scanart SA, which did not have a permanent establishment in the US in any form, could receive the fight income free of all US taxes, even though the income was US-source. Johansson also claimed that he was a Swiss resident even though the great majority of his time had been spent in the US and Sweden during the period under review. The IRS did not agree; it decided to attend the fight and seized the gate receipts under what is known in the US as a jeopardy assessment,[14] thus forcing Scanart SA to go to court to recover the money they considered due to them. It was obvious that, since Scanart SA had no offices or personnel in Switzerland and, in fact, no real identity apart from Johansson, it had been formed specifically to abuse the Switzerland/US tax treaty. The appeal judges, confirming that US tax should be paid, wound up the case in a rather sarcastic manner, noting: 'international trade will not be seriously encumbered by our refusal to grant special tax treatment to one marginally, if at all, Swiss resident, and only technically, if at all, employed by a Swiss paper corporation.'[15]

6.2 TAX SCHEMES

The definition of a tax 'scheme' may vary from country to country. However, it generally means any agreement, whether express or implied and whether legally enforceable or not.

The role of artificial entities and their controllers may call for particular consideration. Where a company is concerned, the company itself will probably be a party to the scheme, its purpose being determined by the collective purpose of its directors or, sometimes, shareholders. However, the directors individually may also be parties, if not otherwise than simply as a result of their involvement as directors. A somewhat similar question may arise in relation to

13. 64-2 USTC 9743.
14. IRC, Section 6861.
15. The *Johansson* case remains good law, and has been followed in *Ross Glove Co. v. Commissioner*, 60 T.C. 569, (T.C. 1973) and *Robinson v. Commissioner*, 44 T.C. 20 (T.C. 1965). The case was also cited in *Del Commer. Properties, Inc. v. Commissioner,* T.C. Memo 1999-411 (T.C. 1999), which was affirmed on appeal by *Del Commer. Properties, Inc. v. Commissioner*, 251 F.3d 210 (D.C. Cir. 2001). In the latter case the Appeal Court affirmed the Tax Court's decision that withholding tax was due in the US on loan payments made to a Canadian affiliate via a Dutch company. The Court found, applying the step-transaction doctrine that the Dutch company was interposed only to benefit from the withholding tax exemption on interest under the Netherlands/US tax treaty.

advisers, particularly when the client of the adviser is relatively unsophisticated and relies heavily on the skill and comprehension of the adviser. In such circumstances, the adviser may well be a party to the scheme.

United Kingdom

Where a scheme consists of a series of steps, it is not normally permissible to isolate particular steps and classify any one of them as a scheme. The whole series of steps must be considered as was demonstrated in the cases of *Peabody*[16] and *Spotless*.[17] However, part of a scheme may be identified as a scheme in itself but only if the circumstances constituting that 'sub-scheme' are capable of standing on their own without being robbed of all practical meaning (*Peabody*).

Schemes have been the centre of a very public debate in the UK between the government and the tax profession.[18] The government's solid desire to stamp out all unacceptable tax avoidance led to the introduction of regulations compelling tax advisers to disclose details of tax schemes that meet certain criteria.[19] These initially include 'Arrangements connected with employment', including payments to trustees (for example an employee benefit trust), the making or releasing of loans, and arrangements involving securities and 'associated rights'. The Regulations are aimed at any arrangements that reduce or defer a tax charge and catch employers, employees and 'any other person' who may be expected to benefit by virtue of another's employment. If a 'scheme' is caught by the Regulations it will be necessary for the adviser to inform HMRC within five days of either him making a notifiable proposal available for implementation or first becoming aware of any transaction forming part of notifiable arrangements. Additionally, arrangements in relation to 'Financial Products' are also caught; again these are widely defined to include loans, shares, derivative contracts and so on. The adviser must provide HMRC with details of the scheme, including an explanation as to how each element is structured and how the tax advantage could be obtained. On receipt of the scheme details, HMRC issue the promoter, i.e. tax adviser, with a reference number. Any client of the adviser who has made use of the scheme must disclose the relevant reference number on their tax return. The introduction of these regulations has caused a debate between accountants and lawyers in respect of professional privilege that lawyers enjoy and which they claim overrides the regulations. To overcome this obstacle, it is the client who must disclose the use of the scheme to HMRC and not the adviser! While the

16. 94 ATC 4663.
17. 93 ATC 4397; 95 ATC 4775.
18. This topic has been touched upon in §1.2.1.
19. Statutory Instrument: Tax Avoidance Schemes (Prescribed Descriptions of Arrangements) Regulations 2004.

regulations are undoubtedly draconian and perhaps a 'step too far' for many, the way in which they were introduced means that there is a certain element of ambiguity that has yet to be tested.

6.3 SUBSTANCE OVER FORM, *FRAUS LEGIS* AND *ABUS DE DROITS*

Like much anti-avoidance legislation, 'substance over form' is now the mantra of tax advisers throughout the world, regardless of whether the jurisdiction in which they operate actually imposes a statutory 'abuse of forms' concept or not. The concepts of *fraus legis* and *abus de droits*, applied in many continental European countries, are essentially a type of substance over form doctrine. Aspects of these doctrines as applied within certain jurisdictions are outlined below.

6.3.1 Belgium

Article 344 of the Income Tax Code (as amended by the Law of 22 July 1993) requires the taxpayer to prove that a tax structure meets his legitimate financial and economic needs, which may include tax benefits but which must not consist solely of such benefits. Advance rulings may be obtained where there is doubt as to the legitimacy of the taxpayer's economic needs.

6.3.2 France

French law recognises the principle of the abuse of rights (*abus de droits*) whereby the true nature or aim of a transaction is disguised in order to avoid altogether or mitigate tax which would have been due if the true nature of the transaction had been shown by the parties. As with other sham transactions and structures in many other European countries, the created form is disregarded for tax purposes and the original form only is considered. This concept, written into the Book of Fiscal Procedures,[20] therefore supports a growing awareness by tax administrations and courts that it is the substance rather than the form of a transaction or structure that is important.

6.3.3 Germany

The concept of abuse of legal forms has also been in existence in Germany for many years, and has been further developed by tax case law. Section 6 of the Steueranpassungsgesetz prevents the reduction or evasion of a person's tax liability by an abuse of forms and legal structures provided by civil law, that is a legal disguise of which the primary *raison d'être* is to avoid tax. Section 42 of the Abgabenordnung 1977, which follows Section 6(1), will disregard the activities of foreign-base companies or foreign trusts which have been created

20. *Livre des Procédures Fiscales*, Article L.64.

for no substantial economic or commercial purpose other than tax avoidance, and which cannot be construed as independent of German beneficial owners.

This general anti-avoidance provision thus attacks letter-box companies and invoicing operations, but genuine foreign companies located in a low-tax regime will not be affected, even if one of the principal reasons for their formation is the reduction of taxes. If an abuse is found to exist, the income or capital which, as a result of the structure, escaped German tax or reduced the level of tax, will then be reallocated to the avoiding taxpayer and full German tax levied accordingly.

6.3.4 The Netherlands

The Netherlands adopts the general approach common to other continental countries. For example, the Dutch Income Tax Law that applies to corporations provides that only those benefits which are derived from the business itself constitute a taxable profit. Hidden dividend distributions or capital contributions are eliminated when arriving at the taxable amount.[21] If a transaction implies a hidden dividend distribution or capital contribution, as would be the case in a transaction carried out between related parties which was not at full market value, the transaction will be ignored for tax purposes and profits restored to the level they would otherwise have been. Dutch courts may rely on this provision (and previous case law) when investigating inter-company pricing policies; it is a generally accepted principle that such transactions must be comparable with transactions between independent parties.

Another example of the general nature of Dutch anti-avoidance legislation is found in Article 31 *Algemene Wet inzake Rijksbelastingen*. This provision applies to all situations where a taxpayer uses artificial legal constructions for the purpose of tax savings, and states that the transaction or structure should be ignored and that tax should be payable as if the artificial transaction had never been implemented. Authorisation from the Ministry of Finance has to be obtained before the tax authorities can invoke Article 31 and the Dutch tax administration has now ceased issuing proceedings under Article 31, relying more on the use of the *fraus legis* provisions.

Dutch courts have established the principle of *fraus legis*, which is similar to the principle of the correct imposition of tax where reliance is placed on an abuse of legal form. This is, however, wider than the principle of correct imposition of tax, since it is not restricted to direct tax only, and permits the tax administration to substitute a separate (normal) transaction in place of the transaction entered into for the purposes of assessing tax liabilities.

Certain aspects of Dutch law have been amended on a specific basis. For

21. Article 3.2, Income Tax Act 2001.

example, Dutch ruling practices have been amended for intermediary finance and royalty companies in measures taking effect from April 2001.[22] The changes are aimed mainly at conduit companies, with the goal of preventing the abuse of the Dutch tax system by publishing a list of 'substance' requirements, which a company must meet to qualify for the advance ruling. The finance and royalty companies must have real substance, local management and control, and a physical presence.

The Minister of Finance has set out the following requirements in respect of substance, which may be compared to the management and control criteria reviewed before:[23]

(a) at least one of the statutory directors with the power to make decisions should be resident in the Netherlands;

(b) the managing directors should have the skills and expertise required to run the business;

(c) the company must have the necessary staff needed to allow it to operate;

(d) the most important management decisions must be taken in the Netherlands;

(e) the main bank account of the company must be situated in the Netherlands;

(f) the company administration must be performed in the Netherlands;

(g) the company must have met its filing obligations and paid any tax due;

(h) the company must be regarded as resident in the Netherlands and must not be deemed resident anywhere else;

(i) the equity of the company must be consistent with the activities it performs.

6.3.5 United Kingdom

Although the UK does not have statutory provisions similar to the abuse of

22. Note that the Dutch State Secretary of Finance published Decree DGB2004/1337M in August 2004 regarding situations where no advance tax ruling will be issued. In general, rulings will not be issued in circumstances where such ruling would be incompatible with good faith in respect of Dutch tax treaty partners, in particular where the interest of a treaty partner is likely to be harmed. An exception to this may occur where the treaty partner is fully aware of all details of a particular structure. In all events, no ruling will be issued in circumstances where the applicants are involved in money laundering, corruption, etc.
23. In §5.1.2.

legal forms concept in Germany and in other continental European countries, it has been veering more towards the concept of substance taking precedence over form when interpreting UK tax law. This trend primarily started with two cases concerning assessments to capital gains tax against which the taxpayers wished to offset with taxable losses pre-arranged through tax avoidance schemes – the *Ramsay* decision[24] and *Eilbeck v. Rawling.*[25]

The decisions of *Bayliss v. Gregory*,[26] *IRC v. Bowater Property Developments Limited*,[27] and particularly *Craven v. White,*[28] have shown that the courts are taking the view that if a series of transactions are be entered into which were preordained in order to produce the required result, and the transactions had no other purpose than tax avoidance, and that it was reasonably certain that the events would take place as planned so that intermediate transactions relied totally on the preceding and succeeding transactions, then the form should be disregarded if the preordained series of events did actually take place. All of the above factors must apply to any given set of circumstances to permit a court to link the transactions together to arrive at a single united whole to which the tax implications thereof could be applied.

The court rejected the Inland Revenue's contention in *Shepherd v. Lyntress* Ltd[29] that the previous tax losses of Lyntress should not be set off by carry-forward against profits subsequently achieved by virtue of a transfer of assets into Lyntress from its new parent company. Although such transfer was followed by a sale, which it was known would result in substantial gains, the transactions must be considered separate and not part of a composite whole.

The question of whether treaty shopping is an abuse of the substance over form doctrine has been raised in cases such as *Padmore v. IRC*[30] and *Strathalmond v. IRC*,[31] and the object and purpose of the relevant treaties seem to have been ignored by the courts. However, continental case law and practice have already had a considerable influence on the UK; there is definitely a trend away from purely literal interpretation of treaties towards looking at the substance itself of particular transactions.

In the UK the courts are usually concerned to reconcile form and substance. These can be two very separate issues and care must be taken so as to

24. Refer to §6.1.3.
25. [1981] STC 174.
26. HL 1988, 62 TC 1.
27. HL 1988, STC 476.
28. HL 1988, 62 TC 1.
29. ChD 1989, 62 TC 495.
30. [1989] STC 493.
31. (1972) 48 TC 537.

discover what the form of a transaction is and what the substance is. In *IR Comrs v. Adam*[32] Lord Clyde stated that:

> *A great deal has been said about form and substance. I think that ... both form and substance must be considered; because the form of the transaction by which [Adam] acquired the right ... may bear very materially on the question of the capital or revenue character of the outlay made to acquire it.*

In conclusion, in *Ramsay*[33] Lord Wilberforce stated that:

> *Given that a document or a transaction is genuine, the court cannot go behind it to some supposed underlying substance ... This is a cardinal principle but it must not be overstated or overextended. Whilst obliging the court to accept documents or transactions, found to be genuine, as such, it does not compel the court to look at a document or a transaction in blinkers, isolated from any context to which it properly belongs. If it can be seen that a document or transaction was intended to have effect as part of* nexus *or series of transactions, or as an ingredient of a wider transaction intended as a whole, there is nothing in the doctrine to prevent it being so regarded; to do so is not to prefer form to substance, or substance to form.*

6.4 GENERAL ANTI-AVOIDANCE RULES (GAAR)

General anti-avoidance rules or GAAR could be likened to the *abus de droits* or *fraus legis* principles, the effect of which would be to catch transactions which would otherwise not be caught under existing legislation. However, the problems encountered with such measures are far-reaching: the tax commissioners are in effect given unfettered discretion in deciding whether certain transactions are tax avoidance-orientated, and to legally define tax avoidance to cover all possibilities, while exempting *bona fide* commercial transactions. GAAR as applied by selected countries is discussed below.

6.4.1 Australia

The courts of Australia have traditionally resisted the temptation to prefer substance over form. Moreover, there are no Australian statutory provisions similar to the abuse of legal forms concept found in continental legal systems. Nonetheless, Australian courts have tended in recent years to strive hard to defeat artificial schemes which, as a matter of form as opposed to substance, comply with the Income Tax Assessment Act 1936 (ITAA). The courts have done this without recourse to the shift in interpretation that has occurred in the UK. However, it should be observed that the general anti-avoidance provision

32. (1928) 14 TC 34 CS.
33. This and subsequent cases have been alluded to in §6.1.3

contained in Part IVA of ITAA requires Australian courts, when deciding whether that anti-avoidance provision applies, to consider, among many other things, the form and substance of the scheme in question.

In the case of *Spotless*,[34] the High Court stated that, had a scheme involving a Cook Islands bank not been entered into, there was a 'reasonable expectation' that tax would have been payable as a result of investing the relevant funds in Australia. The Commissioner identified the tax benefit as the actual amount of Cook Islands interest (less withholding tax) rather than the higher amount of 'notional' Australian interest. It appears that the court considered that the notional amount more accurately reflected the tax benefit but ruled that the Commissioner's quantification was sufficient for GAAR purposes.

The application of GAAR was also considered in the case of *Federal Commissioner of Taxation v. Hart*,[35] in which the High Court ruled that the GAAR provisions should have broader effect than previously thought. The case concerned a 'split loan' scheme, where a loan or credit facility, provided by a financial institution, was split into sub-accounts, one known as a 'private account' and the other as an 'investment account'. Interest due on the investment account was allowed to roll up and was then capitalised, with an equal amount taken from the private account instead. Eventually, all of the interest was due on the capital account, the benefit being that the expected greater investment returns on the capital account could be set off against increased interest deductions.

6.4.2 Canada

Canadian legislation gives the Canada Customs and Revenue Agency potentially very broad discretion to adjust taxes payable using GAAR. To determine if GAAR applies involves a three-stage test:

(a) was the transaction an avoidance transaction?

(b) was there a tax benefit, i.e. was tax was saved or deferred?

(c) if so, were the transactions undertaken primarily for a purpose other than to obtain a tax benefit, i.e. primarily for *bona fide* commercial purposes other than to obtain the tax benefit?

If there was a tax benefit and tax motivation might have been the primary motivation, then the question is asked whether the transactions result in an abuse or misuse of the provisions of the Income Tax Act 1952.

34. 96 ATC 5201.
35. [2004] HCA 26.

In determining purpose, the courts will look at the relevant facts and circumstances at the time of the transactions and not the statements of intention. Where the Minister of National Revenue, at the assessment level, decides that a transaction is an avoidance transaction, he may determine the tax consequences to any person 'as is reasonable in the circumstances' in order to deny the attendant tax benefit.

In determining such consequences once GAAR is applicable, the Minister may, without restriction:

- allow or disallow any deduction or credit;
- allocate any deduction, income or loss to any person;
- recategorise the nature of any amount or ignore any tax effects that would otherwise result from the transaction.

6.4.3 United Kingdom

The UK's HMRC have considered introducing a GAAR, similar to that adopted by Australia and Canada, the aim of which will be to catch all tax avoidance schemes. A consultation document was released on 5 October 1998, but further to this no progress seems to have been made. If this principle were applied in the UK, then the myriad anti-avoidance laws would not be required; for example, instead of having one provision dealing with artificial transactions in securities (such as dividend-stripping operations) and one with artificial transactions in land, *one general provision* would forewarn clients and tax advisers alike that an abuse of forms was unlawful. To a lesser degree there is a form of GAAR, or certainly a limited substance over form doctrine, in existence in the UK when one considers the case law decisions in *Ramsay* and *Furniss* and subsequent cases. As stated above, such cases provide grounds for the UK authorities to disregard transactions as artificial and fiscally ineffective.[36]

The UK has certainly been at the forefront of the fight against tax avoidance; however, recent case law has been of significant benefit to the taxpayer. The seminal case of the 90s, *Willoughby*,[37] illustrated that it is not tax avoidance for an individual to accept a fiscally attractive option as provided by Parliament and thus bearing the economic consequences intended by it. Tax avoidance can therefore only arise where there is no intention by government to confer the created benefit.

36. Contrasting with the comprehensive effect of GAAR are pronouncements in UK tax decisions, including that of Lord Nolan in the Willoughby case referred to in §1.1 and also that in *Ayrshire Pullman Motor Service and Ritchie v. CIR* CS 1929 14 TC 754 (UK): 'No man in this country is under the smallest obligation, moral or other, so to arrange his legal relations to his business or property as to enable the Inland Revenue to put the largest possible shovel in his stores'.
37. Compare §1.1 and the important quotation from the case.

6.5 USE OF LOW-TAX JURISDICTIONS

It has already been seen[38] that it is not improper to keep one's total tax bill as low as possible, making sure that the taxpayer keeps strictly within the law. When dealing with low-tax jurisdictions, the taxpayer and his adviser must be fully conversant with the law, particularly the anti-avoidance provisions prevalent in the tax legislation of most developed countries.

In an attempt to legitimately reduce the increasing burden of corporate and personal taxation at all levels, the international tax consultant may use legal entities recognised broadly within three basic groups of countries:

(a) the first group is generally known as 'offshore jurisdictions', that is, those countries which do not levy taxes at corporate level, but which have not been included in the world's network of double tax treaties;

(b) the second group is low-tax countries, most of which offer special concessions on certain types of income, depending upon their economic requirements and fiscal policy; with a few notable exceptions these countries also have few or no double tax treaties with other countries, and are therefore suitable for certain types of companies only;

(c) the third group is high-tax countries that normally have a very wide range of negotiated double tax treaties, conferring the benefits of these treaties on resident companies and individuals. Many of these offer incentives to manufacturing and trading organisations, particularly as regards investment and small companies' profits; there are also a few countries which offer similar concessions to those found in the other two groups.

The characteristics of offshore jurisdictions, which are frequently used in international tax planning for the jurisdictions' potential of reducing a client's tax burden when his tax affairs are suitably planned, are discussed below.

6.5.1 Characteristics of offshore jurisdictions

The complexity of tax matters in recent years has changed the basic definition of an 'offshore jurisdiction' to some extent. In the present environment, the fundamental characteristics of an offshore jurisdiction might be defined as follows:

(a) there must be a virtual absence of corporate taxation on income and capital, or if resident companies are subject to a tax on income and capital, then

38. In §1.1.1.

there must be concessions offered, entitling certain companies to tax exemption on such income;

(b) if income is to be received from outside the jurisdiction, then either no foreign withholding taxes are levied on such income or, if internal tax legislation of the foreign country requires deduction of tax at source or the imposition of tax on assessable profits, there must be a double tax treaty which reduces such tax to nil or a nominal amount;

(c) there must be no withholding taxes levied by the offshore jurisdiction on distributions or other payments to non-residents;

(d) the tax legislation of the offshore jurisdiction must not include anti-avoidance provisions clawing back any of the above advantages, particularly where the owner of the offshore jurisdiction company is non-resident;

(e) exchange control legislation must not prohibit the free flow of money between group members;

(f) the offshore jurisdiction must be politically and economically stable to ensure the permanence of the group's presence in the country and the security of its assets;

(g) communication to the offshore jurisdiction must be adequate and inexpensive if the company is to be partly managed by non-residents; if it is to be managed locally, there must be the required labour force available who can effectively manage the company.

The above list immediately eliminates many countries commonly referred to as offshore jurisdictions for use by the majority of taxpayers. The use of such jurisdictions is limited since none of these countries has concluded double tax treaties with any other country. Thus, if withholding taxes are levied on dividends, interest, royalties or any other income, such withholding taxes will not be reduced or recovered; however, if the payor company is not obliged to deduct tax at source, then these countries may be used in certain circumstances.

Where no withholding taxes are deducted on royalty or interest payments to non-residents, then a company located in this group of countries may be used as a financing or licensing company. Again, however, the qualification here is that the payment of interest or royalties may not be allowed as a deductible item by the tax authorities of the payor company, which may then defeat the purpose of establishing the recipient in an offshore jurisdiction. Generally speaking, the countries referred to above may be used for passive companies, but are seldom commercially used for active companies.

Such active companies, manufacturing and trading companies, attract much greater non-tax considerations than passive companies, and the offshore jurisdictions are not generally conducive to carrying out such activities within their frontiers. Invoicing operations used to be established in these countries, but with the wealth of anti-avoidance legislation aimed at inter-company pricing policies, such advantages have been gradually whittled away.

[VI.] CASE STUDY 6

'Successful'[39] sham organisations rarely succeed on their own merits. If they succeed, it is mostly because they have evaded detection. The Filipes have managed to create a few sham organisations of their own, resulting from informal discussions with dubious business contacts in smoke-filled bars, and this has nothing to do with their able international tax adviser in London. The following may need to be investigated:

(a) the use of Lucca BV to hold the Lucca Software subsidiaries (Diagram 4);
(b) the use of the BVI company to own the UK property (Diagram 5);
(c) the use of the UK nominee company to extract profits from Lucca Software SpA (Diagram 7);
(d) the use of Opus AG to collect royalties for Paolo's merchandising rights (Diagram 8);
(e) The use of BVI company as an offshore entity (Diagram 5).

Diagram 4

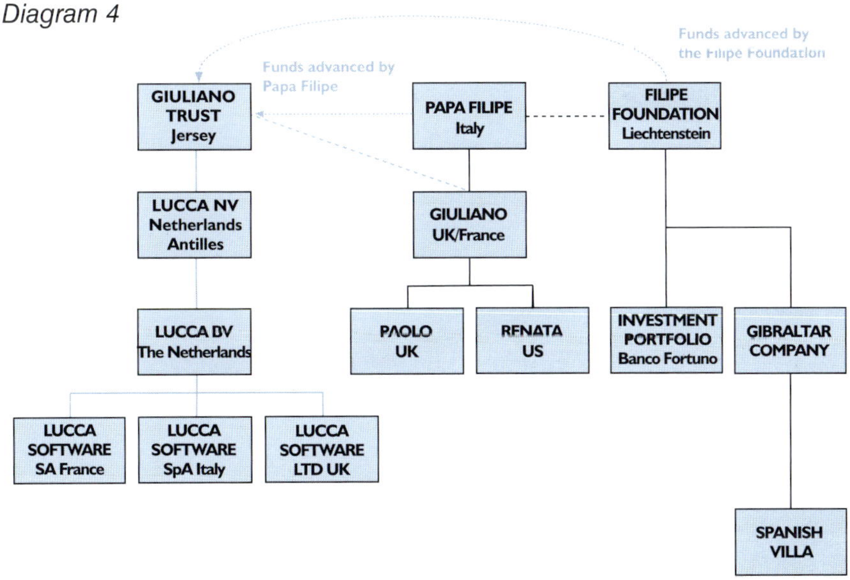

39. This is said slightly tongue-in-cheek.

Diagram 5

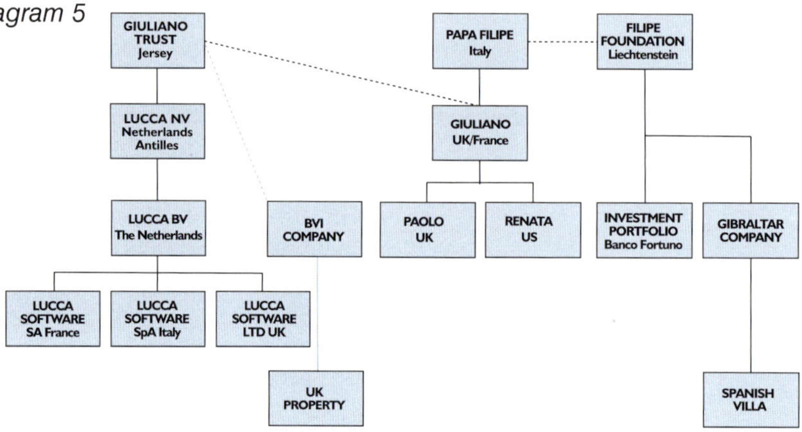

Diagram 7

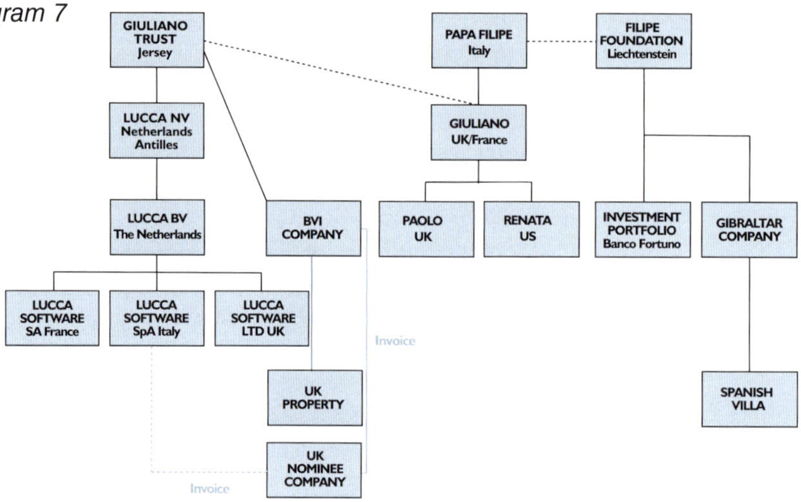

Diagram 8

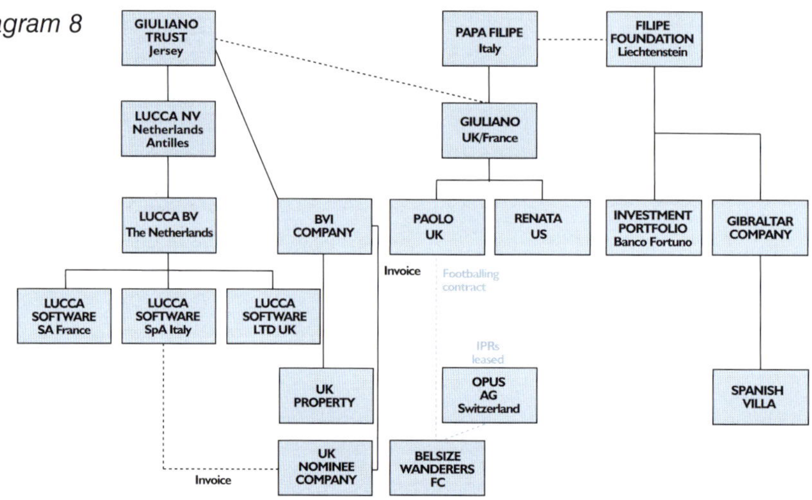

[VI.a] Lucca BV

Maurice Brightman had advised Giuliano to have Lucca BV set up as a holding company for the three subsidiaries in France, Italy and the UK, respectively. Not only was the foreign withholding tax rate reduced in each country under the relevant treaty,[40] but also, under the Dutch qualifying participation privilege, Lucca BV would not be liable to Dutch tax on the foreign dividend income. When Giuliano, shortly after a disagreement with a lady called Griet, mentioned to Maurice that he was thinking of scaling down the Dutch operations of his software group and spending less time in the Netherlands – in fact, possibly not ever setting foot upon Dutch soil again – Maurice reminded Giuliano that based on case law,[41] Lucca BV should be more than a 'shell' company. It should continue playing a real role in the group structure, such as financing the operations or appropriate management activities. 'Perhaps you could continue attending board meetings in Amsterdam but catch the afternoon flight back to London?' Maurice tactfully suggested.

[VI.b] BVI company

The BVI company was established to purchase a house in London in view of Giuliano's move there. It was described in Chapter 3 that Giuliano's idea was to own the BVI company's shares, rather than the house in the UK, thus avoiding UK inheritance tax issues. The BVI company is also being used to extract profits that would otherwise be taxable in Italy as management or consultancy fees. Maurice explained that unless there were genuine services provided under the consultancy fee arrangements, this would represent tax fraud and the prospect of a jail sentence! Maurice did not dare to ask Giuliano whether all of the consultants' names described on the invoice rendered by the BVI company were genuine. Knowledge or even reasonable suspicion of this would, under the new money laundering regulations, have forced Maurice to make a report to the National Criminal Intelligence Service (NCIS) in connection with these transactions. Maurice would not be able to tell Giuliano that he would have to make this report, so instead Maurice strongly argued against any further invoices being rendered by the BVI company for such services.

[VI.c] UK nominee company

The use of the BVI company to issue premium-invoices to Lucca Software SpA via the UK nominee company is likely to enjoy scrutiny by both the Italian and UK authorities. As shown before,[42] HMRC will generally not issue residency certificates for nominee companies to prevent them being used to benefit from the UK's treaty network.

40. Which was relevant before the EU Parent/Subsidiary Directive came into force; compare §3.2.3.
41. Compare §6.1.3.
42. See §5.1.2.

Furthermore, the invoicing transactions, conducted via the UK nominee company to reduce the Italian subsidiary's profits, are classic sham transactions – the BVI company in a low-tax jurisdiction earns an artificial profit as a result of pricing arrangements between related parties, namely Lucca Software SpA and the UK nominee company. The Inland Revenue may, at the very least, want to see cost plus a reasonable service fee left in the UK to be taxed at corporate rates. Moreover, under the EU Mutual Assistance Recovery Directive,[43] the Inland Revenue might inform the Italian tax authorities spontaneously that Italy is suffering a tax loss because of Giuliano's structure. If this is the case, the Mutual Assistance Directive[44] would then enable the Italians to seek recovery of the Italian tax due in the UK.

[VI.d] Opus AG

In connection with Paolo's employment by Opus AG, the Swiss company used to accumulate royalty payments for his merchandising rights, the personal service company rules could apply had Paolo himself set up the company for this purpose. In such a case, and if the company was established with a tax avoidance motive (as perhaps in the *Ingemar Johansson* case), the company could be regarded as a pure fiction, and tax assessed as if the income for the merchandising rights had been received by Paolo personally. Paolo took the trouble to ring Maurice about this. Based on discussions he had with Giuliano on the topic, Maurice had already established that Opus AG was an independent company set up to employ entertainers and sportsmen specifically to exploit their image, merchandising and other rights in consideration for a fee based on such exploitation. As such, the commerciality of the structure could not be attacked, and tax administrations would have to resort to other weapons in their anti-avoidance armoury to attack the structure, if possible.

[VI.e] Use of BVI company as offshore entity

Giuliano was in a tax-planning mood one Saturday afternoon when he made his decision to use the BVI company for the invoicing operations. He was reading a book entitled *Jewels of the Caribbean*, which gave him the idea that the BVI may be just the right place for his own 'offshore entity'. Giuliano learnt that the BVI has an excellent business infrastructure with good telecommunications. English is widely used on the island and the legal system is largely based on English law. Furthermore, large numbers of offshore companies, trusts, banks, insurers and mutual funds on the islands are supported by a well-developed and diverse professional services sector. This is exactly what Giuliano wanted to know! The fact that there are no withholding taxes in the BVI seemed to create a perfect international tax structure as far as Giuliano was concerned. Giuliano also read that the BVI has no exchange controls. This, coupled with the fact that rum is one

43. Compare §1.5.1.
44. Compare §1.4.1.

of the islands' major exports, clinched it for Giuliano. He picked up the phone and got Sophie at SuperTravelAgents to book him a first class plane ticket to the BVI.[45]

[VI.f] Conclusion

Since the trend for tax authorities is to simply ignore sham transactions and apply domestic tax law as if these transactions had not taken place, thus subjecting the taxpayer to the tax that would have been due in the first place plus, potentially, penalties and interest, the taxpayer or tax adviser suggesting such a structure should ask himself before its implementation whether the sham structure is really worth the cost and trouble.

45. The reader may have noticed by now that Giuliano is more than a bit impulsive, and although the BVI certainly has very attractive benefits to offer in terms of offshore tax planning, a more meticulous study of various offshore jurisdictions would have shown Giuliano that there is a myriad of attractive options to choose from.

Chapter 7
What Are the Tax Implications of International Trade?

In Chapter 3 the concept of foreign-source income was examined and how it is taxed locally, and whether the income is from an investment portfolio, rental income from real estate, interest, royalties or personal services income. Parent companies will often incorporate a foreign entity specifically to receive foreign-source income at the lowest possible rate of foreign tax deducted (by withholding or otherwise), or with the intention that the income remains out of the domestic tax net by not remitting such income. Nevertheless, the attribution rules relating to foreign-base income may tax the company (or indeed individual) as if they have received such income, eliminating any tax benefit created by trapping the income within a foreign company.[1]

Another concept which should be considered is whether the company which has been formed for tax planning purposes may itself be taxed in another country as a result of conducting activities there of a nature other than creating passive income which is taxed at source. This is of immediate interest for trading companies, which conduct trading activities in several countries, and particularly relevant are the concepts of 'trading with' or 'trading within' a country. 'Trading with' a country is what virtually all companies involved in

1. Issues in this respect were discussed in detail in Chapter 5.

international trade do: they buy from vendors in one country and sell to purchasers in another country. If they had to file tax returns for every purchase or sale order they entered into with a company based in another country, international trade would soon come to a standstill. As identified in Chapter 4 on double tax treaties, one of the functions of a double tax treaty is to facilitate international trade, allowing companies in one high-tax jurisdiction to trade with companies in another without creating local tax liabilities.

Another possibility in respect of a company's presence within a country's borders is where, for example, a local person is required to develop such international trade. A company may want to expand into the Far East but rather than going to the expense of creating its own subsidiary organisation there, it decides to establish a sales promotion office only, or perhaps appoints a local agent to sell its products in that region. Alternatively, a company may wish to build up a small research and development business in a foreign country, using local consultants, without creating a tax liability in that country for the profits that will be derived from selling the product using such research and development expertise.

'Trading within', on the other hand, denotes a stronger *nexus* with the relevant country – for example, contracts are habitually negotiated and signed within that country's borders, as would be the case where a call centre was established in, say, Ireland to sell software on behalf of a foreign enterprise, or where the risk and responsibilities in respect of a contract are borne in that country. A company trading 'within' a country's border will only escape tax liability there under specific circumstances.

7.1 ENTITY CLASSIFICATION AND GENERAL TAX CHARACTERISTICS

There are a number of different types of commercial undertaking that may be used in order to engage in business. The following provides an outline of the most prevalent forms of business enterprise that are found in a variety of jurisdictions and their legal and tax characteristics, but does not provide a comprehensive list of all available entities.

7.1.1 Sole traders

An individual owning a business as a sole trader has no registration obligations in terms of setting up the business, but conversely does not enjoy any benefits that result from the distinction between his personal and the business's assets.[2] The owner is entitled to all profits of the business. These profits are reportable

2. Such distinction is called 'limited liability' and denotes the protection that an investor enjoys as to his exposure to the claims of creditors. Exposure is limited to the investor's contribution to the business. Limited liability generally is a characteristic of corporate entities only.

on his personal annual income tax return and taxed at graduated rates.[3] Self-employed tax allowances may or may not apply.

7.1.2 Branch operations of foreign companies

A foreign company may decide to establish itself within the borders of a country through a branch, which is carrying on the purchasing and selling activities. For legal purposes, a branch does not usually constitute a legal entity separate from its head office company. However, for tax purposes, branches are generally taxed at domestic corporate tax rates separate from the head office company. Additionally, since dividend withholding tax does not generally apply to local profits upon remittance to the foreign head office company, some countries levy a 'branch profits tax', which has a similar effect to that of a dividend withholding tax.[4]

7.1.3 Trading trusts

Trading trusts may be relatively common, particularly in Australia and, more recently, New Zealand. A trading trust is a trust that is engaged in trade or business. Trading trusts are not separate legal entities, thus the business is actually undertaken in the names of the trustees of the trust. Since the trustees trade on behalf of the beneficiaries and not in their own name, the beneficiaries' individual tax rate will be applicable.

7.1.4 Joint ventures

Joint ventures refer in general to co-operation between businesses, and the constituting entities could take on almost any form. For example, two existing entities (corporate or otherwise) could participate in the capital of another enterprise (corporate or otherwise), usually called the joint venture vehicle. If the joint venture vehicle is incorporated, the joint venture partners hold shares in the corporate joint venture vehicle, which is subject to corporate tax. If the joint venture is unincorporated, the joint venture vehicle is treated as a partnership for tax purposes. Each individual partner of such vehicle is then taxed according to the size of his interest in the vehicle.

The choice of joint venture vehicle will depend upon a variety of different factors, including legal implications, commercial objectives and tax aspects. From a tax point of view, the following matters will have to be considered:

---

3. Thus making this kind of business form fiscally 'transparent', i.e. profits are taxed in the hands of the individuals constituting the business entity only. The entities discussed under §7.1.1 to §7.1.3, as well as §7.1.5, are, generally, transparent for tax purposes. Joint ventures (§7.1.4) may or may not be transparent, depending on the structure of the particular joint venture vehicle.
4. See also the discussion under §7.3 in respect of a branch as a form of permanent establishment as defined in the OECD Model Treaty.

- the tax position of each of the parties, especially if different jurisdictions apply to each and if one regime taxes with reference to residence and the other to source of income;
- the possibility of sourcing major expenditure from a jurisdiction providing the most favourable tax situation;
- the best means to utilise losses and shelter profits;
- the tax consequences of acquiring intellectual property and the payment of royalties.

7.1.5 Unlimited liability partnerships

A partnership, in general, is an agreement between two or more partners with the aim of making a profit. A general partnership creates unlimited liability of the general partners for the partnership's liabilities. A general partnership is transparent for tax purposes, with the profits of the partnership being divided up between the partners in accordance with the partnership agreement and taxed in the hands of each individual.

7.1.6 Hybrid entities

Hybrid entities are those that have the characteristics of both a corporate and non-corporate entity, and as such may often be useful to tax advisers.

Limited partnerships

A limited partnership consists of a 'general partner' and one or more 'limited partners'. The general partner is responsible for managing and administering the partnership, and for all its debts and obligations. The liability of the limited partner is restricted to the amount of capital invested in the partnership. An LP is generally not a legal entity in law and transparent for tax purposes and must generally be registered for the general partner/limited partner distinction to apply. A limited partner may not partake in the management of the LP; if he does, he will normally forfeit his limited liability status.

Limited liability partnerships

Limited liability partnership (LLP) members are generally liable only to an agreed amount, usually the amount of capital contributed. LLPs must have two 'designated members', who have increased responsibilities, e.g. preparing and filing an annual return. LLPs are generally 'bodies corporate' for legal purposes (thereby providing the protection of limited liability to partners) but are usually taxed as partnerships. The motivation behind the initial legislation was that it would benefit those using the vehicle to carry on a 'trade and profession'.[5]

5. In accordance with the Limited Liability Partnership Act 2000 of England and Wales, for example.

Limited liability companies

US limited liability companies (LLCs) combine the benefits of a company and a partnership, as described above, namely the statutory insulation against liability for all investors (relevant for companies) with the elimination of economic double taxation on the earnings of the business and then again on the profits distributed in the form of dividends.

Care must be taken in the setting up of an LLC to make sure that it is within the permissible guidelines to achieve transparent status for US tax purposes. The four relevant guidelines that the IRS views as being corporate characteristics are: limited liability, centralisation of management, continuity of life, and free transferability of stock. To be classified as transparent for tax purposes, the LLC must not possess more than two of the above four characteristics. Thus, the organisation agreement that forms the LLC must be carefully worded to meet the above test, as must any operating agreement further defining the entity's attributes and its members' rights and obligations.

Foreign members of LLCs may be required to file a US income tax return, which is uncommon for stock ownership. On the other hand, some of the benefits of these entities can be summarised as follows:

- the image of a US corporation combined with fiscal transparency;
- no need to disclose accounts to the public, nor a requirement to file a tax return in the US, unless the LLC has US source structure;
- low annual costs of registration (franchise tax).

7.1.7 Limited companies

Limited companies possess legal personality and have capital that is divided into shares. The liability of shareholders does usually not extend beyond the value of their investment in the company. For tax purposes, limited companies are opaque. Shareholders are generally subject to taxation only when they receive a distribution from the company.

A company that is a subsidiary of a limited company (the parent) and effectively controlled by the parent or an affiliate of the parent is generally taxed as a separate legal entity. Differing criteria may be applied to determine what constitutes a subsidiary for tax purposes: this may be a certain holding percentage or the total combined voting power held in the subsidiary. It is generally accepted that, as a separate legal entity, a subsidiary does not of itself create a permanent establishment in its country of residence for a foreign parent.

7.1.8 Protected Cell Companies

Guernsey

Guernsey was at the forefront of the development of the concept of the Protected Cell Company (PCC). A PCC is a single company with multiple classes of share, each with separate characteristics. Crucially, each cell is legally and economically independent of all of the other cells, and so it is possible to create a single PCC with separate cells investing in a diverse and almost unlimited number and category of business or personal interests. Potential investors can then invest in one, several or even all of the cells, with each shareholding in one cell being entirely uncorrelated to the activities of any of the other cells. The benefit of a PCC is that it can be structured in such a way that controlled foreign company and personal attribution provisions, such as Section 13 TCGA 1992 in the UK, are not applicable on the basis that an investor's cell does not represent more than specified limits or thresholds.

7.2 COMMERCIAL LOGIC IN ESTABLISHING ENTITIES

Not only must there be commercial reasons for an actual transaction, but there must also be commercial reasons for incorporating various companies within the structure. If a company has been incorporated in, say, Bermuda by a German company trading in France then, on the face of it, tax avoidance would seem to be the purpose, and little other commercial reason can be attributed to the formation of the Bermudan company.

Suppose that a Luxembourg holding company is owned by a trust as part of an overall tax structure and the company decides to purchase goods from European countries and sell them in the US. It cannot actually trade itself, since its holding company status would be forfeited. Instead, it must select a country in which to incorporate a trading company. Surprisingly enough, commercial logic may often dictate that the Luxembourg holding company should form a Netherlands Antilles trading company. At first glance, it may appear that the motive is purely tax avoidance: provided that the goods are only imported into and directly exported out of the Netherlands Antilles and no sale is effected within the Netherlands Antilles, the concessionary tax rate on trading profits earned by the Netherlands Antilles company may be a third of the normal rates, resulting in an overall effective tax rate of approximately 11%. As a result, 89% of net profits may be distributed to the Luxembourg company without withholding taxes taking a further slice out of the net income after tax, so that the Luxembourg holding company and, by extension, the trust retain a far higher proportion of net profits after all taxes; higher than would have been received from, for example, a Swiss company after the 35% Swiss anticipatory tax on dividends, and certainly higher than if other European companies had been used.

There can, however, be considerable persuasive commercial logic behind incorporating a Netherlands Antilles company:

- the Netherlands Antilles is near the place of eventual sale, the US, so that promotion is easier than if a European country had been used;
- the Netherlands Antilles offers free zone concessions to resident organisations which do not sell within the islands, but only import and re-export, the concessions being that no duty is levied on the goods imported;
- the system of warehousing goods in the Netherlands Antilles is efficient, so that goods may be shipped directly to the Netherlands Antilles for storage prior to sale in the US without incurring heavy additional expenses;
- Netherlands Antilles resident managers and personnel will be able to communicate more easily and might obtain more favourable purchasing arrangements in respect of the Dutch and Belgian products, since Dutch is the national language;
- title to the products passes to the US customer neither in the US nor in Europe; title passes only in the Netherlands Antilles, so that these countries have no power to tax the profits as if the Netherlands Antilles company were trading within those countries, unless it is proved that the Netherlands Antilles organisation is a sham.

There are therefore many commercial reasons, under these particular circumstances, why it is advisable to form a Netherlands Antilles company. It should be stressed that there can be no objection to an international company so conducting its affairs that the least possible tax burden is imposed on profits. Indeed, shareholders often regard it as the duty of corporate management to look for ways of reducing taxation, provided always that these ways cannot be considered a sham and are commercially justifiable.

7.3 DEFINITION OF PERMANENT ESTABLISHMENT

The term 'permanent establishment' (PE) is usually found in unilateral law and double tax treaties and is used to determine a non-resident enterprise's liability to tax in a country. A foreign enterprise is not liable to tax in a state unless it has created a PE in that state.

7.3.1 OECD Model Treaty

As briefly outlined in Chapter 4,[6] Article 5 of the OECD Model Tax Convention on Income and Capital (the OECD Model Treaty)[7] states:

6. In §4.3.1.
7. 2003 Condensed Version.

1. For the purposes of this Convention, the term 'permanent establishment' means a fixed place of business through which the business of an enterprise is wholly or partly carried on.

2. The term 'permanent establishment' includes especially:

a. a place of management;

b. a branch;

c. an office;

d. a factory;

e. a workshop, and

f. a mine, an oil or gas well, a quarry or any other place of extraction of natural resources.

3. A building site or construction or installation project constitutes a permanent establishment only if it lasts more than twelve months.

4. Notwithstanding the preceding provisions of this Article, the term 'permanent establishment' shall be deemed not to include:

a. the use of facilities solely for the purpose of storage, display or delivery of goods or merchandise belonging to the enterprise;

b. the maintenance of a stock of goods or merchandise belonging to the enterprise solely for the purpose of storage, display or delivery;

c. the maintenance of a stock of goods or merchandise belonging to the enterprise solely for the purpose of processing by another enterprise;

d. the maintenance of a fixed place of business solely for the purpose of purchasing goods or merchandise or of collecting information, for the enterprise;

e. the maintenance of a fixed place of business solely for the purpose of carrying on, for the enterprise, any other activity of a preparatory or auxiliary character;

f. the maintenance of a fixed place of business solely for any combination of activities mentioned in subparagraphs a) to e), provided that the overall activity of the fixed place of business resulting from this combination is of a preparatory or auxiliary character.

5. *Notwithstanding the provisions of paragraphs 1 and 2, where a person — other than an agent of an independent status to whom paragraph 6 applies — is acting on behalf of an enterprise and has, and habitually exercises, in a Contracting State an authority to conclude contracts in the name of the enterprise, that enterprise shall be deemed to have a permanent establishment in that State in respect of any activities which that person undertakes for the enterprise, unless the activities of such person are limited to those mentioned in paragraph 4 which, if exercised through a fixed place of business, would not make this fixed place of business a permanent establishment under the provisions of that paragraph.*

6. *An enterprise shall not be deemed to have a permanent establishment in a Contracting State merely because it carries on business in that State through a broker, general commission agent or any other agent of an independent status, provided that such persons are acting in the ordinary course of their business.*

7. *The fact that a company which is a resident of a Contracting State controls or is controlled by a company which is a resident of the other Contracting State, or which carries on business in that other State (whether through a permanent establishment or otherwise), shall not of itself constitute either company a permanent establishment of the other.*

Double tax treaty provisions relating to permanent establishments are therefore designed to give additional protection to taxpayers against the risk of double taxation, while at the same time attempting to reduce tax avoidance possibilities. In the case of companies in high-tax countries trading with other high tax jurisdictions, there will normally be a treaty designed to eliminate juridical double taxation. However, if a company has been formed for tax avoidance purposes, it may be resident in a country which imposes low taxes (or even no tax at all) on trading profits earned abroad, and, in this case, it is improbable that it will enjoy protection under a double tax treaty.

To illustrate the problems of juridical double taxation, Germany may regard trading profits as income effectively connected with a German source, such as an agent, and will therefore subject the trading profits to German tax. The US, on the other hand, may look at where title to the goods has passed as the criterion and, if title passes within the US, then the foreign company may be liable to US tax even though no agent or office is involved. However, this potential problem could be negated by the double tax treaty.

7.3.2 OECD Commentary

The OECD Commentary to its Model Treaty explains how the provisions should be interpreted. With reference to Article 5 it assists the tax adviser's understanding in a number of ways. It outlines the three factors which must be present in order for a permanent establishment to exist, and then considers the question of dependent and independent agents. The three factors essential to a permanent establishment are:

(a) a 'place of business' must exist, for example office premises, a factory or a workshop;

(b) the place of business is fixed, i.e. it exists in a particular place and is not of a temporary nature;

(c) a business of an enterprise is carried on at the fixed place of business.

In respect of the above, the Commentary provides the following guidance:

Place of Business

The Commentary states that a 'place of business' includes 'premises, facilities or installations' which are used to carry on the business of the enterprise, together with an amount of space which is left at the disposal of the business. A permanent establishment may therefore exist in circumstances where an entity merely has unfilled room available to it. It is also of no consequence as to whether the property is owned or rented.

Fixed

The Commentary provides that a 'place of business' must be fixed. A common requirement is therefore that the 'place of business' is linked to a definite 'geographical' site, and under the Commentary this definition may be satisfied in circumstances where, for example, equipment remains in that place.

Permanent

A place of business must be permanent and not just temporary, and it may be noted that a place of business which, when initially set up is of a temporary nature, may become permanent in circumstances where it continues for a period which can no longer be regarded as temporary.

Dependent agents

The Commentary then outlines the position and implications of dependent and independent agents. Under Article 5(5) it is clear that an enterprise may be regarded as having a permanent establishment in a state even though its only presence in that state is a person. For this to be the case the individual must be a 'dependent agent' of the enterprise. The term is well documented and there is a three-part test. First, the dependent agent must have the authority to conclude contracts that bind the foreign enterprise. Secondly, to create a taxable presence or a permanent establishment, the agent must exercise its authority to conclude contracts on a regular basis, i.e. habitually. Finally, the Commentary states that the authority to conclude contracts must be in respect of contracts 'relating to the business proper of the enterprise'.

Independent agents

As if to emphasise the importance of this point, Article 5(6) contains an explanation of the term 'independent agent', the Commentary explaining that a person is an independent agent if 'he is independent of the enterprise both legally and economically, and he acts in the ordinary course of his business when acting on behalf of the enterprise'. This is a very important definition and it is the difference between these two terms that is often of great significance in international tax planning.

7.4 E-COMMERCE

The number of transactions taking place by means of the internet increased phenomenally from the mid-1990s onwards. From tax authorities' perspective, e-commerce had become increasingly important since vast numbers of transactions were taking place within the borders of a particular state, yet with the concepts used to tax 'conventional' transactions not being applicable to assist in determining tax liability.[8]

In January 2001 the OECD published the outcome of discussions on the concept of permanent establishment in the context of what has become known as 'e-tailing'. There is a broad agreement that:

(a) a website cannot, of *itself,* constitute a permanent establishment;

(b) a website hosting arrangement does not usually result in a permanent establishment for the enterprise that carries on business through that website;

(c) an internet service provider will not, except in very unusual circumstances, constitute a dependent agent of another enterprise so as to constitute a permanent establishment of that enterprise;

(d) while a place where computer equipment, such as a server, is located may in certain circumstances constitute a permanent establishment, this requires that the functions performed at that place should be significant as well as an essential or core part of the business activity of the enterprise.

8. Compare, for example, §5.1.2 and §7.3.

The OECD concluded that a server could amount to a permanent establishment, particularly in circumstances where it remains situated in the same place for a period of time; indeed the Committee on Fiscal Affairs determined that a permanent establishment could exist without human presence. With respect to point (d), it was considered that a permanent establishment would not exist in circumstances where the activities were of a 'preparatory or auxiliary' nature. This would need to be established on a case-by-case basis but would usually include:

(a) providing a communications link between suppliers and customers;

(b) advertising goods or services;

(c) relaying information through a mirror server for security and efficiency;

(d) gathering market data for the enterprise;

(e) supplying information.

However, if the above form an 'essential and significant part of the business activity of the enterprise as a whole, or where core functions of the enterprise are carried on through the computer equipment', then the activities would create a permanent establishment if it was considered that the equipment constituted a fixed place of business. An example of the core functions is given where the business of the ISP is to operate its own servers to host websites for enterprises. The operation of the servers is essential for their business and not preparatory or auxiliary. However, the UK authorities have made it clear that servers are not of themselves deemed to be permanent establishments.

Below are a couple of cases which, although they were not decided in respect of internet transactions as such, might be of potential applicability to internet taxation principles.

7.4.1 *Pipeline* case[9]

In this case a Dutch company owned underground pipelines to provide oil in the Netherlands and in Germany. The pipeline at issue was located in Germany and provided oil to Germany companies. The necessary pressure for transporting the oil within Germany was supplied from the Netherlands. The Dutch company had no employees in Germany. Maintenance and repair of the pipeline were done through independent contractors. The German tax authorities assessed net worth tax on the Dutch company on the basis of its pipeline located in Germany. The Dutch company appealed, arguing that since it had no

9. BFH decision of 30 October 1996, II R 12/92.

permanent establishment in Germany, it had no German business assets to be taxed.

The court concluded that the Dutch company had a permanent establishment in Germany by virtue of its pipeline, even for income tax purposes. The court based its decision on the domestic definition of a permanent establishment, which includes any fixed place of business, i.e. a site fixed to the earth's surface, that serves the business activities of the taxpayer. The fact that no employees were involved in running the Dutch company's business in Germany had no bearing on the court's decision.

The court's decision is significant for the purposes of determining the tax liability of, for example, telecommunications companies that also provide internet services. Such companies that own, say, a cable network in Germany may be taxed in that state on principles similar to the *Pipeline* case.

The case is also significant since it found that it was not necessary for there to be 'human intervention' to create a permanent establishment. Since e-tailing is essentially performed without human intervention, one may be unable to argue the absence of a permanent establishment merely because the operation is automatically concluded.

7.4.2 *Quill Corp. v. North Dakota*[10]

The court held that it was unconstitutional for North Dakota to impose state 'use tax' on an out-of-state mail order company that had no physical presence in the state itself. Interestingly the taxpayer did have licensed software in the state which allowed a customer direct access to the taxpayer's stocklist and price guide, and this was held to be insufficient to create a tax *nexus*. While this is not an e-commerce case it is unlikely that if it were, the court would have found any differently on the basis that an Internet transaction could well have even less contact with the state.

7.5 CLEARANCE UNDER ADVANCE TAX RULINGS

Under certain circumstances it may be possible to ask the relevant tax authorities for clearance under a tax ruling, in which case, if approved, the foreign company will run no risk of being taxed on its trading profits earned as a result of trading with that country, provided always that the conditions as set out in the ruling are adhered to. Private rulings[11] may also be granted,

10. 504 U.S. 298 (1992).
11. I.e. rulings taking into account the specific facts and circumstances in respect of a particular taxpayer and providing a binding ruling on the way the tax authorities will treat that particular transaction. This is opposed to public rulings, which have a more general nature.

for example, in respect of controlled foreign company and transfer pricing issues; withholding tax also forms the topic of rulings in many instances.

Where a service or support organisation is set up in a country, for example, to co-ordinate sales, promote products or simply carry out inventory, bookkeeping and debt collection administration on behalf of another company, it is very difficult for any tax regime to determine the taxable profits that should be attributed to the activities of the service organisation. Tax administrations generally accept that the service organisation, which may not conclude any contracts on its own as a principal would, but may only act as a back-up company, earns a deemed profit equal to a mark-up on the arm's-length cost of running the company. In many cases it may be advisable to obtain an advance ruling from the tax authorities, which will specify the expenses that must be taken into account in computing the deemed profits. The mark-up will then be taxed at normal corporate rates.

If there is any question as to where management and control resides and the local tax administration considers it possible that management is effected within its own country, then the total profits of the foreign company, wherever earned, will be brought into the tax net of the country with which it is trading. Thus, a Bahamian company, selling goods to the Netherlands, France, Belgium and Germany may acquire a flat in Amsterdam, for example, as the headquarters of a director of the Bahamian company when he is travelling in Europe. If no application is made for an advance ruling, the Dutch tax administration may later claim that the flat is a permanent establishment of the Bahamian company in the Netherlands and subject the *entire* European trading profits to Dutch corporate tax. Again, if the Bahamian company wishes to trade in the Netherlands and Belgium and employs a resident individual as the sole agent, then even though the Bahamian company negotiates and concludes all trading agreements, the Dutch or the Belgian tax administration may try to assess the entire profits of the Bahamian company to Dutch or Belgian tax on the grounds that management is effected locally, unless a prior advance tax ruling excludes this possibility.

[VII.] CASE STUDY 7

In this chapter, one of the most fundamental concepts of international tax – namely that of 'permanent establishment' – has been outlined. Further episodes in the business ventures of the Filipes may help the reader to become more familiar with certain aspects of the concept and bring them to life:

(a) the opening of the Australian representative office of Lucca Software SpA (Diagram 10);
(b) the appointment of independent agents in Australia and the Far East to sell software systems in the region (Diagram 11);
(c) the creation of a research and development centre, Lucca Developments, in India (Diagram 12).

Diagram 10

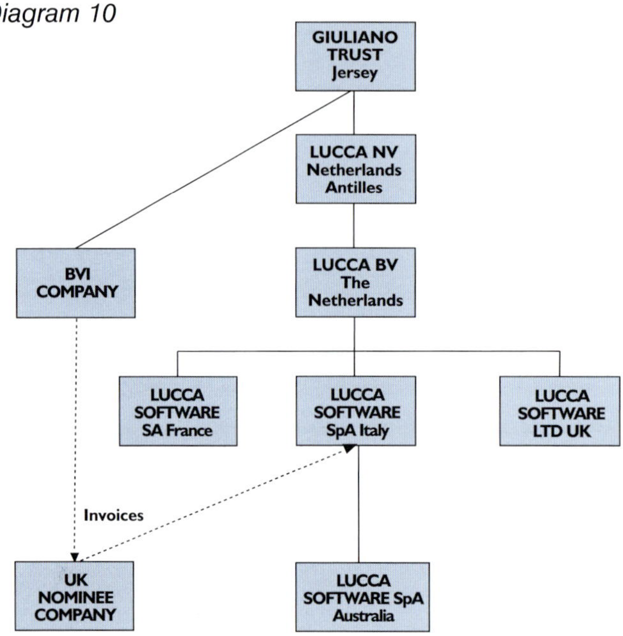

Diagram 11

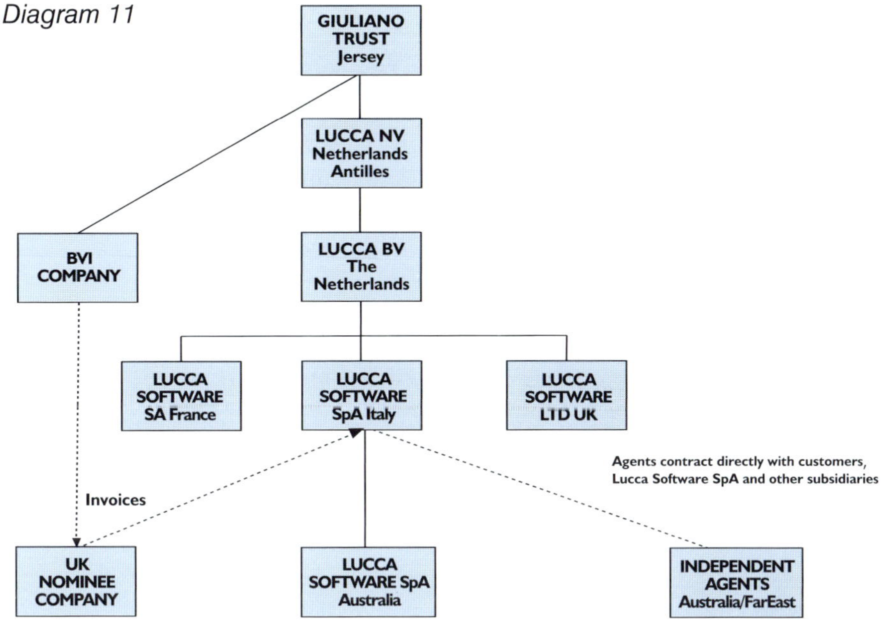

Diagram 12

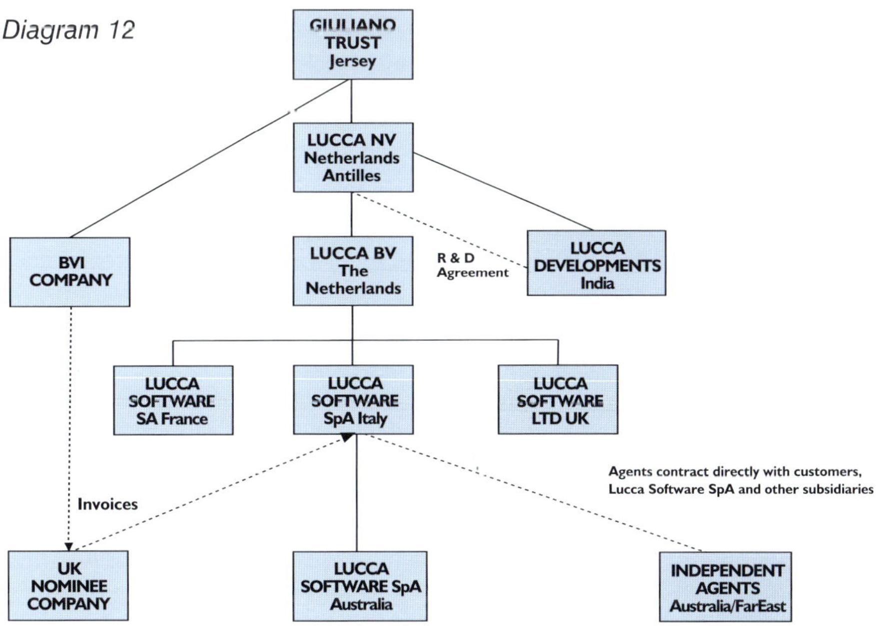

[VII.a] Australian representative office

As part of his plan to expand his software business, Giuliano decided to increase distribution outlets focusing on the Far East, which offers significant sales potential, particularly when Australia and New Zealand are also taken into account. This resulted in the opening of a representative office, Lucca Software SpA (Australia).

The main functions of the representative office are:

(a) to provide a fixed base to store documentation, promotional material etc. and to display them on computers, demonstrating the range of the software to potential clients;
(b) to circulate literature relating to the software to prospective customers in Australia, New Zealand, China and Japan;
(c) to pass on any enquiries or other information which may affect potential sales of the software to Giuliano and his staff in France, Italy and the UK.

In this chapter, the 'permanent establishment' definition of Article 5 of the OECD Model Treaty has been explored. If it is assumed, purely for the purposes of this case study, that Italy and Australia have negotiated a tax treaty that is identical to the OECD Model Treaty, it may be determined how the Australian tax authorities are likely to view the activities of the representative office.

Article 5(2)(c) of the Model Treaty states that a permanent establishment of a foreign entity includes, in particular, 'an office'. Since Lucca Software SpA opened a representative office in Australia, one might be led to believe that a permanent establishment of Lucca Software SpA was created in Australia. However, when the designated activities of the representative office are compared with those outlined in Article 5(4) of the Model Treaty, it may be appreciated that as long as the representative office's activities do not go beyond the scope of the listed activities, no permanent establishment of Lucca Software SpA will be created in Australia, in spite of the fact that it has opened an office there. The representative office's activities relate mainly to storage, display, advertising and information gathering – all activities within the 'preparatory or auxiliary character' allowed in accordance with Article 5(4)(f) of the Model Treaty.

The representative office was inundated with enquiries, to the extent that additional staff had to be employed, mainly technicians who demonstrate software programmes.

Maurice Brightman became concerned when he was contacted from Australia by Bruce, one of the technicians – yes, this international tax adviser's fame reaches far and wide! – with a 'quick question' on the implications of sales of software in Australia. Maurice could not help but wonder what this technician has been up to.

Maurice knew that Giuliano's intention was to avoid a taxable presence in Australia, one of the reasons why his Italian friend opted for a representative office rather than a branch in Australia.[12] Maurice immediately drafted an email to Giuliano, outlining the risk of exposure to Australian taxation if any of the representative office's staff were to engage in concluding software sales contracts in Australia on behalf of Lucca Software SpA.

To: GiulianoFilipe@Lucca.com
Cc: Bruce@LuccaAus.com
Subject: Permanent Establishment Risk

Dear Giuliano,

It has come to my attention that staff of Lucca Software SpA (Australia) might be involved in the negotiation and/or conclusion of sales contracts of the Lucca software in Australia.

The consequence of Article 5(5) of the OECD Model Treaty is that if an employee of the representative office concludes contracts on behalf of the representative office, it would cause such employee to be a dependent agent of Lucca Software SpA and create a permanent establishment of the Italian subsidiary in Australia. The Commentary to the OECD Model states that such a person will create a permanent establishment, as a dependent agent, if he has the authority to conclude contracts to bind the foreign entity (Lucca Software SpA in this case), if the agent exercises such authority on a regular basis, and such contracts relate to the business of the foreign entity. However, based on my experience, the Australian tax authorities often take a stricter approach, and could find a permanent establishment exists even if only one contract had been concluded by the dependent agent. Consequently, I recommend that the technicians and other staff of the representative office are not involved in the sale of the software, but that independent agents are appointed instead to fulfil such a role.

I trust that the above is informative, but please do not hesitate to contact me should you have any questions or comments on the above.

Personal regards,
MB

12. Article 5(2)(b) of the OECD Model Treaty shows that a branch creates a permanent establishment of the foreign entity in the country where the branch is located unless, of course, the branch limits its activities to the 'preparatory or auxiliary activities' outlined in Article 5(4). However, Maurice knows that tax authorities are in many cases not easily convinced that a branch's staff had the discipline to limit activities accordingly.

Giuliano responded by email to thank Maurice for his advice, and issued instructions to all staff of the representative office, and particularly the newly appointed technicians who work closely with prospective clients, to refrain from negotiating or concluding sales agreements for Lucca Software with any potential Australian customer.

[VII.b] Independent agents in Australia and the Far East

The representative office's marketing activities were a huge success – the demand for Lucca software was rising and Giuliano had to appoint a number of independent agents to sell the by now much-coveted software in the region.

After the permanent establishment scare caused by Bruce from Australia, Giuliano thought that it is better to check with Maurice before agreeing particulars with prospective independent agents. Maurice quoted Article 5(6) of the OECD Model Treaty when he explained to Giuliano that when contracts are concluded in the ordinary course of his business by an independent agent, i.e. one who is legally and economically independent of the foreign company, no permanent establishment of the foreign company will be created. Thus, the independent agents concluding contracts on behalf of Lucca Software SpA for the sale of software would not create a permanent establishment of that company in the countries where the sales agreements are concluded.

Giuliano asked Maurice if he would draft some heads of agreement which would clearly show the agent is independent rather than dependent, two terms which, to Giuliano, did not sound that dissimilar to each other. Maurice then drafted the following, to help his client understand how to instruct employees of Lucca Software SpA (Australia) and also independent agents:

MEMORANDUM OF AGREEMENT entered into this .... day of 2005

BY AND BETWEEN:

Lucca Software SpA (Australia), whose registered address is at 41 Gold Coast Road, Brisbane, Qld 100,000, Australia
(hereinafter referred to as 'the Principal')

-and-

[Name of Independent Agent], whose registered address is at ....
(hereinafter referred to as 'the Agent')

WHEREAS:

A. The Principal is engaged in the business of promoting, displaying and demonstrating its software to potential clients in Australia; providing a fixed base to store documentation, etc., circulating literature in relation to the software to prospective clients in the Asia-Pacific region; and passing on enquiries in respect of the software to the management of its head office.

B. Whilst the Principal will largely continue to provide the services in A. above for international business development, the Principal wishes to appoint a person to act as its non-exclusive agent in respect of promoting the Principal's business.

C. For the purposes of clarifying the rights and obligations and specifically for placing on record the manner and basis upon which the Agent will be appointed by the Principal as its agent, the Parties are desirous of reducing to writing the understanding existing between them.

NOW IT IS THEREFORE AGREED as follows:

1. DEFINITIONS

In this Agreement the following expressions shall have the following meanings:

'the Agreement' means this document.

'Gross Sales' mean the total amount of fees payable to the Principal by the client.

2. APPOINTMENT OF THE AGENT

(a) The Principal hereby appoints the Agent, which accepts such appointment accordingly, as its non-exclusive agent to assist the Principal to perform the duties as specified in Clause 4 below.

(b) In rendering the services of an agent for and on behalf of the Principal, the Agent agrees that it shall be bound by the following express limitations, which shall be considered to be material conditions of this Agreement:

(i) The Agent shall assume all rights and duties to that of an agent.

(ii) The Agent shall provide services for the exclusive benefit of the Principal and not in any way for its own benefit and the Agent should at all times represent to third parties that its business is contracted entirely independently.

(iii) In carrying out its duties, the Agent shall specifically advise all third parties that it is entirely independent from the Principal and acting upon a strict mandate.

(iv) The Agent shall be expressly prevented from representing the Principal, entering into agreements on its behalf or binding its credit as against any third parties saving for those instances when given specific authority to do so by the Principal.

3. DURATION

This Agreement shall be deemed to have commenced on the date of signature and shall endure until terminated by one month's written notice given by one party to the other.

4. AGENCY SERVICES

Subject to the terms and conditions of this Agreement, the Agent shall promote the Principal which services shall aim to increase the profitability of the Principal.

5. AGENCY FEES

In respect of the services rendered by the Agent to the Principal as set out herein, the Principal shall pay to the Agent an agency fee equal to 2.5% of all Gross Sales secured by the Agent.

6. CONFIDENTIALITY

The terms of this Agreement are confidential.

IN WITNESS whereof the Parties hereto have executed this Agreement as of the day and year first above written

by [ ]
as witnessed by:

by [ ]
as witnessed by:

[VII.c] R&D centre in India

In order to facilitate the adaptation of Lucca software for users from different backgrounds, Lucca Developments was established in India to serve as the R&D centre. This Indian company charges Lucca NV in the Netherlands Antilles on a basis of all of its operating cost plus 10%.

OECD Model Treaty Article 5(7) explains that the fact that a resident of one state is the subsidiary of a parent company resident in another state does not mean per se that the subsidiary creates a permanent establishment of the parent. Thus, Lucca Developments does not automatically create a permanent establishment of Lucca NV in India.

It has already been considered above what limited functions a representative office may perform under Article 5(4) of the OECD Model Treaty in order not to be labelled as a permanent establishment of its foreign 'head office' entity. Assuming that India follows the guidelines provided by the Model Treaty and the Commentary, Lucca Developments would not create a permanent establishment of Lucca NV *provided that* Lucca Developments' activities are properly charged to Lucca NV on a reasonable basis.

Remuneration by Lucca NV to Lucca Developments involves an operating cost plus 10% arrangement. Provided that 10% is considered a sufficient margin by the Indian tax authorities for the R&D work that is performed by Lucca Developments, the Indian tax authorities should not hold this company liable to more tax than the applicable Indian corporate tax rate applied to the 10% margin.[13]

What if the Indian tax authorities hold that Lucca Developments' R&D activities go beyond the scope of the cost-plus agreement? What if Giuliano decides that he actually wants Lucca Developments' managers to negotiate and conclude contracts with customers in India?

If Lucca Developments' staff were to conclude contracts on behalf of the company, it might no longer be possible to operate on a cost-plus method. The Indian tax authorities would insist on taxing the total profits of the company. Were a tax treaty identical to the OECD Model Treaty in place between the Netherlands Antilles and India, Lucca Developments' adviser could have argued that Article 7 of the treaty should apply. The result of this would be that only so much of Lucca NV's profits as are attributable to Lucca Developments' business would be taxable in India. However, since no treaty is in place, Lucca NV's profits would be left to the mercy of the Indian tax authorities.

[VII.d] Conclusion

Where a company is merely trading *with* another country, it is often possible to limit such company's foreign tax exposure by choosing the entity representing it carefully. However, there is a limit to what a company can do or have done on its behalf without creating a tax liability in a foreign country. In cases where very limited activities in the foreign country is no longer practicable, the company would have to admit that it is trading *within* another country's borders. And that paying foreign tax, like death, is inevitable.

13. More about the cost-plus method of revenue calculation in Chapter 8.

Chapter 8

What are Related-Party Transactions?

This chapter considers how profits of related entities can be adjusted for tax purposes. Previous chapters have considered, among other things, sham structures and whether transactions have any commercial basis, but there may well be situations which involve properly constituted companies and where the transaction is a commercially justifiable one, but where the consideration may not be at a full market value. Pricing arrangements at arm's length between related companies is a fundamental prerequisite of international tax planning. If facts from the case study are looked at, where Lucca Software develops an Indian branch for research and development work, the branch needs to recharge its costs to the group and make a profit. This profit could be based on, say, 5% of costs or 25% of costs. Since the group parent company has control over the agreement that is entered into with the Indian branch, it may naturally wish to restrict the taxable profits to a minimum. Such control means that the inter-company pricing arrangements are not at arm's length, and it is fundamental to tax planning that all transactions, which are not entered into at arm's length, are effected at their full market value.

In a sale and purchase arrangement within a multinational group, for tax purposes the sale or purchase price must therefore be exactly the same as or similar to the price which an independent party would negotiate for purchase or sale with the group company. If a loan is made between members of a group, the rate of interest on the loan must be a commercial one and cannot be insignificant or excessive. Again, if a tax structure is set up which necessitates the payment of an exorbitant royalty from a high-tax country to a low-tax country, the excess over a commercially acceptable royalty will be disallowed as a deductible expense by the tax administration of the high-tax country. As discussed in Chapter 9, the same principles apply to excessive directors' remuneration, management and service fees and similar income items.

8.1 TRANSFER PRICING

8.1.1 Basic concepts

The general concepts explained above fall within the scope of what is called 'transfer pricing'. In general, transfer pricing relates to the method as to how prices should be charged between related parties, particularly between companies within the same group. Often, however, it is difficult to determine what arm's-length prices between related parties should be, since information on comparable transactions in the open market is unavailable. Under such circumstances tax authorities may determine what an arm's-length price would have been using one of the following methods:[1]

(a) the comparable uncontrolled price method (CUP);

(b) the resale price method (RP);

(c) the cost-plus method (CP);

(d) the profit split method (PS);

(e) transactional net margin method (TNM).

Aspects of the various transfer pricing methods are outlined below.

Comparable uncontrolled price method

The CUP method involves investigating the uncontrolled price in respect of the sale of a product or a transfer of services between unconnected parties. The price may need to be adjusted to reflect factors affecting the price of the goods or the services. Where no comparable price can be found, a different method will have to be used.

Resale price method

The RP method starts from the final selling price and subtracts an appropriate gross margin to arrive at a purchase price. This method is suitable where the

1. As provided in the OECD Transfer Pricing Guidelines for Multinational Enterprises and Tax Administrations, which provide guidance on the appropriate pricing of transactions involving the transfer of goods and services between related parties.

reseller has not made substantial modifications to a product. Also, where a seller performs all the functions a distributor would be expected to perform, this method is suitable.

Cost-plus method

The CP method starts by computing the cost of providing the goods or services and adds a mark-up that is deemed appropriate under the particular circumstances. This method is particularly suitable in the manufacture and sale of goods. The size of the mark-up and thus the margin that tax authorities would want to see left within their taxing authority depends, for example, on the nature and complexity of the services rendered – the greater the complexity, the greater the mark-up required.

Profit split method

The PS method examines the profit that has been assigned to each transaction in relation to the value of a given company's real economic contribution to the overall profit on a product. This allocation process is called a 'functional analysis' in which is taken into account the functions performed and risks assumed by each group member.

Transactional net margin method

The TNM method examines the net margin achieved on a particular transaction relative to a base, including turnover, costs or capital used. This information is then compared with the result achieved by independent parties on a similar transaction. This method is lower in priority when compared to the CP or RP methods, and can only be used when the latter two do not apply.

8.1.2 Transfer pricing cases

High-profile cases where an aspect of transfer pricing was the issue include the *Compaq*[2] case, where the US IRS lost against the taxpayer. In this case, the court found that the transfer pricing methodology, the CUP method, was adequate under the circumstances. The IRS argued that its incorrect assessment was based on insufficient information received from Compaq, an argument that the court rejected.

The pharmaceutical group GlaxoSmithKline (GSK) has made headlines for being involved in a spectacular breakdown of competent authority[3] negotiations

2. *Compaq Computer Corp. v. Commissioner,* T.C. Memo. 19990220 (7/2/99).
3. For tax treaty purposes, the Ministers of Finance and their representatives are competent authorities and are those responsible for reaching mutual agreement on certain tax matters.

involving the tax authorities of the UK and the US. The issue was the marketing of intangibles in respect of the promotion of some of the pharmaceutical company's medicines. The IRS argued that GSK underreported the importance of the US in marketing its medicines and also that the company overvalued the R&D taking place in the UK. Therefore, some of the royalties paid by GSK US to the UK parent should be reallocated. GSK has been trying to resolve its disputes with the IRS, a process which broke down when the UK Inland Revenue announced in 2004 that it supported GSK in its contention that no further taxes are due to the IRS.

The Asian unit of the Swiss watchmaker, Swatch, which is registered in the British Virgin Islands, was allegedly involved in manipulating the company's transfer prices in order to reduce its tax liability in the US and other countries. Swatch denied the allegations, stating the transfer pricing policy is a matter of great complexity and involves factors such as currency fluctuation, VAT, a company's distribution structure, etc.

8.2 CONTROLLING PRICES AND PROFIT MARGINS

A multinational organisation will attempt to ensure that profits are earned where taxes are the lowest; few multinational organisations will do anything other than attempt to ensure that this is done. They may not, as discussed in previous chapters, deliberately establish a company in a low or no-tax country simply to act as an intermediary and avoid tax in higher-tax countries. Where there are already many companies within a group, the pricing structures should take into account the differing rates of taxes payable and perhaps existing losses carried forward against which profits could be absorbed without incurring tax liabilities. Provided normal trade is carried out by properly constituted companies, the pricing structures may nevertheless be reviewed by the tax authorities of interested countries.

The tax authorities of most countries are very conscious of the effect of inter-group pricing policies on domestic taxable profits and will attempt to restrict the scope of operation in this respect. Some of the anti-avoidance provisions mentioned in previous chapters are applicable in this context, but more specific legislation also exists in most countries to counteract the effect of pricing policies.

8.3 ADJUSTMENT OF TAXABLE PROFITS

Various tax jurisdictions therefore reserve the power to adjust profits of companies that have been found not to conform to the arm's-length standard. Selected examples of the mechanisms in some jurisdictions are outlined below.

8.3.1 Belgium

Where a Belgian company carries on trade in Belgium or elsewhere, its profits are fully taxable in Belgium. In order to reduce the taxable income of the Belgian company, it is legally possible to structure transactions so that a low-taxed company charges, directly or indirectly, interest on loans to the Belgian company, royalties on a licence given to the Belgian company or charges a higher price on sale of products to the Belgian company (or pays a lower price on purchases from the Belgian company). Several other non-arm's-length transactions are also possible.

However, 'abnormal or gratuitous advantages' are added to the taxable profits of the grantor, unless they are taken into account for determining the taxable income of the beneficiary. This exception does not apply when the beneficiary is a foreign affiliated person, or a foreign branch, or a person enjoying a privileged or tax haven regime.[4]

The cost-plus principle is illustrated in part in the Belgium co-ordination centre regime. Belgium has been the location for co-ordination centres created by large international groups, the major advantages of which include that such centre is taxed on a trimmed down cost-plus principle.[5] Additionally, the qualifying centre, which could be either a Belgian company or a Belgian branch of a foreign company, does not have to withhold tax on profits distributed, nor on interest or royalties paid.

Activities of such co-ordination centres must be restricted to advertising, supply and collection of information, insurance and reinsurance, scientific research, relations with national and international authorities, centralisation of accounting, administration and data processing, centralisation of financial operations and the hedging of risks resulting from fluctuations in foreign exchange, and all activities having a preparatory or auxiliary character for the group's companies.

Co-ordination centres[6] must be recognised by Royal Decree and must employ at least ten persons within two years of commencing operations. A co-ordination centre cannot own shares in any other company, nor act as a cash management centre with funds contributed to it by affiliates, which have borrowed for such purposes. It should be realised that the minimum limits of assets and turnover of the group to which the co-ordination centre belongs restricts the use of such centres to all but the large multinational groups.

4. Code des Impôts sur les Revenus (CIR), Article 26.
5. Generally, the percentage of costs accepted as taxable income of a co-ordination centre in Belgium is around 8% of total expenses and operating cost, but excluding salaries and interest.
6. Royal Decree No. 187 of 30 December 1982.

The Belgian co-ordination centre regime was the subject of a negative European Commission ruling in February 2003. The Commission found that while this system in itself did not necessarily equate to state aid, the application of the scheme resulted in state aid since, among others, a default rate of 8% was used regardless of the services provided. The calculation method allowed certain, but nevertheless substantial, operating costs to be excluded and the centres benefited from certain tax breaks, such as withholding tax exemption on distributed income. The Commission ordered that the scheme be closed to new entrants with immediate effect, with existing entrants benefiting from grandfathering until 2010.

As a result of the Commission's criticism, new rules were proposed concerning co-ordination centres. The Commission partly approved these new rules[7] on the basis that the cost-plus method is based on *all* the centres' operating costs and an 'appropriate mark-up' is applied. In May 2004, Belgium and the Commission reached an agreement according to which Belgium committed to widen the scope of application of the withholding tax exemption currently benefiting solely co-ordination centres to all companies established in Belgium. The co-ordination centres will also in the future be subject to registration duty on contributions, the rate of which will be 0.25% or 0.3% for all companies, instead of the current 0.5%.

8.3.2 France

Article 57 of the CGI[8] restores trading profits to the levels that would have been attained in arm's-length transactions if a French company were owned by, or owned a non-resident company and, between the two companies, sales or purchases at deflated or inflated values have taken place. Article 14 of the Law of Finance 1974 extends Article 57 of the CGI (which basically relates to pricing manoeuvres) so that royalties, fee payments for know-how, interest payments and salaries are very carefully scrutinised to ensure that profits are not being extracted in these forms at the expense of the French entity. If it is discovered, upon investigation, that such payments have not been made under arm's-length conditions, they will not be allowed as deductible items for tax purposes.

The effect of an Article 57 adjustment may be that not only is the excessive payment disallowed for tax purposes, or alternatively an additional assessment rendered on unacceptably low taxable profits, but the difference may be treated as a constructive dividend, even though the dividend has not been declared in conformity with company law. This could then result in French withholding tax being levied on the difference at the standard withholding tax rate of 25%,

7. Press release IP/03/558.
8. Code Générale des Impôts or French Tax Code.

unless this withholding tax rate may be reduced by the provisions of an applicable double tax treaty. However, such treaty provisions may not permit the re-characterisation of the difference as a constructive dividend, and merely treat the difference as falling within the 'other income' article of the treaty, which is only taxable in the country of residence of the recipient. In the event that the dividend article expressly allows constructive dividends to be subject to withholding tax in France, or alternatively that there is no 'other income' article in the relevant double tax treaty, France is entitled to levy withholding tax at the applicable treaty rate.

Article 238A of the CGI places the burden of proof that the transactions are commercially justifiable upon the taxpayer. Thus, if a French resident entity or individual makes payments as described above to an entity in a tax regime which levies substantially lower taxes than French tax,[9] the payment may be added back in the computation of taxable income in France unless the payor proves that the payments correspond with commercially *bona fide* transactions and that the payments are neither excessive nor abnormal.

8.3.3 Germany

Section 1 of the Aussensteuergesetz (AStG) states that profits of internationally related enterprises may be adjusted for German taxation to reflect the amount that would have been earned through dealing with non-related parties. In fact, if a double tax treaty exists between the two countries involved, a provision modelled on Article 9 of the OECD Model Treaty will usually authorise the German tax administration to adjust the profits of the German company if trading has not been effected on a commercially justifiable basis. However, since it is unlikely that a low-tax regime will have a tax treaty with Germany, Section 1 empowers the tax administration to effect profit increases in the absence of commercial transactions, while under another provision of German law, payment of certain items which are not made at arm's length are treated as a hidden distribution of profits (constructive dividend as for France above).

8.3.4 Italy

According to Italian transfer pricing provisions,[10] items contributing to the computation of taxable profits arising from transactions between resident enterprises (individual and corporate) and non-resident companies *only,* which:

(a) are controlled (directly or indirectly) by the resident enterprise; or

(b) control (directly or indirectly) the resident enterprise; or

9. Less than 50% of the French corporate tax rate (2005 Finance Bill).
10. Article 110(7) of the Italian Consolidated Tax Decree (CTD).

(c) are controlled (directly or indirectly) by the same person which controls the resident enterprise;

must be determined on the basis of their 'normal value'.

'Control' should be interpreted extensively to include any form of relevant influence by one enterprise on another enterprise;[11] even in the absence of voting rights over the company.

The provision covers all transactions generating income or expenditure to be taken into account in determining taxable income. Therefore, it includes both sales and purchases of tangible and intangible goods, as well as services, regardless of whether they generate operating income or capital gains.

'Normal value' is defined in Article 9 of the CTD:[12] it is the average price or consideration paid for goods or services of the same or a similar type, in free market conditions and at the same level of commerce, at the time and place at which the goods and services were purchased or performed, or, in absence of such criteria, at the time and place closest thereto. It should be noted that conventional methods are provided in order to determine the 'normal value' of some financial assets. For example, the 'normal value' of shares listed in a stock market is determined on the basis of the last month's average price.

Normal value is determined by the following methods:

(a) the comparable uncontrolled price method is given first priority;

(b) the resale price and/or the cost-plus method may be applied next;

(c) if none of the above is applicable, other methods will be taken into account.

8.3.5 The Netherlands

Article 3.25 of the Dutch Income Tax Law, which also applies to corporations, ascertains profits in accordance with 'sound business practice'. If a transaction is not in accordance with this principle (which would be the case if a transaction carried out between related parties was not at full market value), the transaction will be ignored for tax purposes and profits restored to what they would otherwise have been. The general nature of the Dutch provision can thus possibly be said to offer greater flexibility and possibly greater fairness before the courts.

11. Such as family links or contractual relationships.
12. D.P.R. 22 December 1986, n.917.

8.3.6 United Kingdom

Section 770A of ICTA, in combination with Schedule 28AA, is the provision in UK tax law which specifically controls pricing policies between non-arm's-length companies and allows HMRC to disallow certain prices between related parties. The rules in Schedule 28AA are applicable where a number of conditions have been satisfied, namely:

(a) 'provision' ('the actual provision') has been made between any two persons ('the affected persons');

(b) the actual provision has been implemented through one or a series of transactions;

(c) the actual provision does not conform to the arm's-length standard;

(d) the actual provision may potentially ensure a benefit for UK tax purposes for one or both the affected persons;

(e) one of the affected persons participates in the management, control or capital of the other, or a mutual third party participates in both.

Section 74 of ICTA states what are considered allowable and disallowable expenses and specifically disallows those expenses not wholly and exclusively laid out for the purposes of a trade, profession or vocation. The payment of an excessive price for an article cannot be considered to be wholly or exclusively incurred for the purposes of trade, since an unrelated trader would have bought the same article elsewhere at a lower price.[13]

An early example of a case which invoked Section 770A (or Section 485 as it was then) was *Hoffmann La Roche.*[14] Due to internal pricing arrangements among members of the group, the UK subsidiary paid an excessive price (according to the UK tax authorities) in respect of goods supplied to it. The net result was an assessment under Section 770A, so that Hoffmann La Roche UK incurred heavy additional tax liabilities and, moreover, had to pay substantial sums (representing excess profits obtained as a result of the pricing manoeuvres) to the UK National Health Service.

8.3.7 United States

The transfer pricing policies of multinational organisations are scrutinised by the majority of high-tax countries, and perhaps nowhere more closely than in the

13. To the extent that the profits are calculated relating to a trade carried on by an individual, Section 34 of the Income Tax (Trading and Other Income) Act 2005 applies.
14. Citation unavailable.

US, where the IRS has substantial powers under Section 482 of the IRC and where many court cases have substantiated the effectiveness of US anti-avoidance legislation in respect of pricing manoeuvres. As with Section 770A of ICTA 1988 in the UK, the IRS has the power to reallocate group pricing where the transaction is not commercially acceptable. Section 482 applies even if the companies involved are either both resident in the US or both non-resident.

Regulations under Section 482 lay down certain methods for determining what an arm's-length price is:

(a) comparing prices charged with comparable uncontrolled prices payable for the same goods between parties who are at arm's length; or

(b) ascertaining the actual resale price of the goods and deducting an acceptable profit margin; or

(c) ascertaining the base costs of the products and adding a normal mark-up acceptable within the industry.

Cases will invariably occur where there is no satisfactory evidence of comparable trading or where it is impossible to apply either the resale price or cost-plus methods of calculations. In these situations most jurisdictions adopt any fair and reasonable basis of satisfying their requirements. In particular, they may look to prevailing market conditions and expectations or look to see where the worldwide trading profits are made, to see whether their share of the cake is fair. The IRS, therefore, can reserve a fourth method that is wide in its scope and perhaps subjective in its view. This method provided for under the regulations not only covers prices for products, but also loan interest, royalties, management fees and all other income paid or received by a US or foreign corporation. Even where reallocation is made, but payment of the reallocated amount by a foreign corporation is impossible because of local restrictions, Revenue Ruling 82-45 still entitles the IRS to tax the reallocated amount, although there is still substantial case law authority to the contrary.

An excerpt from the Internal Revenue Field Manual[15] gives some pointers as to what is scrutinised by the IRS for Section 482 reallocations, and some of these are listed below:

- repatriation of foreign profits as loans;
- excessive balances with foreign affiliates without interest payments and where the debt may subsequently be written off;
- absence of expected assets, e.g. patents in the balance sheet;
- hidden research and development expenditure where the asset is not owned by the company or where no royalties are subsequently received;

15. MT 4233-9.

- 'unlikely' recipients of royalties such as Liechtenstein or Swiss companies;
- round sum amounts for royalties, and royalties payable on sale of goods purchased from affiliates;
- payments in respect of expired patents, and payments in respect of trademarks;
- excessive administration costs which may be charged by foreign affiliates;
- non-commercial rates of interest, royalties and other fixed charges;
- sales of partly finished goods which are completed abroad where the major element of profit is retained abroad;
- third party commissions or discounts to foreign affiliates;
- invoices to one party where the actual shipments are to another;
- allocation of remuneration of executives involved in supervising foreign companies charged solely in domestic accounts;
- absence of rental payments incurred by foreign affiliates and full details of the premises occupied may indicate the extent and nature of their activities;
- internal chartering arrangements in shipping groups, which are carefully examined;
- changes in the pattern of accounts such as gross margins, net profits, turnover, debit/credit balances, and accounts with foreign affiliates;
- excessive premiums paid to captive insurance companies.

The above list is not exhaustive, but provides an interesting insight into some of the matters which should be considered by tax practitioners before submitting accounts which may later be scrutinised.

8.4 THIN CAPITALISATION

Thin capitalisation rules are a form of anti-avoidance provision and have been widely introduced by the developed tax authorities of the world. The purpose of the rules is to prevent the creation of a company with loan capital, which, by normal standards, is far greater than the equity capital of the company. The primary benefit of structuring an operation in this way is that large interest payments due on the debt with which the company was created could be used to reduce the profits of that entity. This was often a far more tax-efficient method of profit extraction than the payment of dividends to a parent company out of taxed profits, as interest payments were deducted from pre-taxed profits.

The use of such schemes as a method of transferring profits between countries in a very tax-efficient manner has resulted in the imposition of thin capitalisation rules, which act to restrict the benefits otherwise obtained. Thin capitalisation rules do this by reclassifying the payments of interest as a form of profit distribution. A maximum debt-to-equity ratio is imposed, i.e. by stating the maximum amount of debt that an entity may incur by reference to its equity, usually by considering the equivalent position of an entity operating on an arm's-length basis. In circumstances where the debt-to-equity ratio is greater than the prescribed level, the amount of interest deductible against profits on the excess debt is restricted.

Details of thin capitalisation rules in a selected number of countries are discussed below.

8.4.1 Australia

The government introduced measures in 2001 to improve the rules for allocating income between countries, 'to ensure that Australia receives its appropriate share of tax paid by multinational companies'. The thin capitalisation rules were strengthened to prevent multinationals (both foreign and Australian-based) from reducing their Australian tax by allocating a disproportionate share of debt to their Australian operations.

Thin capitalisation measures apply to the total debt of the Australian operations of multinational groups (including branches of those groups), as follows:

- the rules cover inward investment of foreign multinationals, and include a safe harbour debt-to-equity ratio of 3:1. Interest deductions will be denied to the extent that gearing exceeds the safe harbour ratio;
- where gearing exceeds the safe harbour ratio, multinationals will not be affected by the rules if they can satisfy the arm's-length test (that the gearing could have been borne by an independent entity);
- separate rules apply to financial institutions;
- to facilitate their inclusion in the rules, branches are required to prepare financial accounts for taxation purposes.

8.4.2 Canada

Under general rules, all interest expenses in borrowing money to carry on a business are deductible in computing income. Under the revised thin capitalisation rules (which became effective in 2001), interest on loans received from related non-resident shareholders, directly or indirectly, is deductible provided such loans do not exceed twice the 'tax equity'[16] provided by such shareholders.[17] The excess interest is not, however, re-characterised as a dividend and the excess debt is not re-characterised as equity. The amount of debt is the maximum level incurred during the year and the equity is measured at the year end. The rules specifically prohibit back-to-back loans as a means of circumventing this restriction, although a simple guarantee of indebtedness is not prohibited.

It is important to note that, in applying these rules, the determination of whether a contribution is a loan or debt instrument, as opposed to share capital, is made

---

16. Share capital together with allocable retained earnings measured under generally accepted accounting principles.
17. Those with a 25% or greater interest in any class of shares.

under ordinary principles of commercial law, pursuant to which no contribution would be considered to be share capital unless clearly paid into the company in exchange for stock or specifically designated as a gift or contribution to the capital of the company. A loan made on open account without any terms for repayment would, accordingly, be regarded as a debt instrument, as would a trade account payable.

8.4.3 European Union – general

Having far-reaching impact on the sovereignty of the tax authorities of the EU's member states, the thin capitalisation rules in Germany have been found to be contrary to Article 43 of the EC Treaty (which deals with freedom of establishment). The European Court of Justice held in the case of *Lankhorst-Hohorst v. Finanzamt Steinfurt*[18] that the rules were discriminatory on the grounds that a resident shareholder would have been able to treat the interest as expenditure whereas a non-resident in the same position would in fact be deemed to have received a dividend and been taxed accordingly. The ECJ held that these provisions clearly discriminated against companies established in other EU member states wishing to establish or run a subsidiary in Germany. The German government had unsuccessfully argued that the rule was necessary to prevent tax evasion. This was dismissed on the grounds that the shareholder was, in the case in question, liable to tax in its state of residence. The second unsuccessful argument advanced was based on the necessity to maintain the coherence of the tax system. The result of the case is potentially highly significant and, with increasing judgments of this nature, it has been argued that the ECJ is effectively advancing tax harmonisation through non-democratic means.

8.4.4 Italy

The Italian government introduced[19] thin capitalisation rules at the end of 2003. The rules, outlined in Article 98 of the CTD, are relevant for fiscal years starting from 1 January 2004. The debt-to-equity ratio was set at 4:1; however, for the first year of application of the thin capitalisation rules, the ratio was set at 5:1. The thin capitalisation rules will not apply where the debtor can demonstrate that the excess financing is justified. Where interest has been found to be non-deductible based on exceeding the above ratio, double taxation will be avoided by reclassifying the interest as 'dividend', in which case the 'dividends' will be 95% exempt.[20] The thin capitalisation rules will apply to companies carrying on primarily holding functions.

18. C-324/00.
19. By Legislative Decree 12 December 2003, n.344.
20. Under the participation exemption regime.

8.4.5 United Kingdom

Until the 1992 Finance (No 2) Act, there were no formal thin capitalisation rules in the UK, and the £100 UK company could be capitalised by shareholders' loans without regard to acceptable ratios other than for commercial reasons.

It was often argued by the Inland Revenue that, without a special relationship, a non-resident company would not lend a £100 company £100,000, for example, and therefore the entire interest payment represents an 'excess' payment and should be treated as a distribution. With effect from the 1995 Finance Act, the distribution rules applied to *all* recipients of interest which own more than 75% of the shares of the payor, whether the recipients are non-resident or UK-resident. With effect from 1 April 2004, thin capitalisation rules are included in paragraph 1A of Schedule 28AA[21] as an aspect of the UK's transfer pricing legislation. The 'special relationship' provisions determine that interest may be treated as excessive based on the size of the loan, the rate of the interest and also the question whether the loan would have been made at arm's length on the same terms. Should a loan exceed the amount that would have been granted to a third party borrower, the interest on the excessive part of the loan will not be allowed as a deduction for the borrower.

The Inland Revenue has deliberately avoided introducing debt-to-equity ratios to establish demarcation lines for thin capitalisation situations. This is on the basis that companies may fall within such ratios but not enter into financing arrangements on an arm's-length basis, so that the Inland Revenue may wish to preserve its rights to treat such financing arrangements as falling within the above provisions. For example, companies with existing borrowings at interest rates which are lower than current rates may refinance such loans with inter-company debt at higher rates, still keeping within an acceptable debt-to-equity ratio. This would not necessarily be acceptable to the Inland Revenue as it does not appear to be an arm's-length arrangement to burden the borrower company with higher interest charges. The Inland Revenue has nevertheless in the past commented on a suggested debt-to-equity ratio of 1:1 and an interest cover ratio of 3:1. As stated, it does not want to be bound by such ratios, but it accepts that these ratios are typical of external debt financing in the UK.

8.4.6 United States

The 'earnings stripping provisions' provisions of Section 163(j) of the IRC defer the deductibility of a percentage of the interest paid or payable by a US corporation where (a) that interest is classified as 'disqualified interest'; (b) the paying corporation has 'excess interest expense'; and (c) the debt-to-equity ratio of the payer is in excess of 1.5:1. Disqualified interest is in principle defined as interest that is paid or accrued to a related person that is not subject to US tax. This

21. ICTA 1998.

therefore applies to interest payable under an applicable double tax treaty that may either be exempt from withholding tax or subject to a reduced treaty rate. However, where part of the 30% US withholding tax is still levied under relevant double tax treaties, the proportion of interest equivalent to the ratio of the applicable withholding tax to the standard 30% withholding tax is not considered as disqualified interest, i.e. if the applicable withholding tax under the treaty is 10%, then only two-thirds of the relevant interest will be treated as disqualified interest.

The refusal to allow deductibility in respect of interest is, however, limited to 'excess interest expense', which has been defined as the excess of the company's net interest expense over an amount equal to 50% of the adjusted taxable income of the company together with any excess limitation carried forward from the previous three years.[22] Interest disallowed may, however, be indefinitely carried forward for potential deduction in forthcoming years.[23] These provisions now serve to equate the position with regard to the debt and equity of related parties involving foreign taxpayers, but do not give rise to any tax consequences to the lender upon repayment of such debts.

Although the earnings stripping rules appear to have an adverse effect on foreign investors, they will of course only apply if the ratio of debt-to-equity of the US corporation at the close of the taxable year exceeds the accepted level of 1.5:1. The debt-to-equity ratio is defined as that ratio which the total indebtedness of the company bears to the sum of its cash and all other assets less such total indebtedness.[24] Moreover, the IRS seems to be content to establish the debt-to-equity ratio at the end of the taxpayer's fiscal year, so that movements during the year would be disregarded.

However, in order to avoid artificially decreasing debt or increasing assets prior to the end of each financial year, there is a 90-day rule whereby decreases in debt in the final 90 days of a financial year are disregarded if the amount of debt subsequently increases during the first 90 days of the succeeding accounting period. Similarly, transfers of assets by a related party to the relevant company in the last 90 days of the company's financial year are again disregarded if those or similar assets are transferred back again within the first 90 days of the succeeding accounting period. Nevertheless, it may be beneficial to transfer longer-term assets to a US company in order to avoid the earnings stripping rules. Often these assets may be intangible assets, e.g. technical know-how or other assets which create a royalty stream.

22. IRC, Section 163(j).
23. Hence the deferral of deductibility as opposed to its outright disallowance.
24. IRC, Section 163(j)(2)(C).

[VIII.] CASE STUDY 8

This chapter helps us to understand that although companies within the same group have a certain amount of flexibility in respect of controlling profit margins through intra-group transactions, most tax authorities by no means provide a *carte blanche* in this respect. Consider the following transactions:

(a) thin capitalisation issues relating to Filipe Finance BV (the Netherlands), Lucca Software SA (France), Lucca Software SpA (Italy) and Lucca Software Ltd (UK) (Diagram 13);
(b) transfer pricing issues relating to Lucca Software SA (France), Lucca Software SpA (Italy) and Lucca Software Ltd (UK) (Diagram 7);
(c) transfer pricing issues relating to Lucca Developments India (Diagram 12).

Diagram 7

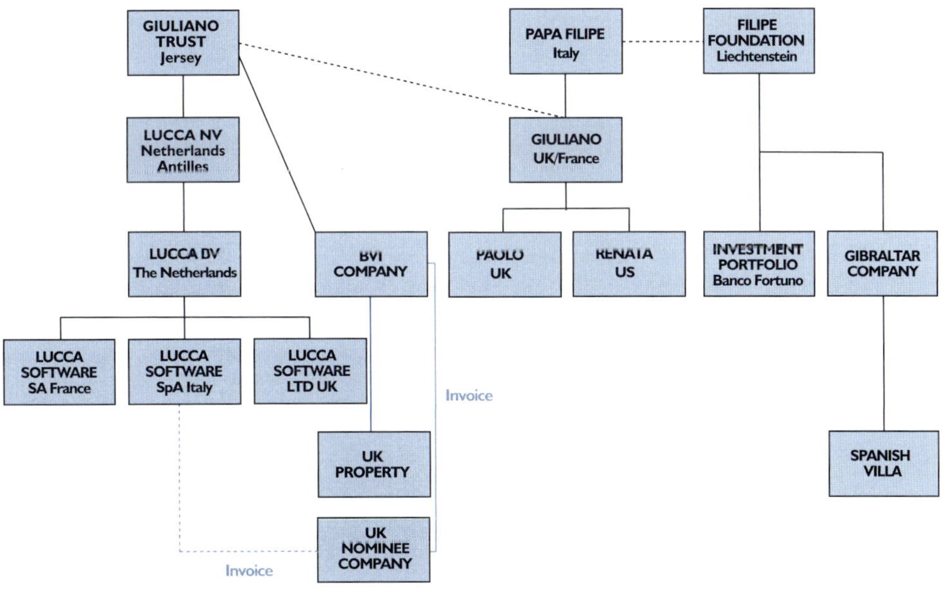

Diagram 12

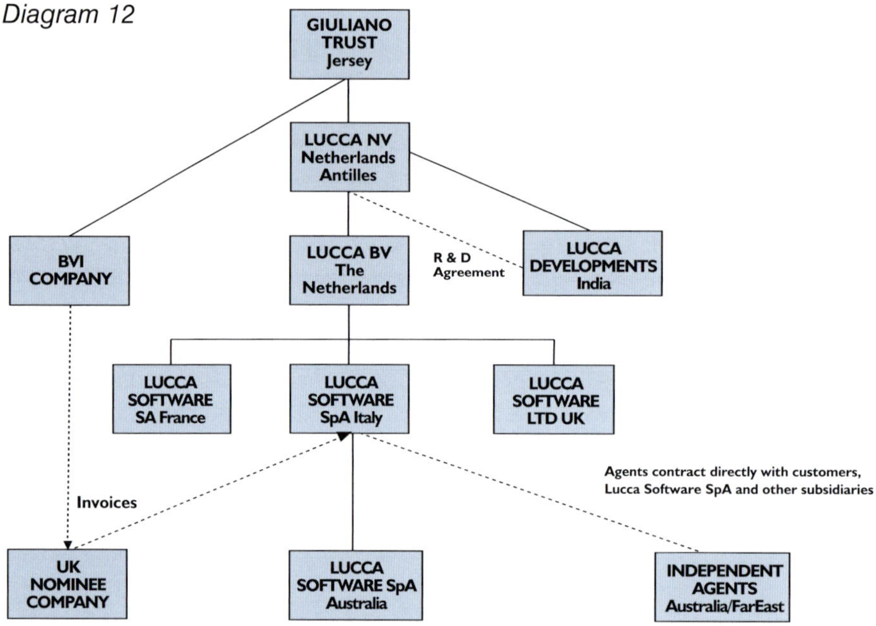

Diagram 13

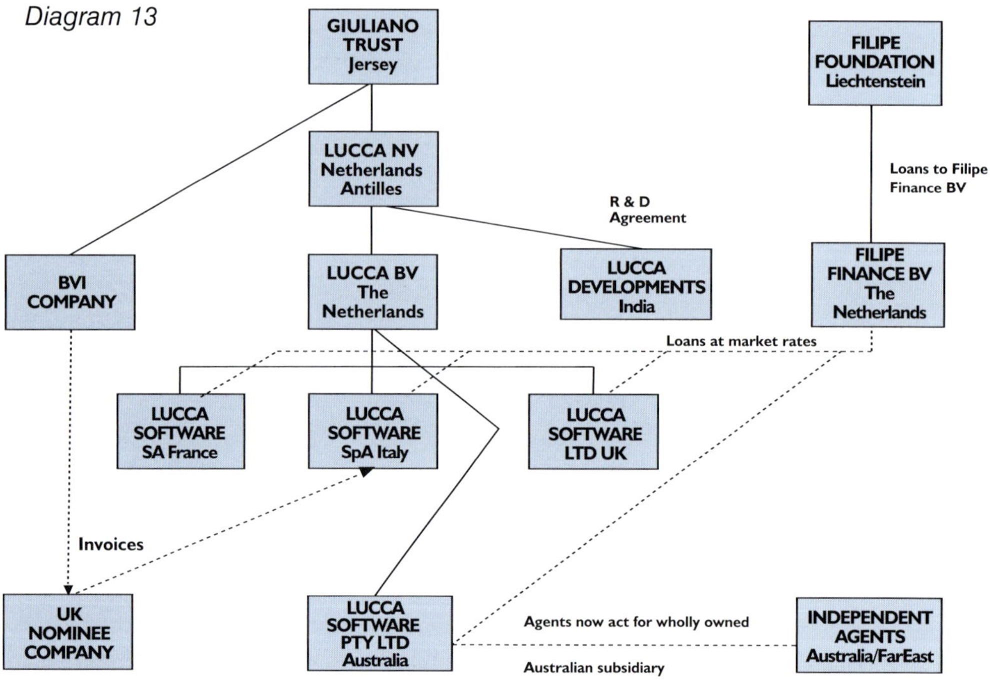

Maurice nearly fell off his chair when he answered the phone one afternoon. Giuliano, calling from what sounded like a swimming pool area, said: 'Maurice, I need your help. I just heard that transfer pricing, whatever that is, may be applicable to my Dutch company. I am tired of always skating on thin ice with tax authorities around the world – I need your advice on potential transfer pricing issues in the European subsidiaries of the business.'

After the conversation, Maurice looked out the window of his office with a distinct feeling of unease. Having resolved to help Giuliano stay clear of trouble Maurice sat down by his PC and drafted a memorandum:

Mr Giuliano Filipe
C/o Jolly Roger Inn
P.O. Box 13
Tortola
British Virgin Islands

URGENT – STRICTLY PRIVATE AND CONFIDENTIAL

Dear Giuliano

Thank you very much for your call this afternoon, and your inquiry relating to thin capitalisation and transfer pricing issues, as discussed. The purpose of this memorandum is to provide a cursory outline of the potential issues you may encounter, and is by no means definitive. In all events, I suggest we arrange a meeting to discuss the issues in greater detail as soon as you are back in the United Kingdom.

Thin capitalisation issues

You mentioned during our conversation that over the past several years, your father has been funding the Lucca software business through the Filipe Foundation via a newly incorporated subsidiary of the foundation, Filipe Finance BV. Filipe Finance BV has then made loans to the three European subsidiaries of your business, Lucca Software SA, Lucca Software SpA, and Lucca Software Ltd, who will pay interest on the loans to this Dutch company.

Outlined below are the potential issues that the respective entities may encounter in turn:

Filipe Finance BV

Thin capitalisation issues will not arise for Filipe Finance BV in the Netherlands, since it is acting as a conduit for the Filipe Foundation loans made through it to the subsidiary companies of Lucca Software BV. There may well be anti-treaty shopping conduit rules, which prevent the interest being received without local withholding taxes in accordance with the terms of a relevant double tax treaty, but these are foreign tax issues. As regards the Netherlands, only in circumstances where finance is being advanced to Lucca Software BV itself, as a holding company entitled to the participation exemption, would a debt-to-equity ratio of 85:15 be relevant. In the absence of any specific legislation, the use of a Dutch conduit financing vehicle such as Filipe Finance BV may be very advantageous.

Lucca Software SA

Any thin capitalisation issues that may crop up in respect of this company are likely to be raised by the French tax authorities, who may query the amount of interest payments from the French subsidiary on loans made by Filipe Finance BV.

French thin capitalisation rules are mainly aimed at denying deductions relating to interest payments to shareholders, particularly controlling shareholders. Since Filipe Finance BV is not a shareholder of any of the subsidiaries in France, Italy, or the UK, the existing French thin capitalisation rules are not applicable to loans from Filipe Finance BV.[25]

The above being said, it is important to keep in mind that the French tax authorities have considerable powers to deny interest deductions on the grounds of 'abnormal financial structuring'. This is closely related to the 'substance versus form' doctrine, under which profits are not allowed to be extracted at the expense of a French entity (and the French fiscus!). You will see in Chapter 6 of *The Principles of International Tax Planning* by *International Fiscal Services*, of which I include a copy, that the French notion of *abus de droits* gives the French tax authorities the powers to ignore any transaction that has been entered into simply to avoid French tax. Additionally, there is a risk that under Article 57 CGI the French tax authorities might reclassify any disallowed interest payment as a constructive dividend, which has withholding tax consequences. Consequently, although there are no debt-to-equity ratios to be kept in mind for the purposes of financing Lucca Software SA, it is advisable not to *abuse* the mechanism of interest payments to Filipe Finance BV in an attempt to reduce the company's taxable profits.

Lucca Software SpA

The Italian authorities will not permit the particular interest rate currently on the Filipe Finance BV loan. In view of the fact that you are developing new Lucca

25. The same may apply to loans from any other related entity, although this is less likely to take place since the intended financing vehicle, after all, is Filipe Finance BV.

software modules in India and licensing these through to the Lucca entities, it may be preferable for you to limit the amount of interest that you charge to the prescribed rate and increase the royalty charges that you intend to make as described below.

Lucca Software Ltd

Although the UK does not have any statutory debt-to-equity ratio (1:1 is used as a guideline, but does not provide a safe harbour), HMRC has the power to deny any excessive interest payments based primarily on the question whether a loan on similar terms would have been made in arm's-length circumstances. Filipe Finance BV is not in a capital relationship with Lucca Software Ltd, but is an associated participator in this connection.

In any event, under Section 770A ICTA[26] HMRC may disallow excessive interest payments by Lucca Software Ltd to Filipe Finance BV. The important thing to consider is the rate of interest that an independent bank would charge Lucca Software Ltd on the same terms and conditions as the loan arrangement from Filipe Finance BV. Thus, you need to consider the relevant security that is afforded under the loan, the term of the loan, repayment conditions, frequency of interest payments or otherwise in order to compare dependent interest rates with non-arm's-length rates.

Transfer pricing issues generally

In this connection and in addition to the thin capitalisation issues as above, transfer pricing rules are aimed at ensuring that transactions between related parties take place 'at arm's length', that is, on a pricing basis as if the transacting parties were not related. Tax authorities around the world, including those in France, Italy and the UK, are concerned that their taxable profits are being eroded to other tax jurisdictions by related parties entering into transactions that reduce the first country's profits. Therefore, as you rightly pointed out during our conversation, Lucca Software SA, Lucca Software SpA, and Lucca Software Ltd should apply pricing arrangements that resemble market values.

For example in France, any excessive price paid for a product purchased from a related entity could be deemed a dividend, with resulting withholding tax consequences. Based on the law, it would be thus recommended that Lucca Software SA, in purchasing or selling any product or service from or to the other entities in the Lucca group, apply arm's-length prices.

Under Italian tax law, transactions between resident and non-resident persons that

26. In combination with Schedule 28AA.

are controlled – directly or indirectly – by the same person that controls the resident enterprise, fall within the scope of the Italian transfer pricing rules. You mentioned during our conversation that the experienced staff of the more established entity, Lucca Software SpA, frequently provide various forms of administrative, technical and development assistance to Lucca Software SA in respect of the Lucca software. The Italian subsidiary then invoices the French subsidiary for such services provided. You will appreciate that the Italian subsidiary is subject to the Italian transfer pricing rules in respect of these transactions. The reasons for this are that these services rendered create taxable income for the Italian subsidiary; furthermore, both Lucca Software SpA, a resident Italian entity, and Lucca Software SA, a non-resident entity, are directly controlled by the same entity, Lucca BV, in the Netherlands.

As a result of the above, the invoices issued by Lucca Software SpA to Lucca Software SA should reflect a 'normal value', which means that the invoice amounts should be at arm's length. This would be determined on the basis of similar services rendered between two parties who compete in the free market and would usually be based on the uncontrolled price method. This means that services rendered by Lucca Software SpA to Lucca Software SA should be priced as if they were not related. Invoices based on time sheets and hourly charges would seem to be appropriate in these circumstances.

Although we have not discussed this issue this morning, I have become aware that the BVI company held by the Giuliano Trust is invoicing Lucca Software SpA via a UK nominee company at a premium for services rendered by staff of the BVI company. As your international tax adviser, I feel I have to point out that the premium paid by Lucca Software SpA is prone to scrutiny by the Italian tax authorities on transfer pricing grounds (if not for artificiality reasons). The transactions meet the typical requirements that might trigger Italian transfer pricing rules – the transactions influence the computation of taxable profits (i.e. deductions from Italian profits for the invoice amounts) between a resident party (i.e. Lucca Software SpA) and a non-resident party (i.e. the BVI company via the UK nominee company), where both parties are indirectly controlled by the same entity (i.e. the Giuliano Trust). In order to ensure that the invoice amounts are acceptable as deductions to the Italian tax authorities, we might need to sit down and determine what would constitute a 'normal value' for such transactions.

In either of the issues pointed out above, we will have to take into account that the services rendered are of a unique nature and that although the Italian tax authorities apply the uncontrolled price method as a matter of priority, this might not be a suitable method in our case. Under the circumstances it would be advisable to have appropriate substantiating documentation in place to convince the Italian tax authorities that the invoice amounts do, indeed, reflect 'normal value' for such transactions.

You mentioned on the phone that you are concerned about UK transfer pricing rules based on the price charged on sales of plastic casings used in assembling floppy disks, manufactured by a division of Lucca Software Ltd, to Lucca Software SA and Lucca Software SpA. The prices of the disks are adjusted to sometimes as low as 22p per casing, in order to keep UK taxable profits as low as possible and to enable Lucca Software SpA to channel its profits to the low-taxed BVI company, as outlined above, rather than to the UK.

In this respect I have to comment that Lucca Software Ltd is at risk of a reallocation of profits in the UK under Section 770A of ICTA 1988. Based on my experience, the current relevant open market price for identical casings is around 92p in the UK. This means that the Inland Revenue may be at liberty to assess an additional 70p per casing as taxable income, if we assume production cost of 12p per casing. You mentioned that Lucca Software Ltd sells around 5 million of these casings a year at prices that do not seem to reflect market value, which could mean additional UK corporate tax payable on around £3,500,000!

To conclude, from our conversation earlier today it was clear that you are aware of the basic theoretical advantages of, for example, extracting profits from a high-tax jurisdiction by means of methods such as interest over-payment or under-charging for products sold. However, since thin capitalisation issues or transfer pricing issues may eliminate the benefits of such structuring, it is highly advisable to remain within the guidelines provided by the relevant tax authority.

Best regards,

Maurice

Chapter 9

What Expenses May Minimise Tax Liabilities?

Tax burdens may be reduced through profit extraction where the profits earned by a company in a high-tax country are moved to another entity whose tax burden is not so onerous. This may be in the form of, say, royalties and licence fees, interest on loans, management fees, service charges, rentals on lease arrangements and property, insurance, director's remuneration and salaries, and any other expenses that may be deductible against profits in the highly taxed company and paid to a non-resident entity. In this respect, the question whether the parties between whom such transactions take place are related is crucial, since if they are, transfer pricing rules apply.[1]

However, domestic laws often provide for the deductibility of certain payments to unrelated or even related parties, and the question frequently asked is whether such expenses are allowable or not. The purpose of this chapter is to outline both cross-border and domestic expenses that may be allowable,[2] and to describe the tax consequences of disallowed expenses.

9.1 FUNDAMENTAL CONSIDERATIONS IN DETERMINING ALLOWABLE EXPENSES

The first vital point to consider is that if the expense is for a *bona fide*

1. Compare Chapter 8 for a detailed discussion.
2. But by no means a *numerus clausus*, since the deductibility of expenses varies greatly from one jurisdiction to the other.

commercial purpose which does not have tax avoidance as the principal object, then this is acceptable to most tax administrations unless the recipient is not only non-resident, but is also located in a blacklisted country.

However, whether or not the tax administration of the country where the company is paying the expenses will allow such expenses to be deductible against the taxable income of that company also depends on a number of other factors. Take, for example, the case of payment of a management fee from a German company to a Swiss company. Here both companies have taxable income, one taxed at, say, 45% (assuming this is the effective German corporate tax rate) and one taxed at, say, 25% (assuming this is the combined federal and cantonal tax rate). Therefore, for every 100 units of profit extracted to Switzerland by way of management fees and other items, there is an apparent saving of 20 units. However, if the German tax administration refuses to allow the expenses as deductible against German profits, then the 45 units of German tax will still be payable on the 100 units of profit extracted through management fees or other charges, yet Swiss tax will also be levied at 25 units on the fees extracted. A total tax charge, therefore, of 70 units is levied on the original 100 units of profit. Even greater penalties may be imposed in Germany, since the German tax administration may regard the expenses paid to the Swiss company as a hidden distribution of profit and consequently subject the amount transferred to dividend withholding tax.

Every payment may therefore be scrutinised to see whether it conforms to the general principle above, and it is folly to base any tax mitigation or tax deferral structure on the deductibility of an item that does not so conform. Even where tax mitigation is not particularly relevant to the transaction, the provisions relating to deductibility of expenses must be borne in mind. For example, the payment by a Belgian subsidiary of an expense that in fact relates to the non-resident shareholder of the Belgian company will not be allowable against taxable income in the Belgian company. In fact, Belgium goes a little further than most countries in that under Article 46 of the Code des Impôts sur les Revenus (CIR), the onus of proof that the expenditure was made in the ordinary course of business and also that it is not unduly high is on the taxpayer.

The general rules under domestic law for the deductibility of expenses in selected jurisdictions are outlined below.

9.1.1 Australia

As is the case in most countries, the Australian tax system provides that the taxable income of a company is to be calculated by deducting from the company's total assessable income all allowable expenses.

The general formula that determines which expenses are allowable provides that all losses and outgoings, to the extent to which they are incurred in gaining or producing assessable income, or are necessarily incurred in carrying on a business for that purpose, are allowable deductions except to the extent to which they are losses or outgoings of capital, or are incurred in relation to the gaining or production of exempt income.[3]

Where expenditure is incurred which is clearly revenue in nature but which is in respect of, for example, a product that will not be wholly completed within one year, the expenditure may need to be apportioned over the fiscal years during which the product will be completed.[4]

9.1.2 Germany

Under Section 160, subsection 1 of the Abgabeordnung, to which Sections 16 and 17 Aussensteuergesetz (AStG) refer, expenses paid to a low-tax country will be deductible only if the taxpayer supplies all the necessary details.[5] All transactions with foreign base companies must be disclosed. Section 1 of the AstG reflects transfer pricing legislation and adjusts the transactions between related enterprises to what would have been paid between non-related companies dealing with each other on an arm's-length basis. Some examples of disallowed expenses included in Section 31, subsection 3 of the Körperschaftsteuer-Richtlinien (KStR) are: excessive director's remuneration or other payments made to a shareholder, loans made at very low interest rates to a shareholder, payment of interest at high rates on loans received from a shareholder, and sales and purchases to and from a shareholder at artificially low or high prices.

9.1.3 The Netherlands

Dutch tax legislation[6] ascertains profits according to the general principle of sound business practice and the courts are able to, and frequently do, amplify this by reference to the deductibility of expenses. Obviously, an excessive payment of, say, a management fee is not in accordance with good business practice and the excess would therefore be disallowed.

9.1.4 United Kingdom

As mentioned in Chapter 8, Section 74 of ICTA provides that no sum shall be deducted in respect of any expenditure which is not wholly and exclusively laid out for the purposes of the particular trade, profession or vocation of the

3. Income Tax Assessment Act 1997, Section 8-(1).
4. Ruling TR94/25.
5. Note that generally, in order to be in line with EU regulations, intra-EU payments, even from high-tax member states to low-tax member states, should be deductible in spite of local legislation stating the contrary.
6. IB (Income Tax Act) 2001, Article 3.25.

taxpayer, a principle which is similar to the corresponding one in Australia. Section 74 continues with specific items that are not deductible against taxable income, specifically mentioning any loss that does not arise out of the particular trade, profession or vocation. Section 74 also covers expenses paid to non-residents and residents of the UK and prevents the excessive payment of interest (if to a non-UK resident), fees, director's remuneration and other items of expenditure, in that the excessive part cannot be considered as expended wholly and exclusively for the purposes of trade.[7]

9.2 REVIEW OF SPECIFIC DEDUCTIONS

The following section outlines some expenses frequently allowed by tax authorities to be set against individual and corporate income.

9.2.1 Individuals

The following list provides examples, albeit not exhaustive, of deductions that are often allowable against individuals' income, gains or estate:

- personal allowances and reliefs;
- standard deductions and exemptions;
- special expenses, e.g. interest paid on certain personal loans and certain insurance premiums;
- expenses in respect of extraordinary burdens, e.g. personal study expenses, provided they specifically relate to the business currently carried on by the individual, not for future business or employment opportunities;
- certain gifts, e.g. to recognised charities;
- capital gains allowances, e.g. the exemption on the sale of one's principal place of residence;[8]
- certain taxes, e.g. state and local income and real property tax in the US;
- interest, e.g. on home mortgages and certain investment interest;
- inheritance tax reliefs, e.g. UK business property relief, which is a deduction of either 50% or 100% made from the value of business property when it is assessed for inheritance tax purposes, or an exemption from tax on the first £275,000 of the estate. Transfers between two UK domiciled spouses are tax free, however;
- special rulings, e.g. the Swedish ruling where, among other reliefs, 25% of the gross salary of expatriates is exempt from income and social security taxes.

9.2.2 Companies

In calculating net profits of a company, which forms the tax base, allowable

7. To the extent that the profits are calculated relating to a trade carried on by an individual, Section 34 of the Income Tax (Trading and Other Income) Act (ITTOIA) 2005 applies.
8. E.g. in the UK, under Section 222 of TCGA 1992.

expenses are deducted from revenues. As a general rule, corporate expenses incurred 'wholly and exclusively' in earning the income are deductible. Disallowed expenses are usually added back to compute the true tax liability.

Management fees

Management fees charged by parent companies to their subsidiaries may be deductible within certain limits.

They must be related to the degree of management exercised in the payor company's business. If a company is actively trading and relies heavily upon personnel seconded to that company by a non-resident or uses the facilities of a non-resident entity,[9] then 'reasonable' management fees will be allowed as deductible expenses. The amount that is considered reasonable is what a non-related company would have charged the local company for the provision of such management services. However, if the local payor company is a passive investment company, then the degree of management required from the non-resident parent is far less and management fees may be entirely disallowed by the local tax administration.

Management fees (or a portion of such fees) chargeable as a result of a relationship between a subsidiary and a foreign parent will generally be disallowed, unless an unrelated party were to similarly pay for such services. The German tax administration, for example, differentiates between management charges paid for controlling the German payor, i.e. stewardship costs, and management charges payable for assisting the German payor to improve its profitability.

The type of expenses that will be considered as reimbursement of stewardship costs and therefore non-deductible will be those payments made in respect of the following:

- group policy control procedures imposed by head office;
- internal reporting requirements, e.g. sales and production reports;
- costs of internal audits;
- other supervisory and co-ordination functions.

On the other hand, the following costs relating to general assistance given to a subsidiary company in terms of local management will be deductible:

- financial services, e.g. arranging loans for subsidiaries, or assisting the subsidiaries in presenting budgets to obtain local financing;
- manufacturing services including plant designs and inspections;

9. Such as secretarial and office services.

- product development services such as clinical trials for products, recommendations relating to quality control and long-term planning relating to production and marketing products;
- operational services, including inventory control, and arranging for market surveys and analyses;
- public affairs services including arranging press releases and official meetings;
- legal services, including trademark co-ordination, ascertaining new product regulations and obtaining necessary approvals, formulating licensing and sales agreements;
- personnel services including staff training and recruitment.

The management contract between the subsidiary and parent company should include the following:

- it should be binding, completed in advance and clearly formulate the method of computing fees;
- it should be observed consistently for several years;
- it must be seen to apply and be beneficial to the payor company;
- it should reflect costs based on generally accepted accounting principles;
- group members sharing costs must have full access to the services concerned; and
- the payor companies must not pay for such services in any other way.

A Dutch holding company, for example, which receives tax-exempt dividend income from a qualifying participation or is treated beneficially on incoming royalties and interest from its licensing and financing operations, will be unable to deduct management fees of any description. Since no expenses relating to the passive operation of the Dutch company are allowed as deductible, it may be more beneficial for them to be charged against other group companies. However, if such expenses do not specifically relate to the activities of those other companies, they too may be disallowed.

General remarks

Generally, management charges will only be accepted if they are specifically seen to be for the benefit of the local company, that the activities have been requested by the local company rather than arbitrarily imposed by the foreign parent company, if the charges can be clearly distinguished and quantified, and are properly substantiated and valued. In order to ensure that this is the case, adequate documentary support should be available in the form of a contract between subsidiary and parent company,[10] relevant telefaxes, memoranda of calls, time sheets showing the amount of time devoted to the management of

10. Or other group management company.

the local company, and in all cases the management charges should be supported by invoices from the management company.

Where management fees are paid, the expenses underlying the fees must be kept on file so that the amount of the fee can be substantiated by invoices, salary time sheets or other documents specifically relating to the payor company's business. They should be billed and paid to the non-resident recipient in the financial year during which they were incurred, the services provided by the non-resident must benefit the payor, and the amount of the fee must not be excessive. A certain profit element may be allowed by the tax administration so that management fees may be the costs incurred by the non-resident recipient, plus say a 10% mark-up, which represents notional profit.

Director's remuneration

The next type of expense that may be considered is director's remuneration paid to resident or non-resident individuals. Certain jurisdictions permit director's remuneration to be paid only to full-time working directors.

Article 39 of the Code Générale des Impôts in France allows director's remuneration to be deductible only if the amount can be related to work effectively performed for the company, provided it is not excessive. In short, the relevant tax administration will use different criteria on which to base their decision whether or not to accept director's remuneration, and may, for example, compare the remuneration with that of the next highest paid person in the company or may compare the remuneration with that of other directors in similar companies or, again, may compare the salary to the company's turnover and see whether it is reasonable. If they decide that the remuneration is excessive, the excess will be added back to the payor company's taxable profits. This may be considered a hidden distribution of profits and, as such, subject to withholding tax.

The same considerations apply to director's remuneration voted in a UK company, except that the UK tax authorities often take a more lenient attitude to director's remuneration than their continental counterparts. Thus, in the UK, director's remuneration may be voted in arrears when the profits of the company are already known. It need not even be paid, but merely credited to a loan account, and any income tax due on the remuneration may be debited to the same loan account and, therefore, paid by the company. Importantly, it is worth noting that if the UK tax authorities decide that the remuneration is excessive, the excess can be written back into the company's tax computation; it is not treated as a distribution of profits as is the case in many other European countries.

Loan interest

A further method used for profit extraction is to pay interest on loans made available by non-resident related entities. For example, if an international group has funds available in a tax haven and uses those funds to lend them to a highly taxed company at a high interest rate, then much of the income obtained as a result of utilising that money in the high-tax country can be extracted to the tax haven in the form of interest. A property may be purchased by a French company, which has received a loan from a Liechtenstein company, so that the rental income is extracted to Liechtenstein in the form of loan interest. Certain countries lay down specific rules as to the maximum rate of interest that may be charged on any loans, while others rely on the general principle of deductibility of expenses as detailed above. The question of thin capitalisation has already been dealt with in Chapter 8 so the following considerations have been limited to loans that do not fall within thin capitalisation prescriptions.

Italy has a maximum rate of interest that may be allowed on any loans so as not to affect the strict usury laws, not therefore a tax restriction. France has a specific maximum rate of interest on loans from shareholders, so that under Article 39 of the CGI the rate must not exceed the Bank of France official rate. In any event, the interest will be disallowed if the loan on which the interest is paid does not exceed the unpaid share capital. In effect, therefore, the share capital must be fully paid up before the shareholders can lend money to the company and receive interest thereon.

In Switzerland, as a rule, only loans granted by shareholders or other related persons may be requalified as equity. If interest is paid on loans that exceed the relevant ratios,[11] the interest may be regarded as a distribution and disallowed as a deduction against corporate taxable profits. Moreover, the distribution tax[12] may be levied on the disallowed payment. In the United Kingdom, reference is made to a 'reasonable commercial rate'. As with excessive director's remuneration, the excess is simply added back to the tax computations of the UK company and is generally not treated as a dividends to the shareholders.

Two further points to be borne in mind when considering lending money to a high-tax country for the purposes of profit extraction are withholding taxes levied on interest payments to non-residents, which may be very considerable unless reduced by double tax treaty provisions, and the use to which the loan is put as to whether or not interest is allowed. For example, the Netherlands does not allow the deduction of interest paid on loans used to acquire interests in subsidiaries since, in view of the qualifying participation privilege, the income received would be exempt. Thus a Dutch holding company that also has trading activities will not be able to offset against trading income interest paid on loans used to finance the acquisition of subsidiaries. In some countries the loan must actually be used by the company if interest is to be allowed and not, for example, used by a subsidiary, irrespective of whether this enables the

11. Compare general discussion on thin capitalisation, §8.4.
12. I.e. a withholding tax of 35%.

subsidiary to distribute income to the parent which is then fully taxed. The parent should, in such circumstances, charge interest to the subsidiary, allowance for which would then be made in the accounts of the subsidiary company which has beneficial use of the money.

Patent royalties and licence fees

A further possibility for profit extraction is through royalties or licence fees paid to a related entity in a low-tax country. Here again, the same considerations apply as previously, and the amount of royalties payable must be no more than would be payable to a non-related patent or licence holder. Very often, taxpayers may contrive to vest the ownership of a patent in an entity established in a tax haven or low-tax country and then charge a royalty for selling or manufacturing the goods covered by the patent at an exorbitant amount in relation to turnover; instances where 30%, 40%, 50% and even higher percentages of sale prices are paid as royalties are not unknown. The drawbacks with the above are:

- if the sale of the patent to the low-tax entity is artificially low in order to restrict the taxable gain arising out of such sale, the true market value of the patent will be substituted;
- the foreign entity may be considered to be managed and controlled by residents of the domestic country, with the result that its full income is liable to domestic tax; and
- the royalties payable by the foreign manufacturing or trading companies will be disallowed in part (and therefore subject to corporate income tax) and the excess may be treated as a constructive dividend and subjected to high withholding taxes.[13]

It should be realised that withholding taxes are often levied on royalties paid by residents of highly taxed countries to recipients in countries that have no applicable double tax treaty, so that the actual amount received by the non-resident will be much lower than originally envisaged.

Insurance premiums paid to captive insurance companies

Another type of expense that may be considered is the payment of insurance premiums to a non-resident entity. Such an entity may be a captive insurance company most probably incorporated as part of a group in a tax haven or low-tax country to receive insurance premiums from companies in the group. The risks against which the group is insured are then reinsured with an independent insurance company and the reinsurance premiums paid out of the premiums received.

13. Compare §9.3 for a more detailed discussion.

The principal advantages of using captive insurance companies are that:

- the premiums paid by the group are paid to a group member so that, until the reinsurance premiums are due (perhaps three months later), the group still has the benefit of the cash. The captive therefore 'captures' the premiums and uses the cash until demanded;
- the captive may provide a way around exchange control laws (if applicable) in that premiums may normally be paid under general licence and the money can be used in an uncontrolled capital market;
- the difference in the premiums is accumulated tax free in the tax haven captive and outside any relevant exchange control net;
- anti-avoidance legislation with regard to captives is traditionally limited and, unless the premium is far higher than would have been paid to a non-related party, the deductibility of insurance premiums is seldom questioned.

Withholding taxes do not normally apply to insurance premiums paid from a high-tax country to a low-tax country.

In 2002 the IRS issued three Revenue Rulings, each concerning captive insurance companies. Revenue Ruling 2002-89 considers whether amounts paid by a US parent to its wholly owned subsidiary are deductible as insurance premiums under Section 162 of the IRC. The ruling describes two situations, under both of which a US parent company pays an arm's-length premium to its wholly owned subsidiary, which deals with its own administration, and maintains its own separate funds. The ruling states that the premiums will not be deductible for income tax purposes in circumstances where the subsidiary earns 90% of its total gross and net premiums from the parent, and the insurance provided by the subsidiary to the parent accounts for 90% of its risk. However, where the premiums paid by the parent amount to less than 50% of the subsidiary's gross or net premium income and equate to less than 50% of its risk, the premiums will be deductible.

Revenue Ruling 2002-90 considers the insurance premiums paid by a group of twelve US subsidiaries to an insurance subsidiary which is a member of the same group. The group insurance subsidiary is incorporated for valid, non-tax purposes and provides cover for the twelve subsidiaries, charging arm's-length premiums; each of the twelve subsidiaries accounts for no less than 5% and no more than 15% of the total risks insured by the insurance subsidiary. The risk of insurance is retained by the insurance subsidiary and does not shift to the parent or other members. The insurance premiums paid by the twelve operating subsidiaries would be deductible under Section 162 of the IRC even though the insurance subsidiary does not provide any cover to third parties.

Revenue Ruling 2002-91 considers the position of insurance premiums paid to a 'group captive', formed by a small number of unrelated companies involved in a highly concentrated industry, where a certain level of insurance is required by regulators. No single unrelated company owns more than 15% of the group insurance company, no company has more than 15% of the voting rights and no single company's risk accounts for more than 15% of the total risk of the group insurance company. Finally, the relationship is carried out on an arm's-length basis. The ruling concluded that the premiums would be deductible and that the 'group' insurance company would be regarded as an insurance company under Section 831 of the IRC.

Other allowable expenses

Although the expenses listed below do not constitute an exhaustive list, they are typical examples of expenses that are often allowed as deductions from income:

- employment-related expenses, e.g. employees' salaries, employers' social security contributions, certain contributions towards pension plans, employees' bonuses and certain employee benefits;
- certain business travel and corporate entertainment expenses;
- certain corporate advertising costs, utilities, supplies and rent;
- service fees, e.g. those paid to accountants and lawyers;
- licensing fees and royalties;
- some taxes incurred in the conduct of a trade or business;
- certain capital costs, i.e. expenses made for items that have useful lives of several years;
- research and development costs incurred in a trade or business;
- bad debt losses if the debt is written off;
- certain payments to trusts, such as UK employee benefit trusts (EBTs). In the case of EBTs, the beneficiaries are usually the company's employees who benefit from deferred compensation paid into the trust. Such payments will become deductible for the payor company once the amounts are distributed to employees.[14]

It should be noted that the rules as to deductibility vary greatly from country to country.

14. In the case of *Macdonald (Inspector of Taxes) v. Dextra Accessories Ltd and Others* [2003] EWHC 872 (Ch), the taxpayer company's right to claim deductions for contributions to an EBT was upheld. The subsequent legislation following the UK 2002 Pre-Budget Report provided that an employer making payments into an EBT will only obtain a deduction where a corresponding payment, which is liable to income tax and national insurance contributions, is made by the employee.

The House of Lords has delivered judgment in *MacDonald (Inspector of Taxes) v. Dextra Accessories Ltd* [2005] UKHL in respect of payments made to EBTs. Section 43 of the Finance Act 1989 denies immediate deduction in calculating profits of employers with regard to remuneration of employees where the remuneration is not paid within nine months. Deduction is postponed until the year when remuneration is actually paid to the relevant employees. Section 43 also encompasses 'potential emoluments': amounts or benefits reserved in the accounts of an employer held by an intermediary. The view taken is that these might become *relevant remuneration*, and a

Continued on facing page...

9.3 CONSTRUCTIVE DIVIDENDS

Where companies have either over-deducted expenses or where profits, but under a different name,[15] are distributed to shareholders, some tax authorities act not only to disallow the deduction, but also to consider the expense or payment as a deemed dividend distribution, subject to local withholding tax – a combined penalty which could cause a significant financial blow.

9.3.1 Switzerland

Where transactions take place between related persons and the Swiss tax authorities consider that excessive expenses have been paid by the Swiss company, such expenses will firstly be disregarded for tax purposes under the Federal Income Tax Law and may also be treated as a constructive dividend and, as such, subject to the 35% Swiss anticipatory tax. A constructive dividend exists where the recipient receives a benefit without giving reasonable commercial consideration in return, where he would not have received the benefit if the transaction had been an arm's-length one, and where the payor is aware that the recipient is receiving a benefit.

Swiss federal, cantonal and municipal tax will then be paid on the excess amount, with the result that the 35% Swiss anticipatory tax may well boost the total Swiss tax bill to more than 65% of the excess. It should be realised that the anticipatory tax is levied on the actual amount paid to the non-resident and not as may be adjusted by additional corporate tax being levied in Switzerland. Thus, the fact that only 70 units may be available out of the excess 100 units paid by the Swiss company once the tax authorities have claimed their 30%, does not alter the position; 100 units were actually transferred and, as such, the constructive dividend must be deemed to be 100 units, subject to the 35% anticipatory tax.

9.3.2 United Kingdom

The UK tax authorities are considerably more lenient in this respect and allow greater flexibility than their continental counterparts. Thus, in the UK, if excessive expenses have been paid and disallowed, the tax authorities simply add back such excessive expenses and adjust profits accordingly. However, the excess paid is not deemed to be a constructive dividend. As noted, an excessive amount paid for director's remuneration will therefore, if disallowed

deduction can only be allowed when a potential emolument becomes relevant remuneration. The court restricted relief from corporation tax for contributions to the EBT in question, as it was deemed they were potential emoluments, even if subsequently loaned to the EBT beneficiaries. This treatment does not apply to contributions made after 26 November 2002, these being governed by Schedule 24 Finance Act 2003.

15. Including through inter-group company pricing mechanisms – see Chapter 8.

by the UK tax authorities, pose no greater problems than if no excess had been paid. Nevertheless, there are other considerations, which may apply to disallowed payments to non-residents, depending on whether they are resident in no-tax, low-tax or high-tax jurisdictions.

[IX.] CASE STUDY 9

In the past, Giuliano has been considerably creative in the type of expenses offset against taxable profits of the Lucca Group. Maurice's personal observation in this respect is that the creativity sometimes required to 'make' expenses fit within the tax law definitions of a particular country, in order to ensure their deductibility, seems to bring out the artist in Giuliano.

In order to see how some of the points made in this chapter affect the Filipes, the following can be looked at:

(a) the creation of licensing structures, in particular licensing intellectual property and sales rights in respect of the Lucca software by Lucca NV (Netherlands Antilles) to Lucca License BV (the Netherlands), and the sub-licensing of such rights by Lucca License BV to Lucca Software Pty Ltd (Australia) (Diagram 14);
(b) Giuliano's home in the UK being held through a BVI company (Diagram 5);
(c) the management fees paid by Lucca BV (the Netherlands) (Diagram 14);
(d) the director's fees paid to Giuliano by Lucca Software SA and Lucca Software Ltd (Diagram 4).

Diagram 4

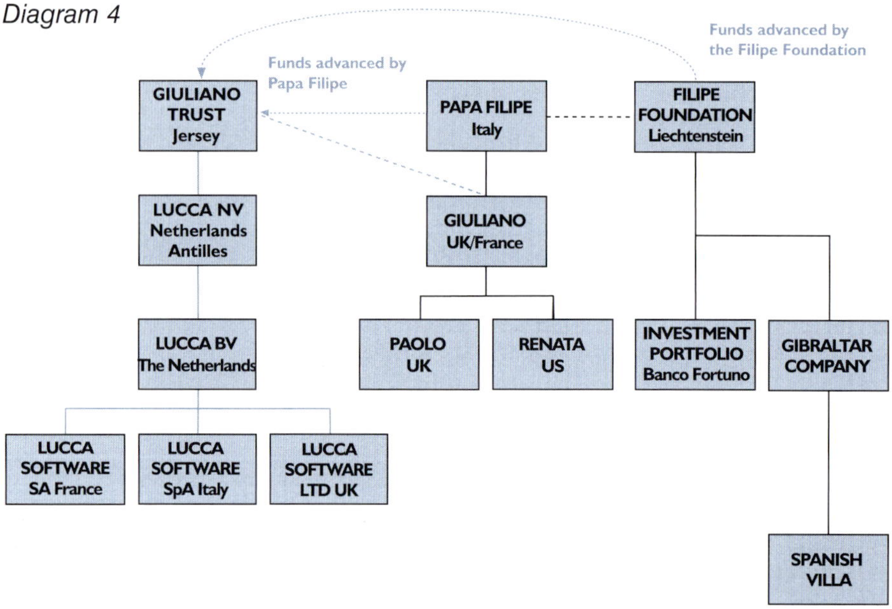

Diagram 5

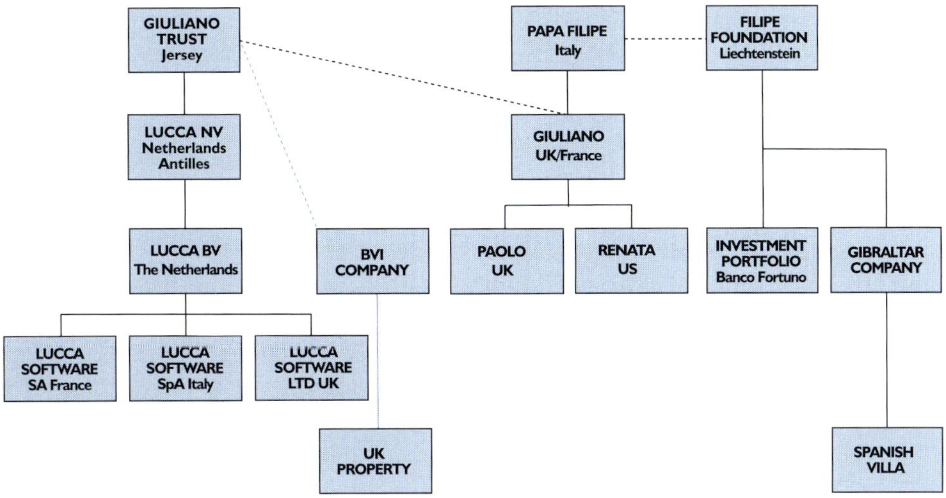

Diagram 14

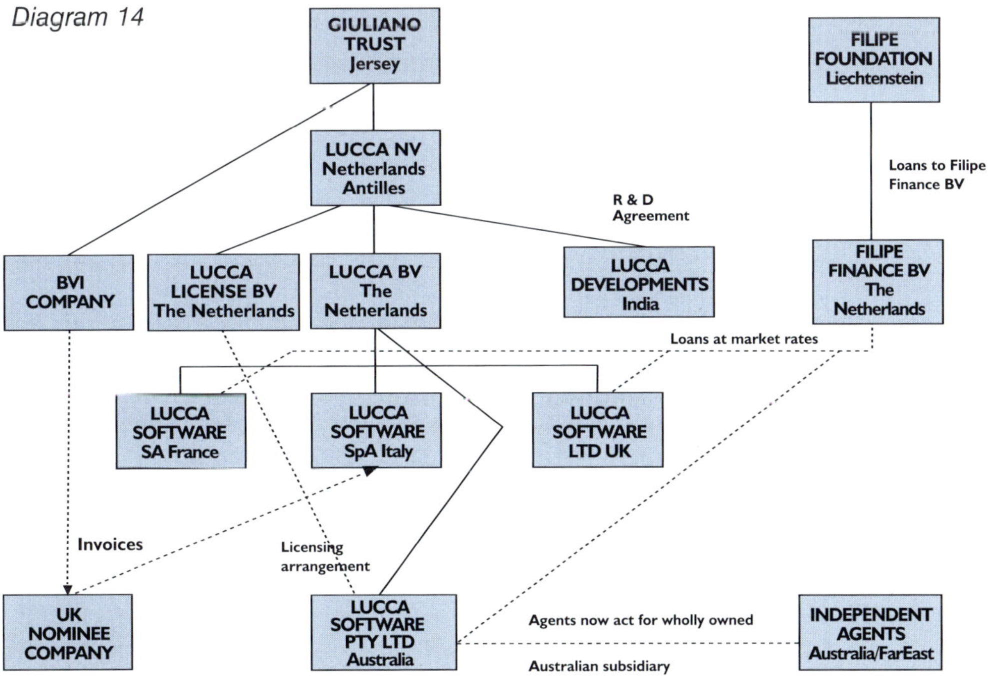

[IX.a] Lucca Software Pty Ltd

The question of whether expenses are deductible in Australia pivots on whether they were necessarily incurred in carrying on a business that produces assessable income. The Lucca sub-licensing structure allows Lucca Software Pty Ltd in Australia to manufacture Lucca software and to sell the software to Australian consumers. These activities produce revenue in Australia, which, after deductions, provides a profit – this is a very successful product after all – on which Australian corporate tax is assessed; thus, Lucca Software Pty Ltd's activities produce assessable income.

The payment of royalties to the foreign licensor company, Lucca License BV, is necessary in order for Lucca Software Pty Ltd to carry on its business – even the Australian tax authorities will have to agree that licences to manufacture and sell valuable products such as Lucca software are not given away for free, not even by companies within the same group. Consequently, the royalty payments to Lucca License BV should be allowable as deductions under Australian tax law, provided, of course, that the amount of the royalty payments conform to the arm's-length principle.[16]

[IX.b] Lucca License BV

The Filipes interposed Lucca License BV to ensure that the Australian/Dutch tax treaty's favourable withholding tax rates on royalties apply to the payments by Lucca Software Pty Ltd.[17]

Once the royalties are received by Lucca License BV, the Dutch tax authorities would generally require a spread of around 7% between the royalty received from Lucca Software Pty Ltd and the royalty paid to Lucca NV. This spread, net of Australian withholding tax, will be subject to Dutch corporate tax at the normal rates. Thus, if the amount of royalties received from Australia is 100, 7 must be left in the Netherlands to be taxed after appropriate deductions; the other 93 can be paid to the original patent owner, Lucca NV.

From the above it is clear that interposing Lucca License BV as a conduit vehicle has two significant advantages: a much lower withholding tax exposure on royalties in Australia than would have been the case had Lucca NV been the direct recipient; and full Dutch taxation on only a fraction of the royalties received from Australia. Were Lucca License BV the actual owner of the intellectual property and sales rights, the full amount of royalties received from Lucca Software Pty would have been subject to Dutch tax.

16. See Chapter 8.

17. I.e. 5%, as opposed to the non-treaty rate, which includes the Netherlands Antilles where Lucca NV is located, of 30%.

[IX.c] Dispute between Lucca Software SpA and Lucca NV/Lucca License BV

The work done by Lucca Developments India mostly relates to translating the software into applicable languages and adapting the software for different accounting systems, and the rights relating to these recent developments vest in Lucca NV based on the contract between Lucca Developments India and Lucca NV.

However, following Giuliano's departure from Italy to the UK, he had offered Matteo Gabrieli, the manager of his Italian company, a profit percentage of income earned by Lucca Software SpA to incentivise him. Clearly, many of the expenses of research and development had been incurred by Lucca Software SpA that, at the time, reduced both taxable profits in Italy and also Matteo's profit participation. Matteo did not now see why he should not benefit from some of the royalty income derived by Lucca License BV for overseas licensing. He demanded that the majority of licence fee income paid by Lucca Software Pty Ltd in Australia be paid to Lucca Software SpA.

Maurice was asked to advise as to which company (Lucca Software SpA or Lucca NV/Lucca License BV) own the intellectual property rights in respect of the software development. Maurice suggested that Lucca NV and Lucca Software SpA agree on what the proportional input of each entity is, and that royalties from Lucca License BV be split into appropriate portions and paid to the relevant entities, based on the agreement and leaving appropriate margins to be taxed in the Netherlands.

Giuliano was concerned that the Italian tax assessment would be much higher because of Matteo's argumentative nature, and he did not want to give in to Matteo just because Matteo wanted to buy a new Lamborghini. The issue was finally settled by a compromise: the agreement Maurice recommended would be put in place, but the lion's share of the royalties would go to Lucca NV, which would then purchase the Lamborghini and let Matteo use it. Maurice tried to explain about employee benefits, customs duties and VAT, but by then neither Giuliano nor Matteo were listening.

[IX.d] UK home held by BVI company

Giuliano's house in the UK is being held through a BVI company – another of Giuliano's 'tax planning' ideas, which actually was sound at the time the UK house was bought. However, Maurice wanted to see an end to this structure – the disadvantages have been outlined in previous chapters.[18] Maurice knew that Giuliano was hoping to retain his UK tax residence and also that he was not using the flat in Paris very much due to his travels to the Caribbean and the Netherlands.

---

18. See, for example, [§III.c], in Chapter 3.

'Why don't you hold the house in your own name?' Maurice asked Giuliano during one of their conversations.

'Ah, but it's being held in a very sophisticated structure as it is...,' Giuliano replied.

'I'm not so sure about that,' said Maurice, and explained about shadow directors and taxable employee benefits. He then asked Giuliano why he would not want to own the house in his own name. 'You will benefit from the provisions of the capital gains laws in the UK – tax-free sale because it's your principal residence – if you simply hold the house in your own name and not bother about the rest.'[19]

'You mean I can sell the house later and not pay tax on a gain...?'

'Yes. It's a personal exemption allowed by the UK government.'

'But I thought personal ownership creates an inheritance tax liability,' said Giuliano.

'Yes, you are quite right, but let's look at the arithmetic. The house is worth £750,000, so, after deduction of the inheritance tax exemption, at a 40% tax rate, the liability could be as much as £200,000. For a man of your age in excellent health, an annual insurance premium for a whole life policy for £200,000 would be approximately £5,000. Compare that to income tax on a deemed benefit in kind which could be £15,000 per annum, plus the costs of running the BVI company and ...'

Maurice allowed this simple solution to sink in, knowing that Giuliano resented paying fees to offshore trust companies almost as much as he resented paying tax. Maurice did add, after a time and so that Giuliano could make an informed decision, that UK stamp duty at 4% would have to be paid on a transfer of the property for the BVI company to Giuliano personally, but Giuliano understood this was a one-off tax liability.

After giving it some thought, Giuliano asked how long it takes to liquidate a BVI company and Maurice knew that he had won another round in tidying up the Filipes' tax affairs.

[IX.e] Management fees paid by Lucca BV

Lucca BV has been paying an amount of management fees to its three subsidiaries for administrative work that was being done in France, Italy and the UK, respectively. Maurice suggested that these functions be centralised within Lucca BV, since the expenses paid to France, Italy and the UK are not deductible for Lucca BV. As an entity that enjoys tax privileges on incoming royalties,[20] none of the management fees it pays will be deductible.

19. In a subsequent memorandum, Maurice clarified that this statement is based on the assumption that Giuliano will spend at least a certain amount of time over a certain number of years living in the house.

20. See [§IX.b].

Moreover, in today's world of requiring commercial substance in relevant entities, Maurice advised Giuliano to employ some of his management staff currently located in France in his Dutch company. Then the position could be reversed and management fees could be charged to the French company, subject to these not being considered stewardship costs. He left Giuliano to consider which of his French employees could be seconded to Lucca BV, knowing the love of his Gallic employees for their native land.

[IX.f] Director's fees paid to Giuliano by Lucca Software SA and Lucca Software Ltd

Giuliano, as one of the directors of Lucca Software SA in France and Lucca Software Ltd in the UK, respectively, is entitled to a substantial amount of director's remuneration. Based on the French rules in respect of director's remuneration, any amount paid to Giuliano has to relate to work actually performed by him to be deductible, provided that the amount is not excessive. Maurice pointed out that the French tax authorities are strict in this respect and that various criteria may be used in determining the 'excessiveness' or not of Giuliano's remuneration, including how Giuliano's salary compares to that of the deputy director (the second-highest paid person in the company) and also to the total turnover of the company. Maurice suggested that Giuliano and the rest of the board keep in mind that should the French tax authorities find that his salary is excessive, that it would be treated as a distribution and subject to withholding tax in France.

As to Giuliano's salary paid by Lucca Software Ltd, Maurice reminded the company's CFO that the UK tax authorities are a little less strict. Nevertheless, should the Inland Revenue learn that excessive salaries have been paid to Giuliano, the excess will be added back into the corporate tax computation.

[IX.g] Conclusion

Even to those with the most basic grasp of taxation matters, the concept of tax-deductible expenses surely rings a bell. After all, an expense that can be shown to be deductible is a much-coveted item in any company's accounts. However, contrary to what Giuliano might want to believe, a fraction more than mere 'creativity' is needed to ensure that expenses are indeed allowed as deductible for tax purposes. In this respect, as always, it is invaluable to have factual knowledge as to what a particular item of expenditure is for, whether it is incurred 'wholly and exclusively' for the purposes of a company's business, and at the correct level for transfer pricing purposes.

Chapter 10
What Other Taxes Need to Be Considered?

As the general rate of direct taxes has fallen throughout the world, with less government reliance on income tax and capital gains tax for raising revenue for local requirements, so the impact of other taxes has increased. Chapter 3[1] discussed the 3% special tax which is imposed when offshore companies are used for real estate investment in certain countries without full declaration of beneficial ownership, inheritance and wealth tax on real estate with a local *situs*, and transfer taxes when real estate is transferred from one party to another. However, the most significant revenue raising tax in most countries is now indirect tax in the form of value added taxation or other similarly named indirect taxes.

10.1 VALUE ADDED TAXES

10.1.1 European Union VAT

Value added tax (VAT) is an indirect tax on the supply of goods and services in the EU by a taxable person. The system is compulsory within the EU, as initially provided by the 1967 Second Council Directive on VAT. Since then the Sixth VAT Directive of 1977[2] has attempted to achieve the harmonisation of VAT, although there are still material differences between the EU countries, in particular with regard to the considerable variation of rates imposed. The

1. In §3.3.
2. As amended and expanded by Directive 91/680 and Directive 92/111.

Thirteenth VAT Directive of 1986,[3] provides for arrangements for the refund of VAT to taxable persons not established in Community territory.

A VAT registration in one EU country can enable the registered person to make claims for VAT incurred elsewhere within the EU. In order to make a claim, the following are required:

(a) a claim form completed in the language of the country where the expenses were incurred;

(b) a certificate confirming VAT registration in the European country of the claimant;

(c) original invoices;

(d) a timely response: the claim must be made within six months of the calendar year in which the expenses are incurred.

In respect of the application of VAT to digital products, new rules were applied in EU member states from 1 July 2003. These products include those which are delivered online, and subscription-based pay-per-view television and radio. Under the Sixth Directive, suppliers based in the EU are not required to charge VAT on products, such as software, sold outside the EU. Suppliers based outside the EU who are supplying business customers in the EU are not required to levy the VAT that the business customer would pay under self-assessment. However, suppliers based outside the EU who supply non-business customers now have to charge VAT. To achieve this, they may register with any EU member state, with VAT then being levied on supplies at the rate of VAT in the country in which the consumer is resident and then redistributed to that state. This is achieved by means of an online registration and VAT return filing system that simplifies compliance. The rules relating to the registration of non-EU based suppliers and the subsequent redistribution of the VAT levied will initially apply for three years and may then be extended or updated. The proposals were initially brought forward by the Commission in 2000 and subsequently amended. Whether it is possible to police such a regime and whether the technology exists to implement it properly remains to be seen.

10.1.2 Interaction between domestic VAT systems and EU VAT

Importation of goods

If the purchases are imports of goods, VAT will be payable on importation by the purchasers themselves, and will be credited as an input tax in the current

3. 86/560/EEC.

quarter's return against VAT due on sales. EU countries allow a postponed accounting system to operate in order to avoid the cash-flow disadvantage of paying VAT on importation and then crediting it only at the end of the current quarter. In the UK, for example, payment may only be deferred until the 15th day of the month following that of importation for non-intra-Community acquisitions, so a cash-flow disadvantage may exist as a result.

However, where goods are imported from outside the EU for trans-shipment outside the UK,[4] the goods may be kept in a bonded warehouse without triggering a VAT liability on importation. Where goods are imported into the UK, for example, without actually being sold to a UK person, the foreign person may himself register for VAT and bring the goods into the UK, and may be required to appoint a VAT fiscal agent.[5] It should be noted that the appointment of such a fiscal agent will not necessarily constitute the creation of a permanent establishment for corporation tax purposes in the UK.

In respect of importation of goods by a VAT registered entity in one EU member state from another EU member state, the EC Sixth Directive as expanded requires VAT to be accounted for by the recipient of the goods in their own country. This is achieved by applying notional VAT at the appropriate rate as part of their VAT return declarations and claiming recovery of this VAT according to their normal VAT recovery rate.

Importation of services

As far as services are concerned, generally speaking VAT is applicable where the supplier is resident,[6] so that such services supplied by a foreign supplier to a UK taxable person, for example, may not be subject to VAT. However, there are certain services which are deemed to be supplied within the UK, even if supplied by a foreign individual or company, and may be summarised as follows:

- services relating to land in the UK;
- transportation services in the UK;
- other services that are physically performed in the UK, including cultural, artistic, sporting and educational services involving the presentation to an audience.

In such cases, the foreign person, if the services exceed the registration threshold, will need to register for VAT and charge VAT to his UK customer.

4. I.e. where the goods will not be used in the UK.
5. Who may be an accountant or lawyer.
6. Where he has established his business or has a fixed establishment from which the service is supplied.

Export of goods and services

As far as the export of goods and services is concerned, such a supply is generally zero-rated. Certainly, this is the case where the exports are to non-EU individuals or companies, as well to EU-registered taxable persons who give their VAT registration number to the UK supplier, for example. However, since 1 January 1993, goods and services supplied to a non-registered person in the EU have been subject to VAT accounted for by the UK supplier.

Telecommunications

Telecommunications services are treated differently for VAT purposes from other services where the place of supply for VAT is normally where the supplier is established, i.e. where it has its fixed place of business. From 1 July 1997, new rules regarding the place of supply of telecommunication services became effective throughout the EU to combat lost VAT on intra-community transactions so that non-EU suppliers will be required to register and charge VAT in the EU country of use of such services, while the recipient of services from EU member state entities accounts for VAT under the reverse charge procedure. The place of supply is now deemed to be the customer's country of residence, so that a UK supplier, for example, is no longer required to account for VAT on such 'exports' to VAT-registered customers in the EU.

VAT groupings

Under Article 4(4) of the Sixth Directive, independent legal persons, including companies, may form a single taxable entity for VAT purposes provided they are closely linked economically and financially in the form of a group. Not all EU member states allow VAT grouping: Austria, Denmark, Germany, Ireland, Finland and the UK being among those that do. In Germany, Austria and the Netherlands, a concept known as *Organschaft* automatically assumes a single entity relationship where two or more entities are so closely connected fiscally, economically and organisationally.

The benefit of a VAT group registration is that the burden of VAT is spread over a number of companies and it also centralises the accounting functions within a group. VAT group treatment is not granted automatically and the following conditions must be met for an application to be considered:

(a) one company in the group must control each of the others; or

(b) one person controls all of them; or

(c) two or more individuals carrying on a business as a partnership control all of them.

Employee expenses

Doubt has been cast upon the deductibility of employee expenses for VAT purposes following the ruling in the case of *Commission of European Communities v. Kingdom of the Netherlands*[7] in which the Dutch tax law allowing a VAT deduction, for input tax purposes, in circumstances where an allowance was paid by employers to employees using a private vehicle for business, was held to be a breach of the Sixth Directive. The Commission's argument centred on the requirement for a taxable person for the deduction to be relevant. The UK supported the Netherlands in the case and the full effect of the decision remains to be seen but the potential is for it to be relatively wide reaching, particularly in the UK where this element is often claimed for a variety of employee expenses. As the European Commission is now taking infraction proceedings against the UK, further developments are expected.

10.1.3 European Union countries

United Kingdom

In addition to VAT being charged on the domestic supply of goods and services within the UK, VAT is also imposed on the importation of goods from outside the EU. The standard rate in the UK is 17.5% of the consideration, but a reduced rate of 5%[8] and a zero rate[9] also apply in respect of certain goods and services. Taxable persons carrying out entrepreneurial activities who are registered for VAT normally have to submit VAT returns each quarter, or monthly returns may be made if a net credit is to be refunded as a result of VAT input taxes exceeding the tax on goods and services supplied. A person is obliged to register or deregister for VAT in the UK if the taxable supplies exceed a certain threshold.[10]

Clearly taxable persons will have purchases as well as sales, on which purchases VAT may be levied by another taxable person. The VAT returns as above would therefore reflect the input VAT as well as the output VAT, and the balance is to be accounted to HMRC or is refundable.

France

VAT in France (*taxe sur la valeur ajoutée* or TVA) is a part-harmonised system which exists in EU countries as a result of the Sixth Directive. An 'entrepreneur'

7. C-338/98.
8. Applies, among other things, to domestic fuel and power, residential conversions and renovations, and energy-saving materials and installation.
9. Including such basic necessities as food, children's clothing, some building services, and the majority of printed material.
10. These thresholds are £60,000 and £58,000, respectively, for 2005/06.

in France is a person who performs independent economic activities. Since 1 April 2000, the standard rate of VAT has been 19.6%; rates of 5.5% and 2.1%[11] are applicable to some services and deliveries of goods. VAT is payable between the 15th and 24th day of the month. The VAT threshold is: (a) €76,300 for taxpayers who deliver goods or who carry out restaurant or lodging activities, and (b) €27,000 for other taxpayers who are deemed to render services, although registration is permitted for a lower turnover provided that, in the case of a foreign person, a fiscal representative is appointed. From 15 September 1999, the rate of VAT applicable to the improvement, development and maintenance of residential premises completed more than two years before the rendering of services has been reduced from the standard rate of 19.6% to 5.5%.

Foreign taxable persons who do not perform independent economic activities within France, but who incur VAT input tax on goods or services supplied in France, may claim a repayment of the input VAT without the need for VAT registration.

The VAT payable on intra-community acquisitions is calculated on the taxable base which includes not only the amount of the invoice but also the costs of transportation and other related costs. In respect of goods supplied from outside the EU, customs duties would also be added to the value of the invoice to arrive at the taxable base.

Germany

Value added tax in Germany (*Umsatzsteuer*) follows the general EU system of value added taxation. The standard rate is 16%, while a reduced rate of 7% applies in respect of certain supplies. Persons carrying out independent economic activities in Germany must file monthly or quarterly VAT returns, depending upon the taxable supplies reported in the preceding year, and must pay with the return the amount of net VAT payable. An annual summary is then prepared at the end of each calendar year.

Foreign taxable persons who do not perform any taxable services or supplies in Germany, but who incur VAT on inputs supplied in Germany, may reclaim such VAT, as is the case in all other EU countries.

The Netherlands

The system of VAT in the Netherlands (*Omzetbelasting* or BTW) is similar to that in other EU countries. Persons carrying out independent economic activities in the Netherlands must register for BTW and submit monthly returns together with the net VAT payable. The current rate is 19%, though as for other

11. For specific medicines repayable to users by the social security system.

EU countries there is a reduced rate of 6% applicable to food and certain pharmaceutical products as well as other basic necessities. Intra-community acquisitions incur VAT, which is due within 15 days after the month in which the acquisition took place.

However, it is worth noting a number of points as regards holding companies. First, a holding company whose sole activities constitute the acquisition and holding of shares and operations concerning the holding of shares is not an entrepreneur for VAT purposes, since this company does not undertake any economic activity. However, if the holding company is directly or indirectly involved in the management of companies, it may be considered an entrepreneur and, as a consequence, deduct input VAT. In general, however, the supply of shares and the services related to shares are exempt from VAT.

10.2 AUSTRALIAN AND CANADIAN GST

10.2.1 Australia

The goods and services tax (GST), which commenced in Australia on 1 July 2000, is a broad-based tax that aims to tax 'private final consumption expenditure'. GST is payable at a flat rate of 10% and is imposed on the supplies of goods, real property, rights and services in Australia and on goods imported into Australia made on or after 1 July 2000. The liability for GST is on the supplier. However, this liability is typically 'passed on' to customers by increasing the price by 10%. There is no statutory right for the supplier to charge an additional amount for GST. Rather, the supplier's right to charge GST arises under the terms of a written agreement or contract.

The GST may apply to supplies made by both residents and non-residents of Australia. Consequently, non-resident organisations that make taxable supplies into Australia need to consider whether or not they are required to register for and return GST in Australia. An entity is required to register for GST in Australia if that entity has an annual turnover of AUD 50,000 or more from supplies that are connected with Australia. An entity which does not reach the AUD 50,000 threshold may elect to register for GST in Australia where it is carrying on an enterprise, even if that enterprise is conducted outside Australia.

GST-registered entities that carry on 'taxable enterprises' can claim 'input tax credits' (effectively a refund) for the GST charged on any acquisitions or purchases made in Australia.

If the GST payable by an entity on its supplies (the GST liability) exceeds the input tax on its acquisitions, then the entity pays the net amount to the Australian Taxation Office. If the GST liability is less than the input tax, then the entity is entitled to a refund from the Australian Taxation Office. The net amount may be adjusted if the supply is cancelled or a discount is given. An input tax credit may only be claimed to the extent of the 'creditable purpose' and if the creditable purpose changes, then the entity may be required to make an adjustment to later GST returns.

GST is imposed on 'taxable supplies' in Australia, which covers virtually all activities in Australia. The entity making the supply is liable to pay the GST in the amount of 10% of the value of the relevant supply. There are two types of non-taxable supplies under the GST:

- 'GST-free' supplies that are not taxed and where an input tax credit is allowed for tax paid on purchases; and
- 'input taxed' supplies that are not taxed and no credit is allowed for tax paid on purchases.

Liability to GST generally arises when an invoice is issued or when any consideration is received, whichever happens first. Most large businesses will account for GST on an invoice basis, as the cash basis is only available where annual turnover is less than AUD 1 million. The GST accounting period is also determined by annual turnover. If an entity's annual turnover is AUD 20 million or more, then it must adopt a monthly tax period. Other entities may use a quarterly tax period, with the option of adopting monthly periods if they wish.

Company groups are allowed to register one representative member in their group allowing intra-group transactions to be ignored for GST purposes. Similar rules for company branches and joint ventures are designed to reduce unnecessary administrative burdens and costs of accounting.

GST base

The GST applies to taxable supplies. Private sales by unregistered people are not taxed.

A taxable supply arises under the following circumstances:

- a supply for consideration;
- in the course of furtherance of an enterprise;
- connected with Australia;
- by a registered entity (or an entity required to be registered).

A 'supply' is very broadly defined, intending to encompass activities as widely as possible. For example, the term 'supply' also captures an 'entry into or release from an obligation' or 'a creation, grant, transfer, assignment or surrender of a right'. The definition of 'supply' does not include money, but does include illegal supplies. Consideration is also very widely defined and includes all forms of payments, acts and forbearances (e.g. barter), whether monetary or non-monetary.

10.2.2 Canada

Unlike the system of value added taxation in EU countries, Canada operates two systems of turnover taxes on the sale or use of goods and services: the goods and services tax (GST) at federal level, a similar value added tax in four provinces and the retail sales tax (RST) in the rest of Canada's provinces. The GST is payable at the rate of 7% in respect of taxable supplies made by registered businesses. As in a VAT system, registered businesses may claim input tax credits on the GST paid by registered businesses on supplies from other Canadian GST registered persons. 'Excluded businesses', such as the financial services and healthcare sectors, are excluded from claiming input tax credits. The net amount of GST after input tax credits will be accounted for in returns filed with Canada Revenue Agency (CRA). Larger taxpayers must file at the latest at the end of the month subsequent to the relevant period. A non-resident person may voluntarily register for GST if supplies of tangible personal property are delivered to him in Canada (such as where goods are imported by the supplier and FOB at the Canadian customer).

Four provinces have a similar value 'harmonised' with the federal GST. All the remaining provinces and territories except Alberta have a retail sales tax (RST) payable by the end-user of goods. There are no input tax credits in respect of RST paid.

The application of the GST to non-resident suppliers will depend largely upon whether the given supplier is a GST registrant. A registrant is a person who is either registered for the GST or is required to register for the GST. A supplier is required to register for the GST if resident in Canada and engaged in a commercial activity or is not resident in Canada but is carrying on business in Canada.

Non-residents of Canada are deemed to be resident in Canada if they maintain a permanent establishment in Canada. A permanent establishment is considered to be any fixed place of business, including branch offices, through which the non-resident makes supplies, or the fixed place of business of another person through whom the non-resident makes supplies. A non-resident who does not have a permanent establishment in Canada will be required to register in the GST system if carrying on any business in Canada. There are also specific mandatory registration rules aimed at particular industries, such as transportation services and non-resident performers. The latter category includes any seminar or event with an admission fee held in Canada and organised by a non-resident. A non-resident carrying on business in Canada must register for the GST and, if the non-resident does not have a permanent establishment in Canada, post security with CRA.

Optional GST registration is available to a non-resident who, in the ordinary course of business, solicits orders for the delivery of goods in Canada, supplies services to be performed in Canada, or supplies intangible property to be used in Canada.

There is a *de minimis* limit so persons whose taxable supplies in a 12-month period are less than C$ 30,000 need not register for GST. This *de minimis* threshold, however, is determined with reference to worldwide supplies, and not only taxable supplies made in Canada. A non-resident who has Canadian sales below the C$ 30,000 threshold will therefore be required to register into the GST system if its worldwide sales exceed C$ 30,000.

Goods and services imported into Canada may be subject to GST on importation. Services imported into Canada are not subject to GST at the border but the recipient of the service will in most cases be required to self-assess the tax to CRA. Except for excluded businesses, the registrant self-assessing GST will be entitled to an offsetting input tax credit and not have any absolute tax cost. The rules with respect to intellectual property are complex and beyond the scope of this brief summary.

10.3 SOCIAL SECURITY TAXES

Social security taxes are a graduated tax based on income earned by individuals, payable by both employers and the employees, and the self-employed. This national system usually provides for old age, disability and unemployment benefits paid out of a trust fund. Indeed, when reviewing the section on personal services companies[12] it may be noted that one of the primary motives for using such entities was the avoidance of UK social security contributions. In fact, the rates in the UK, while having been increased significantly over the past few years, are not nearly as high as in other European countries, particularly the Scandinavian countries. These countries use social security taxes as the means of raising revenue for significant social welfare programmes, and the taxes are therefore clearly identifiable and linked to the services provided.

Some countries have concluded social security agreements (referred to as totalisation agreements), ensuring the applicable individuals remain covered when they move between treaty countries. Agreements can help by adding contributions made to a social security fund or periods of residence in one country to contributions or residency-periods in another treaty country to meet certain minimum qualifying standards. Social security agreements also assist the individual to be able to file claims in respect of the applicable treaty in either of the treaty countries.

It should be noted that it is a fundamental principle of EU law that any individual employee, or his employer, cannot be held liable for social security payments in more than one country in one year.

12. In §3.4.

10.4 CAPITAL TAXES

10.4.1 Capital duty

Some European countries raise revenue through the taxation of capital introduced to business enterprises in the form of capital duty, a tax generally levied on the formation of a company. The tax is usually a percentage of the nominal or issued capital, or both.

The Netherlands is one of a diminishing number of EU countries that levy capital duty. This is not payable on loans (unless these are deemed to be capital contributions), whereas 0.55% capital duty is payable in respect of the subscription of share capital. Additional capital contributions by shareholders are also subject to capital tax even if no additional shares are issued. The capital duty is payable within one month after the capital was contributed, and a capital tax return has to be filed within this one-month period. In order to claim an exemption from capital tax (e.g. in the case of a merger), it is important for the entity issuing the shares to claim this exemption on the tax return;[13] it may be deducted for corporate tax purposes even if the capital increase is not for a purpose which gives rise to taxable income in the Netherlands. A bill has been announced in 2005, which, if passed, will abolish Dutch capital duty from the beginning of 2006.

10.4.2 Stamp duty

Although there is no capital duty in the UK, stamp duty and now stamp duty land tax (SDLT) have both become stealth taxes, which can have a considerable impact on certain transactions.

From 1 December 2003 and following the 2003 Finance Act, the government made major changes to stamp taxes payable on real estate transactions. The scope of UK stamp duty was significantly reduced and SDLT was introduced.

SDLT is wider in its scope than stamp duty because it is a tax on transactions rather than documents and applies to transactions involving UK land. The purchaser is legally obliged to pay the tax and it applies regardless of whether the transaction is evidenced in writing. It is determined by self-assessment and applies wherever there is chargeable consideration for the land transaction, that is any consideration in money or money's worth given directly or indirectly by the purchaser or someone connected with him. At current rates this means that the transfer of UK real estate where the consideration exceeds £500,000 is subject to SDLT at 4% on the total consideration. There are a host of compliance obligations similar to those under corporation tax self-assessment.

13. Which will state nil tax to be paid.

A purchaser is obliged to complete a land transaction return form giving full details of the transaction and submit payment of any SDLT due within 30 days of the effective date of the transaction. If all is in order and the SDLT has been correctly paid, the Inland Revenue will issue an SDLT certificate that is needed to allow registration of the transaction at HM Land Registry. Interest and penalties may be due in respect of any late or underpaid SDLT.

The 2003 legislation effectively dealt a blow to stamp duty mitigation schemes. Over the preceding years, a number of techniques had been developed in order to avoid the payment of stamp duty, generally based on the fact that it is a very old tax and is levied on the stamping of a document. This led to a number of schemes designed to mitigate or avoid payment of stamp duty, including 'resting on contract'[14] or under which documents were executed outside the UK. Such schemes were specifically targeted – and outlawed – by the new legislation, which also sought to simplify the manner in which taxes were calculated and paid.

There is no specific exemption for goodwill. 'Land' also includes goodwill that is attached to and inseparable from the land and therefore any amount that is attributed to such goodwill is within the charge to SDLT. Transfers of debts are not exempt from SDLT but are dealt with in the same way that they were under the old stamp duty regime. Structures designed to avoid payment of stamp duty on the full purchase price – for example by payment of a substantial option price to be deducted from the overall purchase price – will not succeed.

Despite fears that the 2003 legislation would deem the use of a special-purpose vehicle (SPV) redundant, such fears have to date proved unfounded. The use of such vehicles has become more widely publicised in the UK over the past few years. It generally involves the creation of a company, which is then used to purchase the property, instead of the individual purchasing the property personally. The advantage of such a mechanism lies with the reduction of SDLT payable by the next purchaser of the property. Instead of paying SDLT at a rate of 4% on the purchase price, a sale of the shares in the SPV to the purchaser would attract stamp duty only at the rate of 0.5% currently payable.

14. I.e. exchanging contracts without ever actually moving to completion to avoid paying stamp duty on the document that effectively transfers ownership of the property.

X. CASE STUDY 10

This chapter investigates the heavy impact of indirect taxes on the business community in the framework of value added tax in a variety of forms, social security taxes, and stamp duties. To learn something about the impact of these taxes on some of the Filipes' businesses, the following review may be useful:

(a) in France in relation to the sale of Lucca software (Diagram 4);
(b) in the Netherlands in respect of Lucca BV's activities (Diagram 4);
(c) in Australia in relation to the sale of Lucca software (Diagram 14);
(d) social security taxes payable in the UK in respect of earnings of Paolo for Belsize Wanderers and Opus AG (Diagram 8);
(e) capital taxes payable in the Netherlands on additional capital invested into Lucca BV (Diagram 4) and stamp duty on the purchase of the house for Giuliano (Diagram 5).

Diagram 4

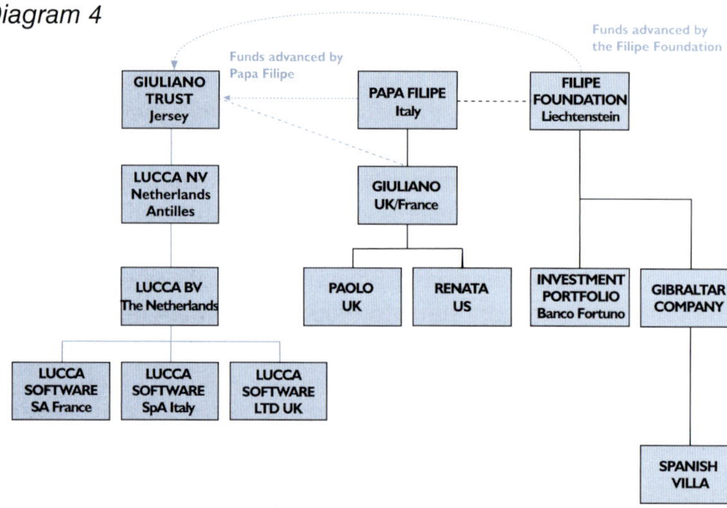

Diagram 5

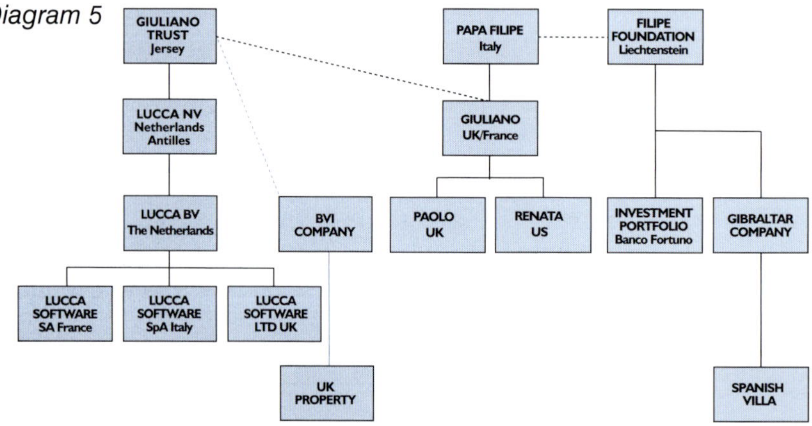

Diagram 8

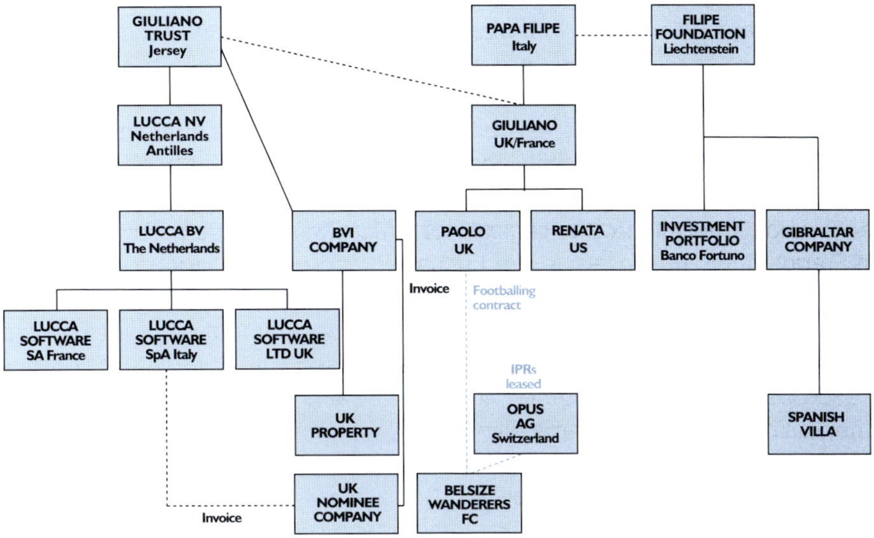

Diagram 14

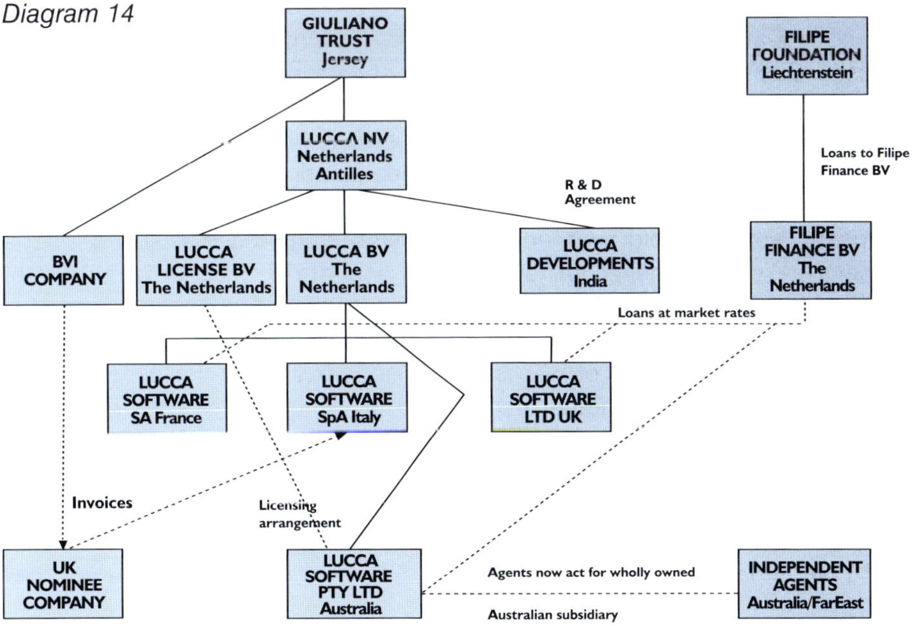

[X.a] France: sale of Lucca software

Lucca Software SA not only manufactures Lucca software in France, but is the hub of the group's e-commerce development. Giuliano, keen to follow in the footsteps of other etail pioneers, was eager to embrace some of this new technology and the tax-saving opportunities. Sales income amounts to around €5 million per year. Since the threshold for VAT purposes for taxpayers delivering goods in France is €76,300 per year, Lucca Software SA is well above the threshold and will have to register for VAT – TVA as it is abbreviated locally – in France.

Giuliano was born with his mother's extrasensory perception. At least, Papa Filipe was convinced that Mama Filipe was blessed with 'the gift' (although as far as Papa Filipe was concerned, it was more a curse than a blessing.) Papa Filipe was convinced that Mama Filipe's 'gift' was responsible for her suspicious looks and remarks that would send a shudder down his spine, as if to confirm his own suspicions about her abilities. Long after she passed away, he could still hear her words: 'Filipe, what have you been up to in Spain?' Giuliano never told Papa Filipe that the smell of Maria Rodrigues' Shalimar was noticeable a mile off, although Papa himself was oblivious to this!

Before you ask yourself what all this has to do with the riveting discipline of VAT, it should be noted that Papa Filipe thought that his son had the same gift. Whether it was 'the gift', or simply his father's business acumen, Giuliano certainly intuitively knew that there was a lot of money to be made from the internet. He made the decision to sell his software through Lucca Software SA's website. Customers from all over the French-speaking world could log on to the website, type in their credit card numbers and then download the software on to their PCs. Before too long, following the launch of the internet software, Lucca Software SA's French accountant called Maurice up, not knowing how to treat the sales for VAT purposes. Maurice explained: 'Montelier, for VAT purposes, software sold over the internet will be treated as the sale of goods. Under the French domestic VAT system, VAT at a rate of 19.6% is payable to the French tax authorities where the software was sold to a French customer. Were the software purchased by a resident of another EU country, the Sixth Directive dictates that the payment of VAT is compulsory, but that if the purchaser is a VAT-registered entity in another EU member state, then the purchaser has to account for the VAT in his own country. Where the purchaser is not a resident of an EU member state, the Sixth Directive dictates that no VAT needs to be charged by the supplier – that is Lucca Software SA – in the EU.'

[X.b] Netherlands: Lucca BV's activities

Persons carrying out economic activities in the Netherlands must register for VAT – BTW as it is called locally – and submit returns on a monthly basis together with the net BTW payable. However, the business of holding companies whose only activities consist of buying and holding shares is not relevant for BTW-purposes, since it is not considered as carrying out economic activities. If the company is to any extent involved in providing other services – management or administration, for example – it may register for BTW in the Netherlands and enjoy input BTW-deductions.

The ever-entrepreneurial Giuliano saw great possibilities in providing services in respect of his software. Since it was important to ensure that Lucca BV in the Netherlands remains a company with clear substance, he decided to set up a Lucca Software Helpline. Friendly and multi-lingual Dutch technicians and IT specialists now assist customers from around the world with their software woes. Maurice thought he was being invaded by Lucca's accountants when, as he put the receiver down from talking to Montelier, the phone rang again. It was Eelko from the Netherlands with a VAT question. He was unsure whether VAT should be levied at all on revenues received from the Helpline's activities since this is, in his mind, clearly not supply of 'goods'. Maurice pointed out that 'services', too, are subject to VAT. And Maurice patiently explained the regime to Eelko, with a distinct feeling of *déjà vu*...

[X.c] Australia: sale of Lucca software

GST is imposed, among other taxes, on the sale of virtually all goods in Australia. The threshold creating a duty for entities to register for GST is an annual turnover of AUD 50,000.

Lucca Software Pty Ltd has, in the true Filipe tradition, become a very profitable business indeed during the relatively short period of its existence. On its software sales its annual turnover exceeded AUD 4 million during 2003. Based on the law, it is clear that the company has a registration obligation in respect of GST.

Giuliano decided that the English-speaking world would be supplied with his software via Lucca Software Pty Ltd's website. Being a scholar at heart, he decided one weekend to study all he could find on the VAT-treatment in the EU resulting from sales into the EU by non-EU sellers. He found out that following the new rules, Lucca Software Pty Ltd would not need to charge VAT if it sells its software to business customers, which was true in most cases. The EU-based purchaser would need to pay the VAT due under a self-assessment system. (He stopped a moment to think about honesty and other good things.) He continued to learn that when the software is sold to a customer who is not a business, Lucca Software Pty Ltd would have to charge VAT. He was cross to learn that a fair amount of red tape was involved (Giuliano, for all his excellent qualities, is an impatient yet efficient man): Lucca Software Pty Ltd would need to register for VAT in any EU member state. VAT would be levied at the rate applicable in the country in which the customer resides and then redistributed to the country of registration. He called Lucca Software Pty's accountant to tell him to start the online registration procedure and to ensure that VAT returns are filed in the Netherlands, where he wants the registration done, on a timely basis.

[X.d] Social security tax

[i.] UK: by Paolo

Both employees and employers contribute to national insurance in the UK. The employee contributes 12.8% of his annual income, while the employer contributes 11% on the employee's annual income. Thus, once Paolo started his glamorous job with Belsize Wanderers FC, both parties are responsible for making NICs – national insurance contributions – at the percentage rates above. Furthermore, Paolo, being a high earner, pays an additional 1% on his annual income over the amount of £30,940. Belsize Wanderers FC is also liable for additional NICs of 12.8% on the tax value of the Mercedes SLK 500 Paolo gets to use for both work and private purposes. However, in respect of any salary received by Paolo from Opus AG for his intellectual property rights, this is outside of the scope of UK national insurance liability.

Here is how Paolo can save on much-dreaded taxes: he is entitled to an annual salary of £3 million. Belsize Wanderers pays this amount to Opus AG, who pays Paolo £1.5 million. Of course, this portion of Paolo's salary is subject to income tax and social security contributions in the UK, which are duly paid on a current basis. The remainder of his annual salary, minus a small fee that Opus AG retains, is paid into an offshore employee benefit trust (EBT). The EBT's funds can be invested and Paolo may receive proceeds from the trustees of the EBT on a discretionary basis. Paolo is protected from the UK's anti-avoidance and attribution rules and he does not incur any withholding tax on the contributions into the EBT nor on receipt of his salary. It's clear to see how this is a win/win situation!

[X.e] Capital and stamp duties

[i.] The Netherlands: additional capital investment into Lucca BV

Papa Filipe – ever-generous and concerned – called Giuliano one Friday evening to ask him whether his son needed any money. Giuliano, not the small boy from the village any longer but a man with an annual income that runs into seven figure amounts in British pounds, found this gesture endearing. Not wishing to discourage Papa, Giuliano suggested that he had been thinking for a while that Lucca BV's business could be expanded significantly if the company could take up some loans. However, Lucca BV is subject to Dutch thin capitalisation rules and would want to stay within an 85:15 debt-to-equity ratio. In order to increase the amount of loans held by Lucca BV, the company could do with a capital injection. Papa and Giuliano agreed that this was a good idea, and that they would decide on the final amount of the capital contribution based on the cost of the transaction. Maurice later told Giuliano that 0.55% of the amount contributed is payable as capital duty in the Netherlands. Giuliano thought long and hard about this. On €1 million offered by Papa as an interest-free loan, he would have to pay 0.55% capital duty in the Netherlands if the Dutch tax administration considered this to be quasi-capital from a party related to the shareholders. However, since the money was to be utilised to build up the UK subsidiary, Giuliano asked Maurice whether it would be okay to have the funds contributed direct to the UK company. Maurice bit his lip, wishing he had thought of this first, and agreed that the €1 million could be advanced to Lucca Software Ltd as redeemable preference share capital without affecting ownership rights of Lucca BV and thereby avoiding €55,000 capital duty in the Netherlands, none being payable in the UK.

[ii.] UK: purchase of house for Giuliano

Giuliano had been contemplating another property acquisition in the UK by the BVI company – a lovely old church at an asking price of £14 million in one of London's most prestigious and established suburbs. He had heard that 4% of the purchase price of the church can be saved if after exchange of contracts the parties never move to completion, called resting on contract. When he ran this idea past Maurice, the latter cautioned Giuliano that under the 2002 Finance Act that was no longer a feasible tax-saving mechanism. Since the 2003 Finance Act, stamp duty land tax has to be paid, at the rate of 4% of the total consideration for the purchase of the property. Late stamping of documents will lead to penalties and will prevent registration of the property in Giuliano's name at HM Land Registry. All property transactions involving the transfer of freehold property are now subject to compulsory registration at HM Land Registry.

[X.f] Conclusion

This chapter has outlined some of the more important aspects relating to taxes other than corporate tax payable on the profits of a company. It has illustrated that the impact of such taxes is significant, not only from an economic viewpoint, but particularly from a compliance viewpoint. Moreover, the responsible international tax adviser will never fail to point out to his client that the impact of these taxes will have to be considered sooner or later in the course of any transaction. All too often these taxes are overlooked, which causes unpleasant results for clients and red faces for tax advisers. Some might call the taxes that are the subject of this chapter 'stealth taxes', although this need not necessarily be so, provided that their impact is not overlooked.

Sources

Andreas Neocleous & Co. *Doing Business in Cyprus*. 2004, Limassol.

Clarke, G. *Offshore Tax Planning*, LexisNexis/Tolley, 10th ed. 2003, London.

International Bureau of Fiscal Documentation. *International Tax Glossary,* IBFD, 1988, Amsterdam.

OECD Model Convention with respect to Taxes on Income and on Capital. © OECD, July 2005. (http://www.oecd.org)

Rohatgi, R. *Basic International Taxation*. Kluwer Law International, 2002, The Hague.

Saunders, R., Dean, M. & Williams, R. *International Tax Systems and Planning Techniques*. Thomson/Sweet & Maxwell, Looseleaf, 2005, London.

Index

Page references to non-textual material such as diagrams are in italic print.